INDIAN UNREST

INDIAN UNREST

VALENTINE CHIROL

GYAN

Published by

Gyan Publishing House
5, Ansari Road
Daryaganj, New Delhi-110002
Phone: 011-47034999, 9811692060
E-mail: books@gyanbooks.com

Distribution Network
gyanbooks.com
India, USA, Canada, UK, Australia, France

ISBN: 978-81-212-8656-5 (PB)
First Published, 1910

2nd Impression 2023

Printed at: Gyan Press, Delhi.

INDIAN UNREST
Author: Valentine Chirol

INDIAN UNREST

By

VALENTINE CHIROL

A Reprint, revised and enlarged, from "The Times," with an introduction by Sir Alfred Lyall

We have now, as it were, before us, in that vast congeries of peoples we call India, a long, slow march in uneven stages through all the centuries from the fifth to the twentieth.
—VISCOUNT MORLEY.

MACMILLAN AND CO., LIMITED
ST. MARTIN'S STREET, LONDON
1910

DEDICATED BY PERMISSION

TO

VISCOUNT MORLEY

AS A TRIBUTE

OF PRIVATE FRIENDSHIP AND

PUBLIC RESPECT

CONTENTS

The numerals above the line in the body of the book refer to notes at the end of the volume.

INTRODUCTION.

By Sir Alfred C. Lyall.

The volume into which Mr. Valentine Chirol has collected and republished his valuable series of articles in *The Times* upon Indian unrest is an important and very instructive contribution to the study of what is probably the most arduous problem in the politics of our far-reaching Empire. His comprehensive survey of the whole situation, the arrangement of evidence and array of facts, are not unlike what might have been found in the Report of a Commission appointed to investigate the causes and the state of affairs to which the troubles that have arisen in India may be ascribed.

At different times in the world's history the nations foremost in civilization have undertaken the enterprise of founding a great European dominion in Asia, and have accomplished it with signal success. The Macedonian Greeks led the way ; they were followed by the Romans ; and in both instances their military superiority and organizing genius enabled them to subdue and govern for centuries vast populations in Western Asia. European science and literature flourished in the great cities of the East, where the educated classes willingly accepted and supported foreign rulership as their barrier against a relapse into barbarism ; nor have we reason for believing that it excited unusual discontent or disaffection among the Asiatic peoples. But the Greek and Roman Empires in Asia have disappeared long ago, leaving very little beyond scattered ruins; and in modern times it is the British dominion in India that has revived and is pursuing the enterprise of ruling and civilizing a great Asiatic population, of developing the political intelligence and transforming the ideas of an antique and, in some respects, a primitive society.

That the task must be one of prodigious difficulty, not always free from danger, has been long known to those who watched the experiment with some accurate foresight of the conditions attending it. Yet the recent symptoms of virulent disease in some parts of the body politic, though confined to certain provinces of India, have taken the British nation by surprise. Mr. Chirol's book has now exhibited the present state and prospect of the adventure; he has examined the causes and the consequences of the prevailing unrest; he has collected ample evidence, and he has consulted all the best authorities, Indian and European, on the subject. His masterly analysis of all this material shows wide acquaintance with the facts, and rare insight into the character and motives, the aims and methods, of those who are engaged in stirring up the spirit of revolt against the British Government. He has pointed to instances where the best intentions of the administrators have led them wrong; his whole narrative illustrates the perils that beset a Government necessarily pledged to moral and material reform, which finds its own principles perverted against its efforts, and its foremost opponents among the class that has been the first to profit by the benefits which that Government has conferred upon them.

The nineteenth century had been pre-eminently an era of the development of rapid and easy communication between distant parts of the world, particularly between Europe and Asia. So long as these two continents remained far apart the condition of Asia was unchanged and stationary ; if there was any change it had been latterly retrogressive, for in India at any rate the eighteenth century was a period of abnormal and extensive political confusion. In Europe, on the other hand, national wealth, scientific discoveries, the arts of war and peace, had made extraordinary progress. Population had increased and multiplied ; and partly by territorial conquests, partly by pacific penetration, the Western nations overflowed politically into Asia during the nineteenth century. They brought with them larger knowledge, novel ideas and manners, which have opened the Asiatic mind to new influences and aspirations, to the sense of needs and grievances not previously felt or even imagined. The effect, as can now be clearly perceived, has been to produce an abrupt transition from old to new ways, from the antique order of society towards fresh models ; and to this may be ascribed the general unsettlement, the uneasy stir, that pervade Asia at the present moment. Its equilibrium has been disturbed by the high speed at which Europe has been pushing eastward ; and the principal points of contact and penetration are in India.

Moreover, towards the latter end of the nineteenth century and in the first years of the present century came events which materially altered the attitude of Asiatic nations towards European predominance. The defeat of the Italians by the Abyssinians in 1896 may indeed be noted as the first decisive victory gained by troops that may be reckoned Oriental over a European army in the open field, for at least three centuries. The Japanese war, in which Russia lost battles not only by land, but also at sea, was even a more significant and striking warning that the era of facile victories in Asia had ended ; since never before in all history had an Asiatic navy won a great sea-fight against European fleets. That the unquiet spirit, which from these general causes has been spreading over the Eastern Continent, should be particularly manifest in countries under European Governments is not unnatural ; it inevitably roused the latent dislike of foreign rule, with which a whole people is never entirely content. Precisely similar symptoms are to be observed in the Asiatic possessions of France, and in Egypt ; nor is Algeria yet altogether reconciled to the *régime* of its conquerors.

That in India the British Government has found the centres of active disaffection located in the Maratha country and in Lower Bengal, is a phenomenon which can be to a large extent accounted for by reference to Anglo-Indian history. The fact that Poona is one focus of sedition has been attributed in this volume to the survival among the Maratha Brahmins of the recollection that "far into the eighteenth century Poona was the capital of a theocratic State in which behind the Throne of the Peshwas both spiritual and secular authority were concentrated in the hands of the Brahmins." The Peshwas, as their title implies, had been hereditary Ministers who governed in the name of the reigning dynasty founded by the famous Maratha leader Sivajee, whose successors they set aside. But before the end of the eighteenth century the secular authority of the Peshwas had become almost nominal, and the real power in the State had passed into the grasp of a confederation of chiefs of predatory armies, whose violence drove the last Peshwa, more than a century ago, to seek refuge in a British camp. The political sovereignty of the Brahmins had disappeared from the time when he placed himself under British protection ; and the Maratha chiefs (who were not Brahmins) only acknowledged our supremacy after some fiercely contested battles ; with the result that they were confined to and confirmed in the possession of the territories now governed by their descendants. But it is quite true that to the memory of a time when for once, and once only, in Indian history, their caste established a great secular dominion, may be ascribed the tendency to disloyalty among the Maratha Brahmins.

The case of Bengal is very different. Poona and Calcutta are separated geographically almost by the whole breadth of India between two seas; yet the historical antecedents of the Bengalees and Marathas are even further apart. The Marathas were the leaders of revolt against the Moghal Empire; they were formidable opponents to the rise of the British power; their chiefs fought hard before yielding to British authority. On the other hand, Lower Bengal belonged to a province that had fallen away from the Moghal Empire, and which was transferred from its Mahomedan Governor to a British General by the result of a single battle at Plassey. The Bengalees took no part in the contest, and they had very good reason for willing acquiescence in the change of masters.

In a comparison, therefore, of the Marathas with the people of Bengal, we have a remarkable instance of the production of similar effects from causes very distinct and dissimilar. In the former case their present unrest may be traced, in a large degree, to the memories of early rulership and to warlike traditions. In the latter case there can be no such recollections, military or political; for the country has had no experience whatever of a state of war, since Lower Bengal is perhaps the only considerable province of India which has enjoyed profound peace during nearly 150 years. It is no paradox to suggest that this prolonged tranquillity has had some share in stimulating the audacity of Bengalee unrest, for the literary classes seem to have no clear notion that the real game of revolutionary politics is necessarily rough and dangerous—certain, moreover, to fail whenever the British Government shall have resolved that it is being carried too far, and must end.

But it is beyond question that the promoters of disaffection on both sides of India have been making strenuous exertions to enlist in the movement the influence of Brahminism; and upon this point the book rightly lays particular stress.

The position and privileges of the Brahmins are rightly

compared to those of the Levites; they are the depositories of orthodox tradition; they preside over and hold (not exclusively) a monopoly for the performance of the sacred rites and offices; and ritual in Hinduism, as in most of the ancient religions, is the essential element; it is closely connected with the rules of caste, which unite and divide innumerable groups within the pale of Hinduism. And in India the peculiar institution of caste, the strict regulation of social intercourse, particularly in regard to intermarriage and the sharing of food, prevails to an extent quite unknown elsewhere in the world. The divisions of caste have always operated to weaken the body politic in India, and thus to facilitate foreign conquest; but, on the other hand, they have opposed a stiff barrier to the invasion of foreign religions, to the fusion of alien races with the Hindu people, and to any success in what may be called national unification.

One can easily understand the formidable power invested by this system in the Brahmins, and the enormous obstacles that it might raise against the introduction of Western ideas, manners, and education. Nevertheless we all know, and we have seen it with real satisfaction, that the Brahmins, very much to the credit of their intelligence and sagacity, have been forward in accepting the new learning, the expansion of general knowledge, offered to them by English schools and Universities; they have acquired our language, they have studied our sciences; they are prominent in the professions of law and medicine, which the English have created; they enter our civil services, they even serve in the Indian Army. Yet their readiness to adopt secular culture does not seem to have abated their religious authority, or to have sensibly weakened their influence over the people at large. And indeed the fact that the Brahmins, with others of the educated classes, should have been able, for their own purposes, to appeal simultaneously to the darkest superstitions of Hinduism and to extreme ideas of Western democracy—to disregard caste rules personally and to stir up caste prejudices among the masses—will not greatly surprise those who have observed the extraordinary elasticity of practical Hinduism, the fictions and anomalies which can be invented or tolerated at need. But the beliefs and practices of popular Hinduism are obviously irreconcilable with the principles of modern civilization ; and the various indications of a desire to reform and purify their ancient religion may be partly due to the perception among educated Hindus that so contradictory a position is ultimately untenable, that the incongruity between sacrifices to the goddess Kali and high University degrees is too manifest.

The course and consequences of the measures taken by the British Government to promote Western education in India has been attentively studied by the author of this volume. It is a story of grave political miscalculation, containing a lesson that has its significance for other nations which have undertaken a similar enterprise. Ignorance is unquestionably the root of many evils ; and it was natural that in the last century certain philosophers should have assumed education to be the certain cure for human delusions ; and that statesmen like Macaulay should have declared education to be the best and surest remedy for political discontent and for law-breaking. In any case it was the clear and imperative duty of the British Government to attempt the intellectual emancipation of India as the best justification of British rule. We have since discovered, by experience, that, although education is a sovereign remedy for many ills—is indeed indispensable to healthy progress—yet an indiscriminate or superficial administration of this potent medicine may engender other disorders. It acts upon the frame of an antique society as a powerful dissolvent, heating weak brains, stimulating rash ambitions, raising inordinate expectations of which the disappointment is bitterly resented. That these effects are well known even in Europe may be read in a remarkable French novel published not long ago, "Les Déracinés," which describes the road to ruin taken by poor collegians who had been uprooted from the soil of their humble village. And in Asia the disease is necessarily much more virulent, because the transition has been more sudden, and the contrast between old ideas of life and new aspirations is far sharper. From the report of an able French official upon the Indo-Chinese Colonies we may learn that the existing system of educating the natives has proved to be mischievous, needing radical reform. Of the Levantine youths in the Syrian towns, the product of European schools, a French traveller writes (1909), "C'est une tourbe de déclassés"; while in China some leaders of agitation for democratic changes in the oldest of all Empires are said to be those who have qualified by competitive examination for public employ, and have failed to obtain it. In every country the crowd of expectants far outnumbers the places available. If, indeed, the Government which introduced Western education into Bengal had been native instead of foreign, it would have found itself entangled in difficulties no less grave than those which now confront the British rulers; and there can be little doubt that it would probably have broken down under them.

The phases through which the State's educational policy in India have passed during the last fifty years are explained at length in this volume. The Government was misled in the wrong direction by the reports of two Commissions between 1880 and 1890, whose mistakes were discerned at the time by those who had some tincture of political prudence. The problem is now to reconstruct on a better plan, to try different lines of advance. But some of us have heard of an enterprising pioneer in a difficult country, who confidently urged travellers to take a new route by assuring them that it avoided the hills on the old road. Whether the hills were equally steep on his other road he did not say. And in the present instance it may not be easy to strike out a fresh path which may be clear from the complications that have been suffered to grow up round our system of Indian education; while no one proposes to turn back. The truth is that in India the English have been throughout obliged to lay out their own roads, and to feel their way, without any precedents to guide them. No other Government, European or Asiatic, has yet essayed to administer a great Oriental population, alien in race and religion, by institutions of a representative type, reckoning upon free discussion and an unrestricted Press for reasonable consideration of its measures and fair play, relying upon secular education and absolute religious neutrality to control the unruly affections of sinful men. It is now seen that our Western ideas and inventions, moral and material, are being turned against us by some of those to whom we have imparted an elementary aptitude for using them. And thus we have the strange spectacle, in certain parts of India, of a party capable of resorting to methods that are both reactionary and revolutionary, of men who offer prayers and sacrifices to ferocious divinities and denounce the Government by seditious journalism, preaching primitive superstition in the very modern form of leading articles. The mixture of religion with politics has always produced a highly explosive compound, especially in Asia.

These agitations are in fact the symptoms of what are said by Shakespeare to be the "cankers of a calm world"; they are the natural outcome of artificial culture in an educational hothouse, among classes who have had for generations no real training in rough or hazardous politics. The outline of the present situation in India is that we have been disseminating ideas of abstract political right, and the germs of representative institutions, among a people that had for centuries been governed autocratically, and in a country where local liberties and habits of self-government had been long obliterated or had never existed. At the same time we have been spreading modern education broadcast throughout the land, where, before English rule, learning had not advanced beyond the stage of Europe in the middle ages. These may be taken to be the primary causes of the existing Unrest; and meanwhile the administrative machine has been so efficiently organized, it has run, hitherto, so easily and quietly, as to disguise from inexperienced bystanders the long discipline and training in affairs of State that are required for its management. Nor is it clearly perceived that the real driving power lies in the forces held in reserve by the British nation and in the respect which British guardianship everywhere commands. That Indians should be liberally invited to share the responsibilities of high office is now a recognized principle of public policy. But the process of initiation must be gradual and tentative; and vague notions of dissolving the British connexion only prove incompetence to realize the whole situation, external and internal, of the country. Across the frontiers of India are warlike nations, who are intent upon arming themselves after the latest modern pattern, though for the other benefits of Western science and learning they show, as yet, very little taste or inclination. They would certainly be a serious menace to a weak Government in the Indian plains, while their sympathy with a literary class would be uncommonly slight. Against intruders of this sort the British hold securely the gates of India; and it must be clear that the civilization and future prosperity of the whole country depend entirely upon their determination to maintain public tranquillity by strict enforcement of the laws; combined with their policy of admitting the highest intellects and capacities to the Councils of the State, and of assigning reasonable administrative and legislative independence to the great provinces in accord with the unity of a powerful Empire.

A. C. LYALL.

CHAPTER I.

A General Survey.

That there is a lull in the storm of unrest which has lately swept over India is happily beyond doubt. Does this lull indicate a gradual and steady return to more normal and peaceful conditions ? Or, as in other cyclonic disturbances in tropical climes, does it merely presage fiercer outbursts yet to come ? Has the blended policy of repression and concession adopted by Lord Morley and Lord Minto really cowed the forces of criminal disorder and rallied the representatives of moderate opinion to the cause of sober and Constitutional progress ? Or has it come too late either permanently to arrest the former or to restore confidence and courage to the latter ?

These are the two questions which the present situation in India most frequently and obviously suggests, but it may be doubted whether they by any means cover the whole field of potential developments. They are based apparently upon the assumption that Indian unrest, even in its most extreme forms, is merely the expression of certain political aspirations towards various degrees of emancipation from British tutelage, ranging from a larger share in the present system of administration to a complete revolution in the existing relations between

Great Britain and India, and that, the issues thus raised being essentially political, they can be met by compromise on purely political lines. This assumption ignores, I fear, certain factors of very great importance, social, religious, and economic, which profoundly affect, if they do not altogether overshadow, the political problem. The question to which I propose to address myself is whether Indian unrest represents merely, as we are prone to imagine, the human and not unnatural impatience of subject races fretting under an alien rule which, however well intentioned, must often be irksome and must sometimes appear to be harsh and arbitrary; or whether to-day, in its more extreme forms at any rate, it does not represent an irreconcilable reaction against all that not only British rule but Western civilization stands for.

I will not stop at present to discuss how far the lamentable deficiencies of the system of education which we have ourselves introduced into India have contributed to the Indian unrest. That that system has been productive of much good few will deny, but few also can be so blind as to ignore the fact that it tends on the one hand to create a semi-educated proletariate, unemployed and largely unemployable, and on the other hand, even where failure is less complete, to produce dangerous hybrids, more or less superficially imbued with Western ideas, and at the same time more or less completely divorced from the realities of Indian life. Many other circumstances also which have helped the promoters of disaffection I must reserve for subsequent discussion. Some of them are economic, such as the remarkable rise in prices during the last decade. This has seriously enhanced the cost of living in India and has specially affected the very classes amongst whom disaffection is most widespread. The clerk, the teacher, the petty Government official, whose exiguous salaries have remained the same, find themselves to-day relatively, and in many cases actually, worse off than the artisan or even the labourer, whose wages have in many cases risen in proportion to the increased cost of living. Plague, which in the course of the last 14 years has carried off over 6,000,000 people, and two terrible visitations of famine have caused in different parts of the country untold misery and consequent bitterness. On the other hand, the growth of commerce and industry and the growing interest taken by all classes in commercial and industrial questions have led to a corresponding resentment of the fiscal restraints placed upon India by the Imperial Government for the selfish benefit, as it is contended, of the British manufacturer and trader. Much bad blood has undoubtedly been created by the treatment of British Indians in South Africa and the attitude adopted in British Colonics generally towards Asiatic immigrants. The social relations between the two races in India itself—always a problem of infinite difficulty—have certainly not been improved by the large influx of a lower class of Europeans which the development of railways and telegraphs and other industries requiring technical knowledge have brought in their train. Nor can it be denied that the growing pressure of office work as well as the increased facilities of home leave and frequent transfers from one post to another have inevitably to some extent lessened the contact between the Anglo-Indian official and the native population. Of more remote influences which have indirectly reacted upon the Indian mind it may suffice for the present to mention the South African War, which lowered the prestige of our arms, and the Russo-Japanese War, which was regarded as the first blow dealt to the ascendency of Europe over Asia, though it may be worth noting that in his novel, "The Prince of Destiny," Mr. Surat Kumar Ghosh lays repeated emphasis on the impression produced in India some years earlier by the defeat of the Italian forces in Abyssinia. Each of the above points has its own importance and deserves to be closely studied, for upon the way in which we shall in the future handle some of the delicate questions which they raise will largely depend our failure or our success in coping with Indian unrest—that is, in preventing its invasion of other classes than those to which it has been hitherto confined. But the clue to the real spirit which informs Indian unrest must be sought elsewhere.

Two misconceptions appear to prevail very widely at home with regard to the nature of the unrest. The first is that disaffection of a virulent and articulate character is a new phenomenon in India; the second is that the existing disaffection represents a genuine, if precocious and misdirected, response on the part of the Western educated classes to the democratic ideals of the modern Western world which our system of education has imported into India. It is easy to account for the prevalence of both these misconceptions. We are a people of notoriously short memory, and when a series of sensational and dastardly crimes, following on a tumultuous agitation in Bengal and a campaign of incredible violence in the native Press, at last aroused and alarmed the British public, the vast majority of Englishmen were under the impression that since the black days of the Mutiny law and order had never been seriously assailed in India, and they therefore rushed to the conclusion that, if the *pax Britannica* had been so rudely and suddenly shaken, the only possible explanation lay in some novel wave of sentiment or some grievous administrative blunder which had abruptly disturbed the harmonious relations between the rulers and the ruled. People had forgotten that disaffection in varying forms and degrees of intensity has existed at all times amongst certain sections of the population, and under the conditions of our rule can hardly be expected to disappear altogether. Whether British statesmanship has always sufficiently reckoned with its existence is another question. More than 30 years ago, for instance, the Government of India had to pass a Bill dealing with the aggressive violence of the vernacular Press on precisely the same grounds that were alleged in support of this year's Press Bill, and with scarcely less justification, whilst just 13 years ago two British officials fell victims at Poona to a murderous conspiracy, prompted by a campaign of criminal virulence in the Press, closely resembling those which have more recently robbed India of many valuable lives.

To imagine that Indian unrest has been a sudden growth because its outward manifestations have assumed new and startling forms of violence is a dangerous delusion ; and no less misleading is the assumption that it is merely the outcome of Western education or the echo of Western democratic aspirations, because it occasionally, and chiefly for purposes of political expediency, adopts the language of Western demagogues. Whatever its modes of expression, its mainspring is a deep-rooted antagonism to all the principles upon which Western society, especially in a democratic country like England, has been built up. It is in that antagonism—in the increasing violence of that antagonism—which is a conspicuous feature of the unrest, that the gravest danger lies.

But if in this respect the problems with which we are confronted appear to me more serious and complex than official optimism is sometimes disposed to admit, I have no hesitation is saying that there is no cause for despondency if we will only realize how strong our position in India still is, and use our strength wisely and sympathetically, but, at the same time, with firmness and consistency. It is important to note at the outset that the more dangerous forms of unrest are practically confined to the Hindus, and amongst them to a numerically small proportion of the vast Hindu community. Not a single Mahomedan has been implicated in, though some have fallen victims to, the criminal conspiracies of the last few years. Not a single Mahomedan of any account is to be found in the ranks of disaffected politicians. For reasons, in fact, which I shall set forth later on, it many be confidently asserted that never before have the Mahomedans of India as a whole identified their interests and their aspirations so closely as at the present day with the consolidation and permanence of British rule. It is almost a misnomer to speak of Indian unrest. Hindu unrest would be a far more accurate term, connoting with far greater precision the forces underlying it, though to use it without reservation would be to do a grave injustice to the vast numbers of Hindus who are as yet untainted with disaffection. These include almost all the Hindu ruling chiefs and landed aristocracy, as well as the great mass of the agricultural classes which form in all parts of India the overwhelming majority of the population. Very large areas, moreover, are still entirely free from unrest, which, except for a few sporadic outbreaks in other districts, has been hitherto mainly confined to three distinct areas—the Mahratta Deccan, which comprises a great part of the Bombay Presidency and several districts of the Central Provinces, Bengal, with the new province of Eastern Bengal, and the Punjab. In those regions it is the large cities that have been the real hot-beds of unrest, and, great as is their influence, it must not be forgotten that in India scarcely one-tenth of the population lives in cities, or even in small townships with more than 5,000 inhabitants. Whereas in England one-third of the population is gathered together in crowded cities of 100,000 inhabitants and over, there are but twenty-eight cities of that size in the whole of India, with an aggregate population of less than 7,000,000 out of a total of almost 300,000,000.

That a movement confined to a mere fraction of the population of India has no title to be called a "national" movement would scarcely need to be argued, even if the variegated jumble of races and peoples, castes and creeds that make up the population of India were not in itself an antithesis to all that the word "national" implies. Nevertheless it would be equally foolish to underrate the forces which underlie this movement, for they have one common *nexus*, and a very vital one. They are the dominant forces of Hinduism—forces which go to the very root of a social and religious system than which none in the history of the human race has shown greater vitality and stability. Based upon caste, the most rigid of all social classifications, Hinduism has secured for some 3,000 years or more to the higher castes, and especially to the Brahmans, the highest of all castes, a social supremacy for which there is no parallel elsewhere. At the same time, inflexibly as they have dominated Hinduism, these higher castes have themselves preserved a flexibility of mind and temper which has enabled them to adapt themselves with singular success to the vicissitudes of changing times without any substantial sacrifice of their inherited traditions and aspirations. Thus it is amongst high-caste Hindus that for the last three-quarters of a century English education has chiefly spread, and, indeed, been most eagerly welcomed; it is amongst them that British administration has recruited the great majority of its native servants in every branch of the public service; it is amongst them also that are chiefly recruited the liberal professions, the Press, the schoolmasters—in fact all those agencies through which public opinion and the mind of the rising generation are most easily moulded and directed. That it is amongst them also that the spirit of revolt against British ascendency is chiefly and almost exclusively rife constitutes the most ominous feature of Indian unrest.

CHAPTER II.

SWARAJ ON THE PLATFORM AND IN THE PRESS.

Before proceeding to describe the methods by which Indian unrest has been fomented, and to study as far as possible its psychology, it may be well to set forth succinctly the political purpose to which it is directed, as far as there is any unity of direction. One of the chief difficulties one encounters in attempting to define its aims is the vagueness that generally characterizes the pronouncements of Indian politicians. There is, indeed, one section that makes no disguise either of its aspirations or of the way in which it proposes to secure their fulfilment. Its doctrines are frankly revolutionary, and it openly preaches propaganda by deed—*i.e.*, by armed revolt, if and when it becomes practicable, and, in the meantime, by assassination, dynamite outrages, dacoities, and all the other methods of terrorism dear to anarchists all over the world. But that section is not very numerous, nor would it in itself be very dangerous, if it did not exercise so fatal a fascination upon the immature mind of youth. The real difficulty begins when one comes to that much larger section of "advanced" politicians who are scarcely less bitterly opposed to the maintenance of British rule, but, either from prudential motives or lest they should prematurely alarm and alienate the representatives of what is called "moderate" opinion, shrink from the violent assertion of India's claim to complete political independence and, whilst helping to create the atmosphere that breeds outrages, profess to deprecate them.

The difficulty is further enhanced by the reluctance of many of the "moderates" to break with their "advanced" friends by proclaiming, once and for all, their own conviction that within no measurable time can India in her own interests afford to forgo the guarantees of internal peace and order and external security which the British *Raj* alone can afford. Hence the desire on both sides to find some common denominator in a nebulous formula which each can interpret as to time and manner according to its own desires and aims. That formula seems to have been discovered in the term *Swaraj*, or self-rule, which, when euphemistically translated into Colonial self-government for India, offers the additional advantage of presenting the political aspirations of Indian "Nationalism" in the form least likely to alarm Englishmen, especially those who do not care or wish to look below the surface and whose sympathies are readily won by any catchword that appeals to sentimental Liberalism. Now if *Swaraj*, or Colonial self-government, represents the *minimum* that will satisfy Indian Nationalists, it is important to know exactly what in their view it really means. Fortunately on this point we have some *data* of indisputable authority. They are furnished in the speeches of an "advanced" leader, who does not rank amongst the revolutionary extremists, though his refusal to give evidence in the trial of a seditious newspaper with which he had been connected brought him in 1907 within the scope of the Indian Criminal Code. Mr. Bepin Chandra Pal, a high-caste Hindu and a man of great intellectual force and high character, has not only received a Western education, but has travelled a great deal in Europe and in America, and is almost as much at home in London as in Calcutta. A little more than three years ago he delivered in Madras a series of lectures on the "New Spirit," which have been republished in many editions and may be regarded as the most authoritative programme of "advanced" political thought in India. What adds greatly to the significance of those speeches is that Mr. Pal borrowed their keynote from the Presidential address delivered in the preceding year by the veteran leader of the "moderates," Mr. Dadabhai Naoroji, at the annual Session of the Indian National Congress. The rights of India, Mr. Naoroji had said, "can be comprised in one word—self-government or *Swaraj*, like that of the United Kingdom or the Colonies." It was reserved for Mr. Pal to define precisely how such *Swaraj* could be peacefully obtained and what it must ultimately lead to. He began by brushing away the notion that any political concessions compatible with the present dependency of India upon Great Britain could help India to *Swaraj*. I will quote his own words, which already foreshadowed the contemptuous reception given by "advanced" politicians to the reforms embodied in last year's Indian Councils Act :—

You may get a High Court judgeship here, membership of the Legislative Council there, possibly an Executive Membership of the Council. Or do you want an expansion of the Legislative Councils ? Do you want that a few Indians shall sit as your representatives in the House of Commons ? Do you want a large number of Indians in the Civil Service ? Let us see whether 50, 100, 200, or 300 civilians will make the Government our own. . . . The whole Civil Service might be Indian, but the Civil servants have to carry out orders—they cannot direct, they cannot dictate the policy. One swallow does not make the summer. One civilian, 100 or 1,000 civilians in the service of the British Government will not make that Government Indian. There are traditions, there are laws, there are policies to which every civilian, be he black or brown or white, must submit, and as long as these traditions have not been altered, as long as these principles have not been amended, as long as that policy has not been radically changed, the supplanting of European by Indian agency will not make for self-government in this country.

Nor is it from the British Government that Mr. Pal looks for, or would accept, *Swaraj* :—

If the Government were to come and tell me to-day " Take *Swaraj*," I would say thank you for the gift, but I will not have that which I cannot acquire by my own hand. . . . Our programme is that we shall so work in the country, so combine the resources of the people, so organize the forces of the nation, so develop the instincts of freedom in the community, that by this means we shall—*shall* in the imperative—compel the submission to our will of any power that may set itself against us.

Equally definite is Mr. Pal as to the methods by which *Swaraj* is to be made "imperative." They consist of *Swadeshi* in the economic domain, *i.e.*, the encouragement of native industries reinforced by the boycott of imported goods which will kill British commerce and, in the political domain, passive resistance reinforced by the boycott of Government service.

They say :—Can you boycott all the Government offices ? Whoever said that we would ? Whoever said that there would not be found a single Indian to serve the Government or the European community here ? But what we can do is this. We can make the Government impossible without entirely making it impossible for them to find people to serve them. The administration may be made impossible in a variety of ways. It is not actually that every deputy magistrate should say : I won't serve in it. It is not that when one man resigns nobody will be found to take his place. But if you create this spirit in the country the Government service will gradually imbibe this spirit, and a whole office may go on strike. That does not put an end to the administration, but it creates endless complications in the work of administration, and if these complications are created in every part of the country, the administration will have been brought to a deadlock and made none the less impossible, for the primary thing is the prestige of the Government and the boycott strikes at the root of that prestige. . . . We can reduce every Indian in Government service to the position of a man who has fallen from the dignity of Indian citizenship. . . . No man shall receive social honours because he is a Hakim or a Munsiff or a Huzur Sheristadar. . . . No law can compel one to give a chair to a man who comes to his house. He may give it to an ordinary shopkeeper; he may refuse it to the Deputy Magistrate or the Subordinate Judge. He may give his daughter in marriage to a poor beggar, he may refuse her to the son of a Deputy Magistrate, because it is absolutely within his rights, absolutely within legal bounds.

Passive resistance is recognized as legitimate in England. It is legitimate in theory even in India, and if it is made illegal by new legislation, these laws will infringe on the primary rights of personal freedom and will tread on dangerous grounds. Therefore it seems to me that by means of the boycott we shall be able to do the negative work that will have to be done for the attainment of *Swaraj.* Positive work will have to be done. Without positive training no self-government will come to the boycotter. It will (come) through the organization of our village life; of our talukas and districts. Let our programme include the setting up of machinery for popular administration, and running parallel to, but independent of, the existing administration of the Government. . . . In the Providence of God we shall then be made rulers over many things. This is our programme.

But Mr. Pal himself admits that even if this programme can be fulfilled, this *Swaraj*, this absolute self-rule which he asks for, is fundamentally imcompatible with the maintenance of the British connexion.

Is really self-government within the Empire a practicable ideal? What would it mean? It would mean either no real self-government for us or no real overlordship for England. Would we be satisfied with the shadow of self-government? If not, would England be satisfied with the shadow of overlordship? In either case England would not be satisfied with a shadowy overlordship, and we refuse to be satisfied with a shadowy self-government. And therefore no compromise is possible under such conditions between self-government in India and the overlordship of England. If self-government is conceded to us, what would be England's position not only in India, but in the British Empire itself? Self-government means the right of self-taxation; it means the right of financial control; it means the right of the people to impose protective and prohibitive tariffs on foreign imports. The moment we have the right of self-taxation, what shall we do? We shall not try to be engaged in this uphill work of industrial boycott. But we shall do what every nation has done. Under the circumstances in which we live now, we shall impose a heavy prohibitive protective tariff upon every inch of textile fabric from Manchester, upon every blade of knife that comes from Leeds. We shall refuse to grant admittance to a British soul into our territory. We would not allow British capital to be engaged in the development of Indian resources, as it is now engaged. We would not grant any right to British capitalists to dig up the mineral wealth of the land and carry it to their own isles. We shall want foreign capital. But we shall apply for foreign loans in the open market of the whole world, guaranteeing the credit of the Indian Government, the Indian nation, for the repayment of the loan, just as America has done and is doing, just as Russia is doing now, just as Japan has been doing of late. And England's commercial interests would not be furthered in the way these are being furthered now, under the conditions of popular self-government, though it might be within the Empire. But what would it mean within the Empire? It would mean that England would have to enter into some arrangement with us for some preferential tariff. England would have to come to our markets on the conditions that we would impose upon her for the purpose, if she wanted an open door in India, and after a while, when we have developed our resources a little and organized our industrial life, we would want the open door not only to England, but to every part of the British Empire. And do you think it is possible for a small country like England with a handful of population, although she might be enormously wealthy, to compete on fair and equitable terms with a mighty continent like India, with immense natural resources, with her teeming populations, the soberest and most abstemious populations known to any part of the world?

If we have really self-government within the Empire, if we have the rights of freedom of the Empire as Australia has, as Canada has, as England has to-day, if we, 300 millions of people, have that freedom of the Empire, the Empire would cease to be British. It would be the Indian Empire, and the alliance between England and India would be absolutely an unequal alliance. That would be, if we had really self-government within the Empire, exactly the relation as co-partners in a co-British or anti-British Empire of the future; and if the day comes when England will be reduced to the alternative of having us as an absolutely independent people or a co-partner with her in the Empire, she would prefer to have us, like the Japanese, as an ally and no longer a co-partner, because we are bound to be the predominant partner in this Imperial firm. Therefore no sane Englishman, politician or publicist can ever contemplate seriously the possibility of a self-governing India, like the self-governing colonies, forming a vital and organic part of the British Empire. Therefore it is that Lord Morley says that so long as India remains under the control of Great Britain the government of India must continue to be a personal and absolute one. Therefore it seems to me that this ideal, the practically attainable ideal of self-government within the Empire, when we analyse it with care, when we study it in the light of common human psychology, when we study it in the light of our past experience of the racial characteristics of the British people, when we study it in the light of past British history in India and other parts of the world, when we study and analyse this ideal of self-government within the Empire, we find it is a far more impracticable thing to attain than even our ideal *Swaraj*.

I have quoted Mr. Pal's utterances at some length, because they are the fullest and the most frank exposition available of what lies beneath the claim to Colonial self-government as it is understood by "advanced" politicians. No one can deny the merciless logic with which he analyses the inevitable results of *Swaraj*, and Englishmen may well be grateful to him for having disclosed them so fearlessly. British sympathizers who are reluctant to look behind a formula which commends itself to their peculiar predilections, naturally dislike any reference to Mr. Pal's interpretation of Indian "self-government," and would even impugn his character in order the better to question his authority. But they cannot get over the fact that in India, very few "moderate" politicians have had the courage openly to repudiate his programme, though many of them realize its dangers, whilst the "extremists" want a much shorter cut to the same goal. It is only by pledging itself to *Swaraj* that the Indian National Congress has been able to maintain a semblance of unity.

Moreover, if any doubt still lingers as to the inner meaning of *Swaraj* and *Swadeshi*, and other kindred war-cries of Indian Nationalism, the language of the Nationalist Press remains on record to complete our enlightenment. However incompatible with the maintenance of British rule may be the propositions set forth by Mr. Bepin Chandra Pal, they contain no incitement to violence, no virulent diatribes against Englishmen. It is in the Press rather than on the platform that Indian politicians, whether "extreme" or merely "advanced," are apt to let themselves go. They write down to the level of their larger audiences. So little has hitherto been done to enlighten public opinion at home as to the gravity of the evil which the recent Indian Press law has at last, though very tardily, done something to repress that many Englishmen are still apparently disposed to regard that measure as an oppressive, or at least dubious, concession to bureaucratic impatience of criticism none the less healthy for being sometimes excessive[1]. The following quotations, taken from vernacular papers before the new Press law was enacted, will serve to show what Lord Morley meant when he said, " You may put picric acid in the ink and the pen just as much as in any steel bomb," and again, " It is said that these incendiary articles are 'mere froth.' Yes, they are froth, but froth stained with bloodshed." Even when they contain no definite incitement to murder, no direct exhortation to revolt, they will show how systematically, how persistently the wells of Indian public opinion have been poisoned for years past by those who claim to represent the intelligence and enlightenment of modern India. Only too graphically also do they illustrate one of the most unpleasantly characteristic features of the literature of Indian unrest—namely, its insidious appeals to the Hindu Scriptures and the Hindu deities, and its deliberate vilification of everything English. Calumny and abuse, combined with a wealth of sacred imagery, supply the place of any serious process of reasoning such as is displayed in Mr. Pal's programme with all its uncompromising hostility.

In the first place, a few specimens of the hatred which animates the champions of *Swaraj*—of Indian independence or, at least, of Colonial self-government. The *Hind Swarajya* is nothing if not plain-spoken :—

> Englishmen ! Who are Englishmen ? They are the present rulers of this country. But how did they become our rulers ? By throwing the noose of dependence round our necks, by making us forget our old learning, by leading us along the path of sin, by keeping us ignorant of the use of arms. . . . Oh ! my simple countrymen ! By their teaching adultery has entered our homes, and women have begun to be led astray. . . . Alas ! Has India's golden land lost all her heroes ? Are all eunuchs, timid and afraid, forgetful of their duty, preferring to die a slow death of torture, silent witnesses of the ruin of their country ? Oh ! Indians, descended from a race of heroes ! Why are you afraid of Englishmen ? They are not gods, but men like yourselves, or, rather, monsters who have ravished your Sita-like beauty [Sita, the spouse of Rama, was abducted by the demon Ravana, and recovered with the help of the Monkey God Hanuman and his army of monkeys]. If there be any Rama amongst you, let him go forth to bring back your Sita. Raise the banner of Swadesh, crying Victory to the Mother ! Rescue the truth and accomplish the good of India.

The Calcutta *Yugantar* argues that "sedition has no meaning from the Indian standpoint."

> If the whole nation is inspired to throw off its yoke and become independent, then in the eye of God and the eye of justice whose claim is more reasonable, the Indian's or the Englishman's ? The Indian has come to see that independence is the panacea for all his evils. He will therefore even swim in a sea of blood to reach his goal. The British

dominion over India is a gross myth. It is because the Indian holds this myth in his bosom that his sufferings are so great to-day. Long ago the Indian Rishis [inspired sages] preached the destruction of falsehood and the triumph of truth. And this foreign rule based on injustice is a gross falsehood. It must be subverted and true *Swadeshi* rule established. May truth be victorious!

The *Gujarat* hails the Hindu New Year which is coming "to take away the curse of the foreigners":—

Oh noble land of the Aryas, thou who wert so great art like a caged bird. Are thy powerful sons, Truth and Love, dead? Has thy daughter Lakshmi plunged into the sea? or art thou overwhelmed with grief because rogues and demons have plundered thee? [" Demons " is the term usually affected by Nationalist journalists when they refer to Englishmen.]

The *Shakti* declares that:—

By whatever names—anarchists, extremists, or seditionists —those may be called who are taking part in the movement for independence, whatever efforts may be made to humiliate and to crush them, however many patriots may be sent to jail, or into exile, yet the spirit pervading the whole atmosphere will never be checked, for the spirit is so strong and spontaneous that it must clearly be directed by Divine Providence.

The following appears in the *Kal* (Poona):—

We Aryans are no sheep. We have our own country, our religion, our heroes, our statesmen, our soldiers. We do not owe them to contact with the English. These things are not new to us. When the ancestors of those who boast to-day of their enterprise and their civilization were in a disgusting state of barbarism, or rather centuries before then, we were in full possession of all the ennobling qualities of head and heart. This holy and hoary land of ours will surely regain her position and be once more by her intrinsic lustre the home of wealth, arts, and peace. A holy inspiration is spreading, that people must sacrifice their lives in the cause of what has once been determined to be their duty. Heroes are springing up in our midst, though brutal imprisonment reduce them to skeletons. Let us devote ourselves to the service of the Mother. A man maddened by devotion will do everything and anything to achieve his ideal. His strength will be adamantine. Just as a widow immolates herself on the funeral pyre of her husband, let us die for the Mother.

The *Dharma* (Calcutta) emphasizes specially the religious side of the movement :—

We are engaged in preaching religion and we are putting our energy into this agitation, looking on it as the principal part of our religion. . . . The present agitation, in its initial stages, had a strong leaven of the spirit of Western politics in it, but at present a clear consciousness of Aryan greatness and a strong love and reverential spirit towards the Motherland have transformed it into a shape in which the religious element predominates. Politics is part of religion, but it has to be cultivated in an Aryan way, in accordance with the precepts of Aryan religion.

Nowhere is the cult of the "terrible goddess," worshipped under many forms, but chiefly under those of Kali and Durga, more closely associated with Indian unrest than in Bengal. Hence the frequency of the appeals to her in the Bengal Press. The *Dacca Gazette* welcomes the festival of Durga with the following outburst :—

Indian brothers ! There is no more time for lying asleep. Behold, the Mother is coming. Oh Mother, the giver of all good ! Turn your eyes upon your degraded children. Mother, they are now stricken with disease and sorrow. Oh Shyama, the reliever of the three kinds of human afflictions, relieve our sorrows. Come Mother, the destroyer of the demons, and appear at the gates of Bengal.

The Barisal *Hitaishi* refers also to the Durga festival, in which the weird and often horrible and obscene rites of *Shakti* worship not infrequently play a conspicuous part :—

What have we learnt from the *Shakti Puja* ? Sooner or later this great *Puja* will yield the desired results. When the Hindus realize the true magnificence of the worship of the Mother, they will be roused from the slumber of ages, and the auspicious dawn of awakenment will light up the horizon. You must acquire great power from the worship of the Mother. Ganesh, the god who grants success, has his seat assigned to him on the left of the great Mother. Why should you despair of obtaining success? Look at Kartiki, the god who is the chief commander of the armies of the gods, who has stationed himself to the right of the Mother; he is coming forward with his bow, to assist you against the demons of sin, who stand in the way of your accomplishing that great object, and as he is up in arms, who can resist?

The *Khulnavasi* breaks out into poetry:—

For what sins, O Mother Durga, are thy sons thus dispirited and their hearts crushed with injustice? The demons are in the ascendant, and constantly triumphing over godliness. Awake, Oh Mother, who tramplest on the demons! Thy helpless sons, lean for want of food, worn out in the struggle with the demons, are struck with terror at the way in which they are being ruled. Famine and plague and disease are rife, and unrighteousness triumphs. Awake, Oh Goddess Durga! I see the lightning flashing from the point of thy bow, the world quaking at thy frowns, and creation trembling under thy tread. Let a river of blood flow, overwhelming the hearts of the demons.

The *Kalyani* chides the Hindus for breaking their *Swadeshi* vows to Durga:—

You have made all sorts of vows to stick to Swadeshi, but you are still using *bilati* [foreign] salt, sugar, and cloths which are polluted with the blood and fat of animals. You swear by the Mother, and then you go and disobey her and defile her temples. Do you know that it is owing to your sins that Mother Durga has not come to accept your worship in Bengal this year? In fact, she is heaving deep sighs of sorrow—sighs which will bring a cataclysmic storm upon you. If you still care to save your country from utter ruin, mend your ways and keep your promises to the Mother.

In other provinces where other deities are more popular it is they who are similarly called in aid. The *Bedari* of Lahore, for instance, reproduces from the Puranas the story of the tyrant Rajah Harnakath, who brought death on himself at the hands of Vishnu for attempting to kill his son Prahlad, whose offence was that he believed in God and championed the cause of justice, in order to liken British statesmen and Anglo-Indian officials to the wicked Rajah and the Indians to Prahlad. As most British statesmen and their representatives abroad are the enemies of liberty and justice and support slavery and oppression, the fall of Great Britain is near at hand, and India will then pass into the possession of her own sons.

The *Prem* of Firozpur is inclined even to give Mr. Keir Hardie a niche in the Hindu Pantheon. Its editor dreamt he was at a meeting in a free and contented country. It was attended by some other Indians, and one of them recited verses bewailing the condition of India, which was once a heaven on earth and was now converted into a hell by its foreign rulers, &c. After prayers had been recited for India, some heavenly beings appeared, one of whom swore to do his best to relieve the sufferings of Indians. The editor learnt on inquiry that the dream country was England, the Indian speaker Bepin Chandra Pal, and the heavenly being Mr. Keir Hardie!

The *Sahaik*, of Lahore, furnishes an apt illustration of the scurrilous abuse and calumny which constitute one of the favourite weapons of Hindu writers. Referring to the Malaria Conference held last year, it begins by remarking that when a famine occurs—

relief works are opened only when the sufferings of the famine-stricken become acute, and their supervision is entrusted to a fat-salaried Englishman who swallows up half the collections, which amount could have fed hundreds of the poor people. Thus also with the forthcoming inquiries concerning malarial fever, which is spreading all over the country. Every Indian knows that, like the plague, this form of fever is due to the poverty and consequent physical weakness of the people. It is, however, to the mosquito that the authorities went for the causes of the disease, just as to the rats for the causes of plague. Different medicines and instruments were invented for extirpating the insect, doctors were also employed, and rewards paid for the writing of books. In this way crores of rupees went into the pockets of English shopkeepers and others. A trial is now being given to quinine, and lakhs-worth sold to Indians, English quinine manufacturers being thus enriched. Again a commission is about to sit on the heights of Simla. The commissioners will enjoy feasts and dances and drink brandy which will cost poor natives lakhs of rupees, and afterwards they will devise means to develop the trade in quinine or other drugs.

The Ranjpur *Vartabaha* writes that in the local charitable dispensary a surgical operation was performed on a patient who died in two hours, and that a similar operation on a pregnant woman resulted in her death. It adds, with delicate sarcasm, that "the Chief Medical Officer should get his salary increased." The idea that Englishmen deliberately want to depopulate India is one that is sedulously propagated. Thus the *Jhang Sial* jeers at British "generosity," which has "converted India, one of the richest countries in the world, into the land of the starving," and British "wisdom" for wishing to "starve out the natives and reign over empty brick and mortar buildings."

The *Akash* (Delhi), referring to the pension granted to the widow of Sir W. Curzon Wyllie, asks whether "the English can hold up their heads after this. Even their widows are fed by India. A nation whose widows are fed by another should never boast that it is an Imperial and self-respecting nation."

In the same spirit another Punjab paper argues ironically from the speech of a Mahomedan member of the Punjab Legislative Council in condemnation of Dhingra that "all the white-skinned Europeans, including the English rulers of India, must be the lowest born people in the world, seeing that they are in the habit of killing natives every day."

No public servants who venture to discharge their duty loyally fare worse at the hands of the Nationalist Press than Judges—especially if they are Indians. Mr. Justice

Davar was the Parsee Judge who sentenced Tilak. The *Kesari* declared that "he had already settled the sentence in his own mind after a careful consideration of external circumstances," and "had made himself the laughing-stock of the whole world, like the meddlesome monkey in the fable who came to grief in trying to pull out the peg from a half-sawed beam." Now the *Kesari* was Tilak's own paper, and he was convicted on two seditious articles that had appeared in its columns, but the *Kal*, another Poona sheet, also maintained that everything was done on a prearranged plan. "There is no sense in saying that Mr. Tilak was sentenced according to law. There was mockery of justice, not justice." It added that "if the Hindus are to suppose Mr. Tilak guilty because an English Court of Justice had condemned him, Christians will have to forswear Christ because He was crucified by a Roman Court." The *Karnatak Vaibhav* recalled the story of the notorious washerman who, by scandalizing Rama, had been immortalized in the Ramayana. In the same way the names of Strachey—who sentenced Tilak at his first trial in 1897—and Davar would be remembered as long as history endured.

Quotations could be multiplied *ad infinitum* and *ad nauseam* from the same papers—I have given only one from each—and from scores of others. These will suffice to show what the freedom of the Press stood for in India, in a country where there is an almost superstitious reverence for, and faith in, the printed word, where the influence of the Press is in proportion to the ignorance of the vast majority of its readers, and where, unfortunately, the more violent and scurrilous a newspaper becomes, the more its popularity grows among the very classes that boast of their education. They are by no means obscure papers, and some of them, such as the *Kal*, the *Hind Swarajya*, and especially the *Yugantar*, which became at one time a real power in Bengal, achieved a circulation hitherto unknown to the Indian Press. Can any Englishman, however fervent his faith in liberty, regret that some at least of these papers have now disappeared either as the result of prosecutions under the Indian Criminal Code or from the operation of the new Press Law? The mischief they have done still lives and will not be easily eradicated. It is the fashion in certain quarters to reply :—"But look at the Anglo-Indian newspapers, at the aggressive and contemptuous tone they assume towards the natives of India, at the encouragement they constantly give to racial hatred." Though I am not concerned to deny that, in the columns of a few English organs, there may be occasional lapses from good taste and right feeling, such sweeping charges against the Anglo-Indian Press as a whole are absolutely grotesque, and its most malevolent critics would be at a loss to quote anything, however remotely, resembling the exhortations to hatred and violence which have been the stock-in-trade not only of the most popular newpapers in the vernaculars, but of some even of the leading newspapers published in English, but edited and owned by Indians.

Even such extracts as I have given above from vernacular newspapers do not by any means represent the lengths to which Indian "extremism" can go. They represent merely the literature of unrest which has been openly circulated in India. There is another and still more poisonous form which is smuggled into India from abroad and surreptitiously circulated.

CHAPTER III.

A Hindu Revival.

Thirty years ago, when I first visited India, the young Western-educated Hindu was apt to be, at least intellectually, *plus royaliste que le roi*. He plucked with both hands at the fruits of the tree of Western knowledge. Some were enthusiastic students of English literature, and especially of English poetry. They had their Wordsworth and their Browning Societies. Others steeped themselves in English history and loved to draw their political inspiration from Milton and Burke and John Stuart Mill. Others, again, were the humble disciples of Kant and Schlegel, of Herbert Spencer and Darwin. But whatever their special bent might be, the vast majority professed allegiance to Western ideals, and if they had not altogether—and often far too hastily—abjured, or learned secretly to despise, the beliefs and customs of their forefathers, they were at any rate anxious to modify and bring them into harmony with those of their Western teachers. They may often have disliked the Englishman, but they respected and admired him ; if they resented his frequent assumption of unqualified superiority, they were disposed to admit that it was not without justification. The enthusiasm kindled in the first half of the last century by the great missionaries, like Carey and Duff, who had made distinguished converts among the highest classes of Hindu society, had begun to wane ; but if educated Hindus had grown more reluctant to accept the dogmas of Christianity, they were still ready to acknowledge the superiority of Western ethics, and the Brahmo Samaj in Bengal, the Prarthana Samaj in Bombay, the Social Reform movement which found eloquent advocates all over India, and not least in Madras, and other agencies of a similar character for purging Hindu life of its more barbarous and superstitious associations, bore witness to the ascendency which Western standards of morality exercised over the Hindu mind. Keshub Chunder Sen was not perhaps cast in so fine a mould as Ram Mohan Roy or the more conservative Dr. Tagore, but his ideals were the same, and his life-dream was to find a common denominator for Hinduism and Christianity which should secure a thorough reform of Hindu society without denationalizing it.

Nor were the milder forms of political activity promoted by the founders of the Indian National Congress inconsistent with the acceptance of British rule or with the recognition of the great benefits which it has conferred upon India, and least of all with a genuine admiration for Western civilization. For many of them at least the political boons which they craved from their rulers were merely the logical corollaries of the moral and intellectual as well as of the material boons which they had already received. The fierce political agitation of later years denies the benefits of British rule and even the superiority of the civilization for which it stands. It has invented the legend of a golden age, when all the virtues flourished and India was a land flowing with milk and honey until British lust of conquest brought it to ruin. No doubt even to-day there are many eminent Hindus who would still rely upon the older methods, and who have sufficiently assimilated the education they have received at the hands of Englishmen to share wholeheartedly the faith and pride of the latter in British ideals of liberty and self-government, and to be honestly convinced that those ideals might be more fully realized in the government of their own country if British administrators would only repose greater confidence in the natives of India and give them a larger share in the conduct of public affairs. But men of this type are now to be found chiefly amongst the older generation.

No one who has studied, however scantily, the social and religious system which for the sake of convenience we call Hinduism will deny the loftiness of the philosophic conceptions which underlie even the extravagances of its creed or the marvellous stability of the complex fabric based upon its social code. It may seem to us to present in many of its aspects an almost unthinkable combination of spiritualistic idealism and of gross materialism, of asceticism and of sensuousness, of overweening arrogance when it identifies the human self with the universal self and merges man in the Divinity and the Divinity in man, and of demoralizing pessimism when it preaches that life itself is but a painful illusion, and that the sovereign remedy and end of all evils is non-existence. Its mythology is often as revolting as the rigidity of its caste laws, which condemn millions of human beings to such social abasement that their very touch—the very shadow thrown by their body—is held to pollute the privileged mortals who are born into the higher castes. Nevertheless, Hinduism has for more than thirty centuries responded to the social and religious aspirations of a considerable fraction of the human race. It represents a great and ancient civilization, and that the Hindus should cling to it is not surprising. Nor is it surprising that after the first attraction exerted by the impact of an alien civilization equipped with all the panoply of organized force and scientific achievements had worn off, a certain reaction should have ensued. In the same way it was inevitable that, after the novelty of British rule, of the law and order and security for life and property which it had established, had gradually worn away, those who had never experienced the evils from which it had freed India should begin to chafe under the restraints which it imposed. What is disheartening and alarming are the lengths to which this reaction has been carried. For among the younger generation of Hindus there has unquestionably grown up a deep-seated and bitter hostility not only to British rule and to British methods of administration, but to all the influcnces of Western civilization, and the rehabilitation of Hindu customs and beliefs has proceeded *pari passu* with the growth of political disaffection.

Practices which an educated Hindu would have been at pains to explain away, if he had not frankly repudiated them thirty years ago, now find zealous apologists. Polytheism is not merely extolled as the poetic expression of eternal verities, but the gods and goddesses of the Hindu pantheon are being invested with fresh sanctity. The Brahmo Samaj is still a great influence for good, but it appears to be gradually losing vitality, and though its literary output is still considerable, its membership is shrinking. The Prarthana Samaj is moribund. The fashion of the day is for religious "revivals," in which the worship of Kali, the sanguinary goddess of destruction, or the cult of Shivaji-Maharaj, the Mahratta chieftain who humbled in his day the pride of the alien conquerors of Hindustan, plays an appropriately conspicuous part. The Arya-Samaj, which is spreading all over the Punjab and in the United Provinces, represents in one of its aspects a revolt against Hindu orthodoxy, but in another it represents equally a revolt against Western ideals, for in the teachings of its founder, Dayanand, it has found an aggressive gospel which bases the claims of Aryan, *i.e.*, Hindu, supremacy on the Vedas as the one ultimate source of human and Divine wisdom. The exalted character of Vedantic philosophy has been as widely recognized among European students as the subtle beauty of many of the Upanishads, in which the cryptic teachings of the Vedas have been developed along different and often conflicting lines of thought to suit the eclecticism of the Hindu mind. But the Arya-Samaj has not been content to assert the ethical perfection of the Vedas. In its zeal to proclaim the immanent superiority of Aryan civilization—it repudiates the term Hindu as savouring of an alien origin—over Western civilization, it claims to have discovered in the Vedas the germs of all the discoveries of modern science, even to wireless telegraphy and aeroplanes.

Just as the political agitation in India has derived invaluable encouragement from a handful of British members of Parliament and other sympathizers in Europe and America, so this Hindu revival has been largely stimulated and to some extent prompted by Europeans and Americans. Not only the writings of English and German scholars, like Max Müller and Deutsch, helped enormously to revive the interest of educated Hindus in their ancient literature and earlier forms of religion, but it was in the polemical tracts of European writers that the first protagonists of Hindu reaction against Christian influences found their readiest weapons of attack. The campaign was started in 1887 by the Hindu Tract Society of Madras, which set itself first to inflame popular fanaticism against the missionaries, who, especially in the south of India, had been the pioneers of Western education. Bradlaugh's text-books and the pamphlets of many lesser writers belonging to the same school of thought were eagerly translated into the vernacular, and those that achieved the greatest popularity were books like "The Evil of Continence," in which not only Christian theology, but Christian morality was held up to scorn and ridicule. The advent of the theosophists, heralded by Madame Blavatsky and Colonel Olcott, gave a fresh impetus to the revival, and certainly no Hindu has done so much to organize and consolidate the movement as Mrs. Annie Besant, who, in her Central Hindu College at Benares and her Theosophical

Institution at Adyar, near Madras, has openly proclaimed her faith in the superiority of the whole Hindu system to the vaunted civilization of the West. Is it surprising that Hindus should turn their backs upon our civilization[2] when a European of highly-trained intellectual power and with an extraordinary gift of eloquence comes and tells them that it is they who possess and have from all times possessed the key to supreme wisdom ; that their gods, their philosophy, their morality are on a higher plane of thought than the West has ever reached ? Is it surprising that with such encouragement Hinduism should no longer remain on the defensive, but, discarding in this respect all its own traditions as a non-proselytizing creed, should send out missionaries to preach the message of Hindu enlightenment to those still groping in the darkness of the West ? The mission of Swami Vivekananda to the Chicago Congress of Religions is in itself one of the most striking incidents in the history of Hindu revivalism, but it is perhaps less wonderful than the triumph he achieved when he returned to India accompanied by a chosen band of eager disciples from the West.

There are, indeed, endless forms to this revival of Hinduism—as endless as to Hinduism itself—but what it is perhaps most important for us to note is that, wherever political agitation assumes the most virulent character, there the Hindu revival also assumes the most extravagant shapes. Secret societies place their murderous activities under the special patronage of one or other of the chief popular deities. Their vows are taken " on the sacred water of the Ganges," or " holding the sacred Tulsi plant," or " in the presence of Mahadevi " —the great goddess who delights in bloody sacrifices. Charms and amulets, incantations and imprecations, play an important part in the ceremonies of initiation. In some quarters there has been some recrudescence of the *Shakti* cultus, with its often obscene and horrible rites, and the unnatural depravity which was so marked a feature in the case of the band of young Brahmans who conspired to murder Mr. Jackson at Nasik represents a form of erotomania which is certainly much more common amongst Hindu political fanatics than amongst Hindus in general.

By no means all, however, are of this degenerate type, and the *Bhagvat Gita* has been impressed into the service of sedition by men who would have been as incapable of dabbling in political as in any other form of crime, had they not been able to invest it with a religious sanction. There is no more beautiful book in the sacred literature of the Hindus ; there is none in which the more enlightened find greater spiritual comfort ; yet it is in the *Bhagvat Gita* that, by a strange perversion, the Hindu conspirator has sought and claims to have found texts that justify murder as a divinely inspired deed when it is committed in the sacred cause of Hinduism. Nor is it only the extremists who appeal in this fashion to Hindu religious emotionalism. It is often just as difficult to appraise the subtle differences which separate the "moderate" from the "advanced" politician and the "advanced" politician from the extremist as it is to distinguish between the various forms and gradations of the Hindu revival in its religious and social aspects. But it was in the court-yard of the great temple of Kali at Calcutta in the presence of "the terrible goddess" that the "leaders of the Bengali nation," men who, like Mr. Surendranath Banerjee, have always professed to be "moderates," held their chief demonstrations against "partition" and administered the *Swadeshi* oath to their followers. Equally noteworthy is the part played by the revival of Ganpati celebrations in honour of Ganesh, the elephant-headed god, perhaps the most popular of all Hindu deities, in stimulating political disaffection in the Deccan.

Hand in hand with this campaign for the glorification of Hinduism at the expense of Western civilization there has been carried on another and far more invidious campaign for the vilification of everything British. The individual Englishman is denounced as a bloodsucker and a tyrant ; his personal integrity is impugned and derided ; his methods of administration are alleged to be wilfully directed to the impoverishment, and even to the depopulation, of India ; his social customs are traduced as depraved and corrupt ; even his womenfolk are accused of common wantonness. This systematized form of personal calumny is a scarcely less significant feature of the literature of Indian unrest than its appeals to the Hindu scriptures and to the Hindu deities and its exploitation of the religious sentiment for the promotion of racial hatred. *Swadeshi* and *Swaraj* are the battle-cries of this new Hindu " nationalism," but they mean far more than a mere claim to fiscal or even political independence. They mean an organized uplifting of the old Hindu traditions, social and religious, intellectual and moral, against the imported ideals of an alien race and an alien civilization, and the sincerity of some, at least, of the apostles of this new creed cannot be questioned. With Mr. Arabindo Ghose, they firmly believe that " the whole moral strength of the country is with us, justice is with us, nature is with us, and the law of God, which is higher than any human law, justifies our action."

This is a grave phenomenon not to be contemptuously dismissed as the folly of ill-digested knowledge or summarily judged and condemned, in a spirit of self-righteousness, as an additional proof of the innate depravity and ingratitude of the East. It undoubtedly represents a deep stirring of the waters amongst a people endowed with no mean gifts of head and heart, and if it has thrown up much scum, it affords glimpses of nobler elements which time may purify and bring to the surface. Nor if our rule and our civilization are to prevail must we be unmindful of our own responsibility or forget that our presence and the influences we brought with us first stirred the waters.

The part played by Brahmanism in Indian unrest is far more conspicuous in some parts of India than in others, and for reasons which are generally not far to seek. Wherever it has been most active, it connotes perhaps more than anything else the reactionary side of that unrest. Though there have been and still are many enlightened Brahmans who have cordially responded to the best influences of Western education, and have worked with admirable zeal and courage to bridge the gulf between Indian and European civilization, Brahmanism as a system represents the antipodes of all that British rule must stand for in India, and Brahmanism has from times immemorial dominated Hindu society —dominated it, according to the Hindu Nationalists, for its salvation. "If," writes one of them, "Mother India, though reduced to a mere skeleton by the oppression of alien rulers during hundreds of years, still preserves her vitality, it is because the Brahmans have never relaxed in their devotion to her. She has witnessed political and social revolutions. Famines and pestilence have shorn her of her splendour. But the Brahmans have stood by her through all the vicissitudes of fortune. It is they who raised her to the highest pinnacle of glory, and it is they whose ministrations still keep up the drooping spirits of her children."

The Brahmans are the sacerdotal caste of India. They are at the same time the proudest and the closest aristocracy that the world has ever seen, for they form not merely an aristocracy of birth in the strictest sense of the term, but one of divine origin. Of the Brahman it may be said as of no other privileged mortal except perhaps the Levite of the Old Testament : *Nascitur non fit.* No king, however powerful, can make or unmake a Brahman, no genius, however transcendent, no services, however conspicuous, no virtues, however pre-eminent, can avail to raise a Hindu from a lower caste to the Brahman's estate. In early times the caste laws must have been less rigid, for otherwise there would only be

Aryan Brahmans, whereas in the South of India there are many Brahmans of obviously Dravidian stock. But to-day not even the Brahmans themselves can raise to their own equal one who is not born of their caste, though by the exercise of the castely authority they can in specific cases outcaste a fellow-Brahman who has offended against the immutable laws of caste, and, except for minor transgressions which allow of atonement and reinstatement, when once outcasted he and his descendants cease for ever to be Brahmans. The Brahmans might be at a loss to make good their claim that they date back to the remote ages of the Vedas. But a good deal more than two thousand years have passed since they constituted themselves the only authorized intermediaries between mankind and the gods. In them became vested the monopoly of the ancient language in which all religious rites are performed, and with a monopoly of the knowledge of Sanskrit they retained a monopoly of learning long after Sanskrit itself had become a dead language. Like the priests who wielded a Latin pen in the Middle Ages in Europe, they sat as advisers and conscience-keepers in the councils of every Hindu ruler. To the present day they alone can expound the Hindu scriptures, they alone can approach the gods in their temples, they alone can minister to the spiritual needs of such of the lower castes as are credited with sufficient human dignity to be in any way worthy of their ministrations.

In the course of ages differences and distinctions have gradually grown up amongst them, and they have split up into innumerable septs and sub-castes. As they multiplied from generation to generation an increasing proportion were compelled to supplement the avocations originally sacred to their caste by other and lowlier means of livelihood. There are to-day over 14 million Brahmans in India, and a very large majority of them have been compelled to adopt agricultural, military, and mercantile pursuits which, as we know from the Code of Manu, were already regarded as, in certain circumstances, legitimate or excusable for a Brahman even in the days of that ancient law-giver. In regard to all other castes, however, the Brahman, humble as his worldly *status* may be, retains an undisputed pre-eminence which he never forgets or allows to be forgotten, though it may only be a pale reflection of the prestige and authority of his more exalted caste-men—a prestige and authority, be it added, which have often been justified by individual achievements. How far the influence of Brahmanism as a system has been socially a good or an evil influence I am not concerned to discuss, but, however antagonistic it may be at the present moment to the influence of Western civilization, it would be unfair to deny that it has shown itself and still shows itself capable of producing a very high type both of intellect and of character. Nor could it otherwise have survived as it has the vicissitudes of centuries.

Neither the triumph of Buddhism, which lasted for nearly 500 years, nor successive waves of Mahomedan conquest availed to destroy the power of Brahmanism, nor has it been broken by British supremacy. Inflexibly as he dominates a social system in all essentials more rigid than any other, the Brahman has not only recognized the need of a certain plasticity in its construction which allows for constant expansion, but he has himself shown unfailing adaptability in all non-essentials to varying circumstances. To the requirements of their new Western masters the Brahmans adapted themselves from the first with admirable suppleness, and when a Western system of education was introduced into India in the first half of the last century, they were quicker than any other class to realize how it could be used to fortify their own position. The main original object of the introduction of Western education into India was the training of a sufficient number of young Indians to fill the subordinate posts in the public offices with English-speaking natives. The Brahmans responded freely to the call, and they soon acquired almost the same monopoly of the new Western learning as they had enjoyed of Hindu lore through the centuries. With the development of the great administrative services, with the substitution of English for the vernacular tongues as the only official language, with the remodelling of judicial administration and procedure on British lines, with the growth of the liberal professions and of the Press, their influence constantly found new fields of activity, whilst through the old traditional channels it continued to permeate those strata of Hindu society with which the West had established little or no contact.

Nevertheless the spread of Western ideas and habits was bound to loosen to some extent the Brahmans' hold upon Hindu society, for that hold is chiefly rooted in the immemorial sanctity of custom, which new habits and methods imported from the West necessarily tended to undermine. Scrupulous—and, according to many earnest Englishmen, over-scrupulous—as we were to respect religious beliefs and prejudices, the influence of Western civilization could not fail to clash directly or indirectly with many of the ordinances of Hindu orthodoxy. In non-essentials Brahmanism soon found it expedient to relax the rigour of caste obligations, as for instance to meet the hard case of young Hindus who could not travel across the "black water" to Europe for their studies without breaking caste, or indeed travel even in their own country in railways and river steamers without incurring the pollution of bodily contact with the "untouchable" castes. Penances were at first imposed which had gradually to be lightened until they came to be merely nominal. Graver issues were raised when such ancient customs as infant marriage and the degradation of child widows were challenged. The ferment of new ideas was spreading amongst the Brahmans themselves. Some had openly discarded their ancestral faith, and many more were moved to search their own scriptures for some interpretation of the law less inconsistent with Western standards. It seemed at one moment as if, under the inspiration of men like Ranade in the Deccan and Tagore in Bengal, Brahmanism itself was about to take the lead in purging Hinduism of its most baneful superstitions and bringing it into line with the philosophy and ethics of the West. But the liberal movement failed to prevail against the forces of popular superstition and orthodox bigotry, combined with the bitterness too frequently resulting from the failure of Western education to secure material success or even an adequate livelihood for those who had departed from the old ways. Though there have been and still are many admirable exceptions, Brahmanism remained the stronghold of reaction against the Western invasion. Of recent years, educated Brahmans have figured prominently in the social and religious revival of Hinduism, and they have figured no less prominently, whether in the ranks of the extremists or amongst the moderate and advanced politicians, in the political movement which has accompanied that revival.

CHAPTER IV.

Brahmanism and Disaffection in the Deccan.

Fundamental as is the antagonism between the civilization represented by the British *Raj* and the essential spirit of Brahmanism, it is not, of course, always or everywhere equally acute, for there is no more uniformity about Brahmanism than about any other Indian growth. But in the Deccan Brahmanism has remained more fiercely militant than in any other part of India, chiefly perhaps because nowhere had it wielded such absolute power within times which may still be called recent. Far into the eighteenth century Poona had been the capital of a theocratic State in which behind the throne of the Peshwas both spiritual and secular authority were concentrated in the hands of the Brahmans. Such memories are slow to die and least of all in an ancient and conservative country like India, and there was one sept of Brahmans, at any rate, who were determined not to let them die.

The Chitpavan Brahmans are undoubtedly the most powerful and the most able of all the Brahmans of the Deccan. A curious legend ascribes their origin to the miraculous intervention of Parashurama, the sixth Avatar of the god Vishnu, who finding no Brahmans to release him by the accustomed ritual from the defilement of his earthly labours, dragged on to shore the bodies of fourteen barbarians that he had found washed up from the ocean, burnt them on a funeral pyre and then breathed life and Brahmanhood into their ashes. On these new made Brahmans he conferred the name Chitpavan, which means "purified by fire," and all the land of the Konkan from which, by a bolt from his arrow, he caused the sea for ever to recede. Every Chitpavan to-day claims descent from one or other of the fourteen divinely Brahmanized barbarians, whom some believe to have been hardy Norsemen driven in their longships on to the sandy shores of what is now the Bombay Presidency. At any rate, as has been well said of them, Western daring and Eastern craft look out alike from the alert features and clear parchment skin and through the strange stone-grey eyes of the Chitpavan. It was not, however, till about two centuries ago that the Chitpavan Brahmans began to play a conspicuous part in Indian history, when one of this sept, Balaji Vishvanath Rao, worked his way up at the Court of the Mahratta King Shahu to the position of Peshwa, or Prime Minister, which he succeeded even in bequeathing to his son, the great Bajirao Balaji, who led the Mahratta armies right up to the walls of Delhi. Bajirao's son not only succeeded as Balaji II., but on the death of King Shahu disposed of his Royal master's family by a bold Palace conspiracy and openly assumed sovereign powers. The crushing defeat of Panipat brought him to his grave, and though the dynasty was still continued, and regained some of its lustre under Madhao Rao I., the Peshwas subsequently became little more than *rois fainéants* in the hands of their Ministers, and especially in those of the great Regent Nana Phadnavis. He, too, was a Chitpavan Brahman, and it was under his reign that his fellow caste-men acquired so complete a monopoly of all the chief offices of State that the Mahratta Empire became essentially a Chitpavan Empire. The British arms ultimately defeated the dreams of universal dominion which, in the then condition of India, the Chitpavans might well have hoped to establish on the ruins of the great Moghul Empire. But Br.tish rule did not destroy their power. They were quick to adapt themselves to new conditions and above all to avail themselves of the advantages of Western education. Their great administrative abilities compelled recognition, and Chitpavans swarm to-day in every Government office of the Deccan as they did in the days of Nana Phadnavis. They sit on the Bench, they dominate the Bar, they teach in the schools, they control the vernacular Press, they have furnished almost all the most conspicuous names in the modern literature and drama of Western India as well as in politics. Of the higher appointments held by natives in the Presidency of Bombay, the last census tells us that the Hindus held 266 against 86 held by Parsees and 23 held by Mahomedans, and that out of those held by the Hindus, more than 72 per cent. were held by Brahmans, though the Brahmans form less than one-fourteenth of the total Hindu population of the province. All Brahmans are not, of course, Chitpavans, but the Chitpavans supply an overwhelming majority of these Government officials, and their ascendency over every other Brahman sept in Maharashtra is undisputed. From the Deccan, moreover, their influence has spread practically all over India and, especially, in the native States, which have recruited amongst the Chitpavans some of their ablest public servants. Amongst Chitpavans are to be found many of the most enlightened and progressive Indians of our times and many have served the British *Raj* with unquestioned loyalty and integrity. But amongst many others—perhaps indeed amongst the great majority—there has undoubtedly been preserved for the last hundred years from the time of the downfall of the Peshwa dominion to the present day, an unbroken tradition of hatred towards British rule, an undying hope that it might some day be subverted and their own ascendency restored. Not to go back to the exploits of Nana Sahib, himself a Chitpavan, and his followers during the Mutiny, or to the Ramoshi rebellion round Poona in 1879, it was in Poona that the native Press, mainly conducted by Brahmans, first assumed that tone of virulent hostility towards British rule and British rulers which led to the Press Act of 1879, and some of the worst extracts quoted at that time by the Government of India in support of that measure were taken from Poona newspapers. It was in Poona that some years later the assassination of two English officials by a young Chitpavan Brahman was the first outcome of a fresh campaign, leading directly to political murder. It was by another Chitpavan Brahman that Mr. Jackson was murdered last December at Nasik; his accomplices were with one exception Chitpavan Brahmans, and to the same sept of Brahmans belong nearly all the defendants in the great conspiracy trial now proceeding at Bombay.

But if there were already, more than 20 years ago, wild and irreconcilable spirits bent on fomenting disaffection, there were amongst the Deccanee Brahmans themselves a small intellectual *élite* who, though by no means servile apologists of British rule, fully realized that their primary duty was not to stir up popular passion against alien rulers, but to bring Hindu society into closer communion with the higher civilization which those rulers, whatever their shortcomings, undoubtedly represented. Conspicuous amongst such men was Mahadev Govind Ranade. Equally conspicuous in the opposite camp was a man of a very different stamp, Bal Gangadhar Tilak, who was destined to become one of the most dangerous pioneers of disaffection. It was a Hindu gentleman and a Brahman who told me that if I wanted to study the psychology of Indian unrest I should begin by studying Tilak's career. "Tilak's onslaught in Poona upon Ranade, his alliance with the bigots of orthodoxy, his appeals to popular superstition in the new Ganpati celebrations, to racial fanaticism in the 'Anti-Cow-killing Movement,' to Mahratta sentiment in the cult which he introduced of Shivaji, his active propaganda amongst schoolboys and students, his gymnastic societies, his preaching in favour of physical training, and last but not least his control of the Press and the note of personal violence which he imparted to newspaper polemics, represent the progressive stages of a highly-organized campaign which has served as a model to the apostles of unrest all over India." This was a valuable piece of advice, for, if any one can claim to be truly the father of Indian unrest, it is Bal Gangadhar Tilak. The story of his initial campaign in the Deccan, though it dates back to the closing decades of the last century, is still well worth studying, and has, in fact, never received adequate attention, for on the one hand it pricks the shallow view that Indian unrest is merely an echo of the Japanese victories in Manchuria, and, on the other hand, it illustrates clearly the close connexion that exists between the forces of Indian political disaffection and those of social and religious reaction, whilst the methods which he employed and the results which attended his activity have been reproduced with singular fidelity in subsequent phases of the movement.

When Tilak entered upon public life in the early eighties, the Brahmans of the Deccan were divided into two camps, one of which, headed at first by the late Mr. Justice Ranade, consisted of a small intellectual *élite*, who held, without forgoing their right to criticize British administrators or to promote political reforms by constitutional methods, that Indians of all creeds, including the Hindus, should begin by reforming their own social institutions, and bring them into greater harmony with Western standards. Tilak, a Chitpavan Brahman of considerable erudition, who had graduated with honours at Bombay, had, however, inherited his full share of Chitpavan hostility to British ascendency. He was also by temperament and ambition impatient of all restraint, and jealous of the commanding authority which a man like Ranade owed quite as much to the nobility of his character as to his social position and force of intellect. In opposition to Ranade, with whom he had at first co-operated as an educationist, Tilak drifted rapidly into the reactionary camp. The battle was first engaged over the control of the Poona Sarvajanik Sabha and the Education Society, two progressive associations which, though mainly composed of Brahmans, included a sprinkling of Mahomedans and of non-Brahman Hindus. Tilak had thrown himself into journalism, and after the repeal of the Indian Press Law on the return of a Liberal Administration to office at home in 1881, he had been amongst the first to revive the incendiary methods which it had temporarily and very successfully checked. His first onslaught upon Ranade's position, however, failed, and instead of supplanting him, it was he who was compelled in 1890 to sever his connexion with the Education Society.

Tilak's defeat was short lived. The introduction of the Age of Consent Bill, in 1890, to mitigate the evils of Hindu child-marriage, gave him a fresh opening. Ranade, discouraged and alarmed by the violence of the Tilak party, had by this time retired from the forefront of the fray, but in Dr. Bhandarkar, Mr. Justice Tilang, Mr. A. K. Nulkar, Mr. (now Sir N. G.) Chandavarkar, and other courageous Hindu reformers, with whom Mr. Gokhale was always ready to co-operate against the forces of religious superstition, he had left disciples ready to carry on the good fight. Tilak raised against them a storm of passion and prejudice. In the columns of the *Kesari*, of which he had become sole proprietor, he denounced every Hindu who supported the measure as a renegade and a traitor to the cause of Hinduism, and thus won the support of conservative orthodoxy, which had hitherto viewed with alarm some of his literary excursions into the field of Vedantic exegesis. With the help of the brothers Natu, who were the recognized leaders of Hindu orthodoxy, he carried his propaganda into the schools and colleges in the teeth of the Moderate party, and, proclaiming that unless they learnt to employ force the Hindus must expect to be impotent witnesses of the gradual downfall of all their ancient institutions, he proceeded to organize gymnastic societies in which physical training and the use of more or less primitive weapons were taught in order to develop the martial instincts of the rising generation.

If amongst many Brahmans of Maharashtra hatred of the British is the dominant passion, amongst the Mahratta population at large whatever there is of racial and religious jealousy is mainly directed against the Mahomedans. This is partly, no doubt, a legacy of the old days of Mahomedan supremacy. In 1893 some riots in Bombay of a more severe character than usual gave Tilak an opportunity of broadening the new movement by enlisting in its support the old anti-Mahomedan feeling of the people. He not only convoked popular meetings in which his fiery eloquence denounced the Mahomedans as the sworn foes of Hinduism, but he started an organization known as the "Anti-Cow-Killing Society," which was intended and regarded as a direct provocation to the Mahomedans, who, like ourselves, think it no sacrilege to eat beef. In vain did liberal Hindus appeal to him to desist from these inflammatory methods. Their appeals had no effect upon him, and merely served his purpose by undermining the little authority they still possessed. Government had forbidden Hindu processions to play music whilst passing in front of Mahomedan mosques, as this was a fertile cause of riotous affrays. Tilak not only himself protested against this "interference with the liberties of the people," but insisted that the Sarvajanik Sabha should identify itself with the "national" cause and memorialize Government for the removal of a prohibition so offensive to Hindu sentiment. The Moderates hesitated, but were overawed by popular clamour and the threats of the Tilak Press. The Mahomedans and a few other members repudiated the memorial and resigned. Tilak, though not yet in absolute control of the Sabha, became already practically its master. No one knew better than he how to compel submission by packed meetings and organized rowdyism.

Tilak's propaganda had at the same time steadily assumed a more and more anti-British character, and it was always as the allies and the tools of Government, in its machinations against Hinduism, that the Hindu reformers and the Mahomedans had in turn been denounced. In order to invest it with a more definitely religious sanction, Tilak placed it under the special patronage of the most popular deity in India. Though Ganesh, the elephant-headed god, is the god of learning whom Hindu writers delight to invoke on the title-page of their books, there is scarcely a village or a frequented roadside in India that does not show some rude presentment of his familiar features, usually smeared over with red ochre. Tilak could not have devised a more popular move than when he set himself to organize annual festivals in honour of Ganesh, known as Ganpati celebrations, and to found in all the chief centres of the Deccan Ganpati societies, each with its *mela* or choir recruited among his youthful bands of gymnasts. These festivals gave occasion for theatrical performances [3] and religious songs in which the legends of Hindu mythology were skilfully exploited to stir up hatred of the "foreigner" —and *mlenccha*, the term employed for "foreigner," applied equally to Europeans and to Mahomedans—as well as for tumultuous processions only too well calculated to provoke affrays with the Mahomedans and with the police, which in turn led to judicial proceedings that served as a fresh excuse for noisy protests and inflammatory pleadings. With the Ganpati celebrations the area of Tilak's propaganda was widely increased.

But the movement had yet to be given a form which should directly appeal to the fighting instincts of the Mahrattas and stimulate active disaffection by reviving memories of olden times when under Shivaji's leadership they had rolled back the tide of Musulman conquest and created a Mahratta Empire of their own. The legends of Shivaji's prowess still lingered in Maharashtra, where the battlemented strongholds which he built crown many a precipitous crag of the Deccan highlands. In a valley below Pratabghar the spot is still shown where Shivaji induced the Mahomedan general, Afzul Khan, to meet him in peaceful conference half-way between the contending armies, and, as he bent down to greet his guest, plunged into his bowels the famous "tiger's claw," a hooked gauntlet of steel, while the Mahratta forces sprang out of ambush and cut the Mahomedan army to pieces. But if Shivaji's memory still lived, it belonged to a past which was practically dead and gone. Only a few years before an Englishman who had visited Shivaji's tomb had written to a local newspaper calling attention to the ruinous condition into which the people of Maharashtra had allowed the last resting-place of their national hero to fall. Some say it was this letter which first inspired Tilak with the idea of reviving Shivaji's memory and converting it into a living force. Originally it was upon the great days of the Poona Peshwas that Tilak had laid the chief stress, and he may possibly have discovered that theirs were not after all names to conjure with amongst non-Brahman Mahrattas, who had suffered heavily enough at their hands. At any rate, Tilak brought Shivaji to the forefront and set in motion a great "national" propaganda which culminated in 1895 in the celebration at all the chief centres of Brahman activity in the Deccan of Shivaji's reputed birthday, the principal commemoration being held under Tilak's own presidency at Raighar, where the Mahratta chieftain had himself been crowned. What was the purpose and significance of this movement may be gathered from a *Shlok* or sacred poem improvised on this occasion by one of Tilak's disciples who was soon to acquire sinister notoriety.

Let us be prompt like Shivaji to engage in desperate enterprises. Take up your swords and shields and we shall cut off countless heads of enemies. Listen! Though we shall have to risk our lives in a national war, we shall assuredly shed the life-blood of our enemics.

It was on the occasion of the Shivaji "coronation festivities" that the right—nay, the duty—to commit murder for political purposes was first publicly expounded. With Tilak in the chair, a Brahman professor got up to vindicate Shivaji's bloody deed :—

Who dares to call that man a murderer who, when only nine years old, had received Divine inspiration not to bow down before a Mahomedan Emperor? Who dares to condemn Shivaji for disregarding a minor duty in the performance of a major one? Had Shivaji committed five or fifty crimes more terrible, I would have been equally ready to prostrate myself not once but one hundred times before the image of our lord Shivaji . . . Every Hindu, every Mahratta must rejoice at this spectacle, for we too are all striving to regain our lost independence, and it is only by combination that we can throw off the yoke.

Tilak himself was even more outspoken :—

It is needless to make further researches as to the killing of Afzul Khan. Let us even assume that Shivaji deliberately planned and executed the murder. Was the act good or evil? This question cannot be answered from the standpoint of the Penal Code or of the laws of Manu or according to the principles of morality laid down in the systems of the West or of the East. The laws which bind society are for common folk like you and me No one seeks to trace the genealogy of a Rishi or to fasten guilt upon a Maharaj. Great men are above the common principles of morality. Such principles do not reach to the pedestal of a great man. Did Shivaji commit a sin in killing Afzul Khan? The answer to this question can be found in the Mahabharata itself. The Divine Krishna teaching in the Gita tells us we may kill even our teachers and our kinsmen, and no blame attaches if we are not actuated by selfish desires. Shivaji did nothing from a desire to fill his own belly. It was in a praiseworthy object that he murdered Afzul Khan for the good of others. If thieves enter our house and we have not strength to drive them out, should we not without hesitation shut them in and burn them alive? God has conferred on the *mlencchas* (foreigners) no grant of Hindustan inscribed on imperishable brass. Shivaji strove to drive them forth out of the land of his birth, but he was guiltless of the sin of covetousness. Do not circumscribe your vision like frogs in a well. Rise above the Penal Code into the rarefied atmosphere of the sacred Bhaghavad Gita and consider the action of great men.

In the reflected blaze of this apotheosis of Shivaji, Tilak stood forth as the appointed leader of the "nation." He was the triumphant champion of Hindu orthodoxy, the high-priest of Ganesh, the inspired prophet of a new "nationalism," which in the name of Shivaji would cast out the hated *mlencchas* and restore the glories of Mahratta history. The Government feared him, for people could put no other construction on the official confirmation of his election when he was returned in 1895 as a member of the Bombay Legislative Council—above all, when inside tho Council-room he continued with the same audacity and the same impunity his campaign of calumny and insult. His activity was unceasing. He disdained none of the arts which make for popularity. His house was always open to those who sought in the right spirit for assistance or advice. He had absolute control of the Sabha and ruled the municipality of Poona. In private and in public, through his speeches and through his newspapers, he worked upon the prejudices and passions of both the educated and the uneducated, and especially upon the crude enthusiasm of the young. Towards the end of 1896 the Deccan was threatened with famine. Hungry stomachs are prompt to violence, and Tilak started a "no-rent" campaign. Like all Tilak's schemes in those days it was carefully designed to conceal as far as possible any direct incitement to the withholding of land revenue. His missionaries went round with a story that Government had issued orders not to collect taxes where the crops had fallen below a certain yield. The *rayats* believed them, and when the tax-gatherer arrived they refused payment.

Trouble then arose. Outrages such as the mutilation of the Queen's statue at Bombay, the attempt to fire the Church Mission Hall, the assaults upon "moderate" Hindus who refused to toe the line, became ominously frequent. Worse was to follow when the plague appeared. The measures at first adopted by Government to check the spread of this new visitation doubtless offended in many ways against the customs and prejudices of the people, especially the searching and disinfection of houses, and the forcible removal of plague-patients even when they happened to be Brahmans. What Tilak could do by secret agitation and by a rabid campaign in the Press to raise popular resentment to a white heat he did. The *Kesari* published incitements to violence which were put into the mouth of Shivaji himself [4]. The inevitable consequences ensued. On June 27, 1897, on their way back from an official reception in celebration of Queen Victoria's Diamond Jubilee, Mr. Rand, an Indian civilian, who was President of the Poona Plague Committee, and Lieutenant Ayerst, of the Commissariat Department, were shot down by Damodhar Chapekur, a young Chitpavan Brahman, on the Ganeshkind road. No direct connexion has been established between that crime and Tilak. But, like the murderer of Mr. Jackson at Nasik last winter, the murderer of Rand and Ayerst—the same young Brahman who had recited the *Shlok*, which I have quoted above, at the great Shivaji celebration—declared that it was the doctrines expounded in Tilak's newspapers that had driven him to the deed. The murderer who had merely given effect to the teachings of Tilak was sentenced to death, but Tilak himself, who was prosecuted for a seditious article published a few days before the murder, received only a short term of imprisonment, and was released before the completion of his term under certain pledges of good behaviour which he broke as soon as it suited him to break them.

Thus ended the first campaign of Indian unrest, which, even in its details, has served as an incitement and a model to all those who have conducted subsequent operations in the same field.

The Poona murders sent a thrill of horror throughout India and caused a momentary sensation even in England. But though Government was not wholly blind to the warning, it could not decide what ought to be done, and beyond tinkering at one or two sections of the Criminal Code bearing on Press offences, it did nothing until history had repeated itself on a much larger scale. Tilak was generously released from prison before the expiration of his sentence, and his release was construed in the Deccan as a fresh triumph. He was acclaimed by his followers as a "national" martyr and hero. After a short "rest-cure" in a sanatorium Tilak returned to the *Kesari*, which, in the hands of his coadjutors, two other Chitpavan Brahmans, Mr. Kelkar and Mr. Khadilkar, had lost nothing of its vitriolic pungency in his absence. The celebration with renewed pomp in 1900 of Shivaji's "birthday" at Raighar marked the resumption of Tilak's operations. I need not stop to recount all the incidents of this second campaign in the Deccan, in which Ganpati celebrations, Shivaji festivals, gymnastic societies, &c., played exactly the same part as in the first campaign. For three or four years the Tai Maharaj case, in which, as executor of one of his friends, Shri Baba Maharaj, a Sirdar of Poona, Tilak was attacked by the widow and indicted on charges of forgery, perjury, and corruption, absorbed a great deal of his time, but, after long and wearisome proceedings, the earlier stages of the case ended in a judgment in his favour which was greeted as another triumph for him, and not unnaturally though, as recent developments have shown, quite prematurely,[5] won him much sympathy, even amongst those who were politically opposed to him. But throughout this ordeal Tilak never relaxed his political activity either in the Press or in the manifold organizations which he controlled.

His influence, moreover, was rapidly extending far beyond Poona and the Deccan. He had at an early date associated himself with the Indian National Congress, and he was secretary of the Standing Committee for the Deccan. His Congress work had brought him into contact with the politicians of other provinces, and upon none did his teachings and his example produce so deep an impression as upon the emotional Bengalees. He had not the gift of sonorous eloquence which they possess, and he never figured conspicuously as an orator at the annual sessions of Congress. But his calculating resourcefulness and his indomitable energy, even his masterfulness, impressed them all the more, and in the two memorable sessions held at Benares in 1905 and at Calcutta in 1906, when the agitation over the Partition of Bengal was at its height, his was the dominant personality, not at the tribune, but in the lobbies. He had been one of the first champions of *Swadeshi* as an economic weapon in the struggle against British rule, and he saw in the adoption of the boycott, with all the lawlessness which it involved, an unprecedented opportunity of stimulating the active forces of disaffection. As far as Bengal was concerned, an "advanced" Press which always took its cue from Tilak's *Kesari* had already done its work, and Tilak could rely upon the enthusiastic support of men like Mr. Bepin Chandra Pal and Mr. Arabindo Ghose, who were politically his disciples, though their religious and social standpoints were in many respects different. Mr. Surendranath Banerjee, who subsequently fell out with Tilak, had at first modelled his propaganda very largely upon that of the Deccan leader. Not only had he tried to introduce into Bengal the singularly inappropriate cult of Shivaji, but he had been clearly inspired by Tilak's methods in placing the *Swadeshi* boycott in Bengal under the special patronage of so popular a deity as the "terrible goddess" Kali. Again, he had followed Tilak's example in brigading schoolboys and students into youthful gymnastic societies for purposes of political agitation. Tilak's main object at the moment was to pledge the rest of India, as represented in the Congress, to the violent course upon which Bengal was embarking. Amongst the "moderate" section outside Bengal there was a disposition to confine its action to platonic expressions of sympathy with the Bengalees and with the principle of *Swadeshi*—in itself perfectly legitimate—as a movement for the encouragement of native industries. At Benares in 1905 the Congress had adopted a resolution which only conditionally endorsed the boycott, and the increasing disorders which had subsequently accompanied its enforcement had tended to enhance rather than to diminish the reluctance of the Moderate party to see the Congress definitely pledged to it when it met at the end of 1906 in Calcutta. The "advanced" party led by Mr. Bepin Chandra Pal had put forward Tilak's candidature to the presidency, and a split which seemed imminent was only avoided by a compromise which saved appearances. Sir Pherozeshah Mehta, a leading Parsee of Bombay, who had been drawn into co-operation with the Congress under the influence of the political Liberalism which he had heard expounded in England by Gladstone and Bright, played at this critical period an important part which deserves recognition. He was as eloquent as any Bengalee, and he possessed in a high degree the art of managing men. In politics he was as stout an opponent of Tilak's violent methods as was Mr. Gokhale on social and religious questions, and he did perhaps more than any one else to prevent the complete triumph of Tilakism in the Congress right down to the Surat upheaval. Thanks largely to his efforts, the veteran Mr. Naoroji was elected to the chair at Calcutta. None could venture openly to oppose him, for he was almost the father of the Congress, which in its early days had owed so much to the small group of liberal Parsees whom he had gathered about him, and his high personal character and rectitude of purpose had earned for him universal respect. Nevertheless, a resolution as amended by Tilak was adopted which, without mentioning the word "boycott," pledged the Congress to encourage its practice. But there was considerable heartburning, and the Moderates were suspected of contemplating some retrograde move at the following annual session. Tilak was determined to frustrate any such scheme, and before the Congress assembled at Surat he elaborated at a Nationalist conference, with Mr. Arabindo Ghose in the chair, a plan of campaign which was to defeat the "moderates" by demanding, before the election of the president, an undertaking that the resolutions of the Calcutta conference should be upheld. The plan, however, was only half successful. The first day's proceedings produced a violent scene in which the howling down of Mr. Surendranath Banerjee by the "advanced" wing revealed the personal jealousies that had grown up between the old Bengalee leader on the one hand and Tilak and his younger followers in Bengal on the other. The second day's proceedings ended in still wilder confusion, and after something like a free fight the Congress broke up after an irreparable rupture, from which its prestige has never recovered.

Tilak's own prestige, however, with the "advanced" party never stood higher, either in the Deccan or outside of it. In the Deccan he not only maintained all his old activities, but had extended their field. Besides the *Kal*, edited by another Chitpawan Brahman, and the *Rashtramat* at Poona, which went to even greater lengths than Tilak's own *Kesari*, lesser papers obeying his inspiration had been established in many of the smaller centres. A movement had been set on foot for the creation of "national" schools, entirely independent of State support, and therefore of State supervision, in which disaffection could, without let or hindrance, be made part and parcel of the curriculum. Such were the schools closed down last year in the Central Provinces and this year at Telegaon. The great development of the cotton industry during the last ten years, especially in Bombay itself—which has led to vast agglomerations of labour under conditions unfamiliar in India—had given Tilak an opportunity of establishing contact with a class of the population hitherto outside the purview of Indian politics. There are nearly 100 cotton spinning and weaving mills, employing over 100,000 operatives, congregated mostly in the northern suburbs of the city. Huddled together in huge tenements this compact population affords by its density, as well as by its ignorance, a peculiarly accessible field to the trained agitator. Tilak's emissaries, mostly Brahmans of the Deccan, brought, moreover, to their nefarious work the added prestige of a caste which seldom condescends to rub shoulders with those whose mere contact may involve " pollution." In this, as in many other cases, politics were closely mixed up with philanthropy, for the conditions of labour in India are by no means wholly satisfactory, and it would be unfair to deny to many of Tilak's followers a genuine desire to mitigate the evils and hardships to which their humbler fellow-creatures were exposed. Prominent amongst such evils was the growth of drunkenness, and it would have been all to his honour that Tilak hastened to take up the cause of temperance, had he not perverted it, as he perverted everything else, to the promotion of race-hatred. His primary motives may have been excellent, but he subordinated all things to his ruling anti-British passion, whilst the fervour of his philanthropic professions won for him the sympathy and co-operation of many law-abiding citizens who would otherwise have turned a deaf ear to his political doctrines. He must have had a considerable command of funds for the purposes of his propaganda, and though he doubtless had not a few willing and generous supporters, many subscribed from fear of the lash which he knew how to apply through the Press to the tepid and the recalcitrant, just as his gymnastic societies sometimes resolved themselves into juvenile bands of dacoities to swell the coffers of *Swaraj*. Not even Mr. Gokhale with all his moral and intellectual force could stem the flowing tide of Tilak's popularity in the Deccan ; and in order not to be swept under he was perhaps often compelled like many other

Moderates to go further than his own judgment can have approved. Tilak commanded the allegiance of barristers and pleaders, schoolmasters and professors, clerks in Government offices—in fact, of the large majority of the so-called educated classes, largely recruited amongst his own and other Brahman castes; and his propaganda had begun to filter down not only to the coolies in the cities, but even to the rayats, or at least the head-men in the villages.

More than that. From the Deccan, as we have already seen in his relations with the Indian National Congress, his influence was projected far and wide. His house was a place of pilgrimage for the disaffected from all parts of India. His prestige as a Brahman of the Brahmans and a pillar of orthodoxy, in spite of the latitude of the views which he sometimes expressed in regard to the depressed castes, his reputation for profound learning in the philosophies both of the West and of the East, his trenchant style, his indefatigable activity, the glamour of his philanthropy, his accessibility to high and low, his many acts of genuine kindliness, the personal magnetism which, without any great physical advantages, he exerted upon most of those who came in contact with him, and especially upon the young, combined to equip him more fully than any other Indian politician for the leadership of a revolutionary movement.

The appeal which Tilak made to the Hindus was twofold. He taught them, on the one hand, that India, and especially Maharashtra, the land of the Mahrattas, had been happier and better and more prosperous under a Hindu *raj* than it had ever been or could ever be under the rule of alien "demons"; and that if the British *raj* had at one time served some useful purpose in introducing India to the scientific achievements of Western civilization, it had done so at ruinous cost, both material and moral, to the Indians whose wealth it had drained and whose social and religious institutions it had undermined, and on the other hand he held out to them the prospect that, if power were once restored to the Brahmans, who had already learnt all that there was of good to be learnt from the English, the golden age would return for gods and men. That Tilak himself hardly believed in the possibility of overthrowing British rule is more than probable, but what some Indians who knew him well tell me he did believe was that the British could be driven or wearied by a ceaseless and menacing agitation into gradually surrendering to the Brahmans the reality of power, as did the later Peshwas, and remaining content with the mere shadow of sovereignty. As one of his organs blurted it out :—" If the British yield all power to us and retain only nominal control, we may yet be friends."

Such was the position when, on June 24, 1908, Tilak was arrested in Bombay on charges connected with the publication in the *Kesari* of articles containing inflammatory comments on the Muzafferpur outrage, in which Mrs. and Miss Kennedy had been killed by a bomb—the first of a long list of similar outrages in Bengal. Not in the moment of first excitement, but weeks afterwards, the *Kesari* had commented on this crime in terms which the Parsee Judge, Mr. Justice Davar, described in his summing up as follows :—" They are seething with sedition ; they preach violence ; they speak of murders with approval ; and the cowardly and atrocious act of committing murders with bombs not only meets with your approval, but you hail the advent of the bomb into India as if something had come to India for its good." The bomb was extolled in these articles as " a kind of witchcraft, a charm, an amulet," and the *Kesari* delighted in showing that neither the " supervision of the police " nor " swarms of detectives " could stop " these simple playful sports of science." Whilst professing to deprecate such methods, it threw the responsibility upon Government, which allowed " keen disappointment to overtake thousands of intelligent persons who have been awakened to the necessity of securing the rights of

Swaraj." Tilak spoke four whole days in his own defence—21½ hours altogether—but the jury returned a verdict of "Guilty," and he was sentenced to six years' transportation, afterwards commuted on account of his age and health to simple imprisonment at Mandalay.

The prosecution of a man of Tilak's popularity and influence at a time when neither the Imperial Government nor the Government of India had realized the full danger of the situation was undoubtedly a grave measure of which a weaker Government than that of Bombay under Sir George Clarke might well have shirked the responsibility. There were serious riots after the trial. From the moment of his arrest Tilak's followers had put it about amongst the mill-hands that he was in prison because he was their friend and had sought to obtain better pay for them. Some of his supporters are said to have declared during the trial that there would be a day's bloodshed for every year to which he might be sentenced by the Court, and, as a matter of fact, he was sentenced to six years' imprisonment and the riots lasted six days. The rioting assumed at times a very threatening character. The European police frequently had to use their revolvers, and the troops had several times to fire in self-defence. But rigorous orders had been issued by the authorities to avoid as far as possible the shedding of blood, and both the police and the military forces exercised such steady self-restraint that casualties were relatively few, and the violence of the mob never vented itself upon the European population of the city. The gravity of the disturbances, however, showed the extent and the lawless character of the influence which Tilak had already acquired over the lower classes in Bombay, and not merely over the turbulent mill-hands. In the heart of the city many Hindu shops were closed "out of sympathy with Tilak," and the most violent rioting on one day occurred amongst the Bhattias and Banias employed in the cloth market, who had hitherto been regarded as very orderly and rather timid folk.

The trouble in Bombay was certainly not a sudden and spontaneous outburst of popular feeling. It bore throughout the impress of careful and deliberate organization. By a happy combination of sympathy and firmness Sir George Clarke had, however, won the respect of the vast majority of the community, and though he failed to secure the active support which he might have expected from the "moderates," there were few of them who did not secretly approve and even welcome his action. Its effects were great and enduring, for Tilak's conviction was a heavy blow—perhaps the heaviest which has been dealt—to the forces of unrest, at least in the Deccan; and some months later one of the organs of his party, the *Rashtramat*, reviewing the occurrences of the year, was fain to admit that "the sudden removal of Mr. Tilak's towering personality threw the whole province into dismay and unnerved the other leaders."

The agitation in the Deccan did not die out with Tilak's disappearance, for he left his stamp upon a new generation, which he had educated and trained. More than a year after Tilak had been removed to Mandalay, his doctrines bore fruit in the murder of Mr. Jackson, the Collector of Nasik—a murder which, in the whole lamentable record of political crimes in India, stands out in many ways pre-eminently infamous and significant. The chief executive officer of a large district, "Pundit" Jackson, as he was familiarly called, was above all a scholar, devoted to Indian studies, and his sympathy with all forms of Indian thought was as genuine as his acquaintance with them was profound. His affection for the natives was such as, perhaps, to blind him to their faults, and like the earliest victims of the Indian Mutiny he entertained to the very last an almost childlike confidence in the loyalty of the whole people. Only a few days before his death he expressed his conviction that disaffection had died out in Nasik, and that he could go anywhere and at any hour without the slightest risk of danger. That he was very generally respected and even beloved by many there can be no doubt, and there is no reason to question the sincerity of the regrets which found expression on the announcement of his impending transfer to Bombay in a series of farewell entertainments, both public and private, by the inhabitants of the city. Only two days before the fatal 21st of December, an ode in Marathi addressed to him at a reception organized by the Municipal Council dwelt specially upon his gentleness of soul and kindliness of manner.

Yet this was the man whom the fanatical champions of Indian Nationalism in the Deccan singled out for assassination as a protest against British tyranny. The trial of the actual murderer and of those who aided and abetted him abundantly demonstrated the cold-blooded premeditation which characterized this crime. Numerous consultations had taken place ever since the previous September between the murderer and his accomplices as to the manner and time of the deed. It was repeatedly postponed because the accomplices who belonged to Nasik were afraid of rendering active assistance which might compromise them, though they were ready enough to arm the hand of the wretched youth from Aurungabad who had volunteered to strike the blow. Ready as he was to kill any Englishman, he himself had some misgivings as to the expediency of selecting a victim whose personal qualities were so universally recognized, and these misgivings were only allayed by the assurance that all that was mere hypocrisy on poor Jackson's part. It was the news of Jackson's approaching departure for Bombay that finally precipitated the catastrophe. The murderer practised carefully with the pistol given to him and other precautions were taken so that, even if the first attempt was foiled, Jackson should not escape alive from the theatre—the native theatre which he had been asked to honour with his attendance. So the young Chitpavan Brahman, Ananta Luxman Kanhere, waylaid the Englishman as he was entering, shot him first in the back, and then emptied the contents of his revolver upon him, as he turned round. Mr. Jackson fell dead in front of the friends who were accompanying him, two young English ladies and a young civilian of his staff, who had only joined a month before from England and faced without flinching this gruesome initiation into the service. It all happened in a moment, and the native Deputy Collector, Mr. Palshikar, who leapt forward to Mr. Jackson's assistance, was only able to strike down the murderer and tear from him the second weapon with which he was armed. Thanks also to Mr. Palshikar's presence of mind, information was at once sent to the railway station and the escape of some of the accomplices prevented, whose confessions materially helped in promoting the ends of justice.

But besides the facts which were brought out in evidence during the trial at Bombay, there are some features connected with the crime to which attention may be usefully directed, as they lie outside the province of the Law Courts. In the first place, it must be noted that not only the murderer but the majority of those implicated in the crime were Chitpavan Brahmans, and at the same time they were the strange products both of the Western education which we have imported into India and of the religious revivalism which underlies the present political agitation. They were certainly moral, if not physical, degenerates, and most of them notoriously depraved, none bearing in this respect a worse character than the actual murderer. I happened, when at Nasik, to see the latter whilst he was performing his ablutions in front of the Government building in which he was confined. Four policemen were in charge of him, but he seemed absolutely unconcerned, and after having washed himself leisurely, proceeded to discharge his devotions, looking around all the while with a certain self-satisfied composure, before returning to his cell. His appearance was puny, undergrown, and effeminate, and his small, narrow, and elongated head markedly prognathous, but he exercised over some of his companions a passionate, if unnatural, fascination which, I have been told by one who was present at the trial, betrayed itself shamelessly in their attitude and the glances they exchanged with him during the proceedings. Distorted pride of race and of caste combined with neuroticism and eroticism appear to have co-operated here in producing as complete a type of moral perversion as the records of criminal pathology can well show.

What are the secret forces by which these wretched puppets were set in motion ? Their activity was certainly not spontaneous. Who was it that pulled the strings ? There is reason to believe that the revolver with which the murder was committed was one of a batch sent out by the Indian ringleaders, who until the murder of Sir W. Curzon-Wyllie, had their headquarters at the famous "India House," in Highgate, of which Swami Krishnavarma was originally one of the moving spirits. Upon this and other cognate points the trial of Vinayak Savarkar, formerly the London correspondent of one of Tilak's organs and a familiar of the "India House," and of some twenty-five other Hindus on various charges of conspiracy which is now proceeding in the High Court of Bombay, may be expected to throw some very instructive light.

The atmosphere of Nasik was no doubt exceptionally favourable for such morbid growths. For Nasik is no ordinary provincial town of India. It is one of the great strongholds of Hinduism. Its population is only about 25,000, but of these about 9,000 belong to the Brahmanical caste, though only about 1,000 are Chitpavan Brahmans, the rest being mainly Deshastha Brahmans, another great sept of the Deccanee sacerdotal caste. It is a city of peculiar sanctity with the Hindus. The sacred Godavery—so sacred that it is called there the *Ganga*—*i.e.*, the Ganges—flows through it, and its bathing *ghats* which line the river banks and its ancient temples and innumerable shrines attract a constant flow of pilgrims from all parts of India. Indeed, many of the great Hindu houses of India maintain there a family priest to look after their spiritual interests. Nasik was, moreover, a city beloved of the Peshwas, and next to Poona preserves, perhaps, more intimate associations with the great days of the Mahratta Empire than any other city of the Deccan. But though no doubt these facts might account for a certain latent bitterness against the alien rulers who dashed the cup of victory away from the lips of the Mahrattas, just as the latter were establishing their ascendency on the crumbling ruins of the Moghul Empire, they do not suffice to account for the attitude of the people generally in presence of such a crime as the assassination of Mr. Jackson. For if murder is a heinous crime by whomsoever it may be committed, it ranks amongst Hindus as specially heinous when committed by a Brahman. How is it that in this instance, instead of outcasting the murderer, many Brahmans continued more or less secretly to glorify his crime as "the striking down of the flag from the fort"? How is it that, when there was ample evidence to show that murder had been in the air of Nasik for several months before the perpetration of the deed, not a single warning, not a single hint, ever reached Mr. Jackson, except from the police, whose advice, unfortunately, his blindly trustful nature led him to ignore to the very end? How is it that, even after its perpetration, though there was much genuine sympathy with the victim and many eloquent speeches were delivered to express righteous abhorrence of the crime, no practical help was afforded to the authorities in pursuing the ramifications of the conspiracy which had "brought disgrace on the holy city of Nasik"?

All this opens up wide fields for speculation, but there is one point which a statement solemnly made by the murderer of Mr. Jackson has placed beyond the uncertainties of speculation. In reply to the magistrate who asked him why he committed the murder, Kanhere said :—

> I read of many instances of oppression in the *Kesari*, the *Rashtramat*, and the *Kal* and other newspapers. I think that by killing *sahibs* [Englishmen] we people can get justice. I never got injustice myself nor did any one I know. I now regret killing Mr. Jackson. I killed a good man causelessly.

Can anything be much more eloquent and convincing than the terrible pathos of this confession ?[6] The three papers named by Kanhere were Tilak's organs. It was no personal experience or knowledge of his own that had driven Kanhere to his frenzied deed, but the slow persistent poison dropped into his ear by the Tilak Press. Though it was Kanhere's hand that struck down "a good man causelessly," was not Tilak rather than Kanhere the real author of the murder ? It was merely the story of the Poona murders of 1897 over again.

Other incidents besides the Nasik tragedy have occurred since Tilak's conviction to show how dangerous was the spirit which his doctrines had aroused. One of the gravest, symptomatically, was the happily unsuccessful attempt to throw a bomb at the Viceroy and Lady Minto whilst they were driving through the streets of Ahmedabad during their visit to the Bombay Presidency last November. For that outrage constituted an ominous breach of all the old Hindu traditions which invest the personal representative of the Sovereign with a special sanctity.

But in spite of spasmodic outbreaks, of which we may not yet have seen the end, aggressive disloyalty in the Deccan has been at least temporarily set back since the downfall of Tilak. The firmer attitude adopted by the Government of India and such repressive measures as the Press Act, combined with judicious reforms, have done much ; but it was by the prosecution of Tilak that the forces of militant unrest lost their ablest and boldest leader—perhaps the only one who might have concentrated their direction, not only in the Deccan, but in the whole of India, in his own hands and given to the movement, with all its varied and often conflicting tendencies, an organization and unity which it still happily seems to lack.

CHAPTER V.

Poona and Kolhapur.

It is not, after all, in British India (*i.e.*, in that part of India which we directly administer) that the Brahmanical and reactionary character of Indian unrest, at any rate in the Deccan, can best be studied. There it can always be disguised under the "patriotic" aspects of a revolt against alien rule. To appreciate its real tendencies we must go to a Native State of the Deccan about 100 miles south of Poona. Kolhapur is the most important of the Native States under the charge of the Bombay Government, and its ruler is the only ruling Mahratta chief who can claim direct descent from the great Shivaji, the "Shivaji-Maharaj" whose cult Tilak made one of the central features of his political propaganda. He is the "Chhatrapati Maharajah," and is acknowledged to be as such the head of the Mahratta Princes of India. One would have thought that such a lineage would have sufficed in itself to invest the Maharajah of Kolhapur with a certain measure of sanctity in the eyes of Tilak and his followers. Far from it. His Highness is an enlightened ruler and a man of great simplicity of character. He takes a keen interest in the administration of his State, and has undertaken, at no small cost to his Exchequer, one of the most important irrigation works yet attempted in any Native State. But he committed what Tilak and his friends regarded as two unforgivable offences : he fought against the intolerance of the Brahmans and he is a faithful friend and ally of the British *Raj*. Hence they set in motion against him, the descendant of Shivaji, in his own State, exa tly the same machinery of agitation and conspiracy which they have set in motion against British rule in British India.

It is a curious and most instructive story. There had been long minorities in Kolhapur, and, especially during the more or less nominal reign of the present Maharajah's predecessor, Sh vaji IV., who ultimately went mad, the Prime Minister, a Chitpavan Brahman of Ratnagiri, acquired almost supreme power in the State, and filled every important post with his fellow caste men, of whom he introduced more than a hundred into the public service. Under Chitpavan rule the interests of the people of the soil were systematically neglected in Kolhapur, as they had been throughout the Deccan in the later days of the Chitpavan theocracy at Poona, and privileges and possessions were showered upon members of the favoured caste. On his accession in 1894 the present Maharajah appointed as his Prime Min'ster, with a view to very necessary reforms in the administration, a Kayastha Prabhu, Rao Bahadur Sabnis, who, though a high-caste Hindu, was not a Brahman. There has long been great rivalry between the Brahmans and the Prabhus, who belong mostly to the moderate progressive school of Hinduism. The appointment of Mr. Sabnis, besides portending unpalatable reforms, was therefore in itself very unwelcome to the Ko hapur Brahmans, amongst whom one of the most influential, Mr. B. N. Joshi, the Chief Judge, was a personal friend of Tilak. Consternation increased when the young Maharajah announced his intention of promoting to positions of trust such non-Brahmans as should be found capab e of filling them and actually started educating non-Brahmans for the purpose. In order to put pressure upon their ruler, the Brahmans had recourse to one of the most powerful weapons with which the semi-religious, semi-social structure of Hinduism has armed them. They questioned his caste and refused to recite at certain religious ceremonies in his family the Vedic hymns, to which as a Kshatriya (*i.e.*, as a member of the "twice-born" caste ranking next to the Brahmans) his Highness claimed to be traditionally entitled. The stalwart Brahmans of the Deccan allege, it seems, that in this *Kali Yuga*, or Age of Darkness, there can be no Kshatriyas, since there is no room for a warrior caste in the orthodox sense under an alien rule, and that therefore the Hindus who are neither Brahmans nor pariahs can at best be Shudras—a "clean" caste, but not even entitled to wear the "sacred thread" reserved for the highest castes.

The Maharajah remained firm, for this insult, though aimed chiefly at him, affected equally all high-caste Mahrattas who were not Brahmans. To their credit be it said, several of the more progressive Brahmans, braving the pressure of their fellow caste-men at Poona and in Kolhapur itself, stood by his Highness. The dispute was aggravated when the Rajpadhya—the family priest of the Kolhapur ruling family—himself refused the Vedic ritual to his Highness, even when two Judges, both Brahmans, who were appointed to form with him a committee of three to decide the issue, pronounced in favour of the Maharajah's claim. His Highness then took the case to the Sankeshwar Shankaracharya, the highest religious authority with jurisdiction in such matters. But the feud only grew the more bitter, as, owing to the death of the incumbent of that high office, rival candidatures were put forward to the succession by the Maharajah's supporters on the one hand and by Tilak and his friends on the other. To the present day the feud continues, and the present Shankaracharya is not recognized by the Poona school of Brahmans. Nor is he likely to be, as he has had the unique courage publicly to condemn as a Brahman the murder of Mr. Jackson by Brahmans.

I have already remarked with reference to the Nasik tragedy that, if murder is a heinous crime by whomsoever committed, it ranks amongst Hindus as specially heinous when committed by a Brahman; and I have asked several Brahmans how it is that instead of outcasting the murderer many Brahmans continue more or less secretly to glorify his crime. Some have admitted that there is a strong case for the public excommunication of Brahmans guilty of political murder, some have regretted that no such action has ever been taken by the caste authorities, some have argued that caste organization has been so loosened that any collective action would be impracticable. Only in Kolhapur has a Brahman, qualified to speak with the highest religious authority in the name of Hindu sacred law, been found to have in this respect the courage of his convictions. This Brahman was no less a personage than the Shankaracharya of the Karveer Petha, who took the very noteworthy step of issuing a proclamation solemnly reprobating the murder committed by a Brahman "in the holy city of Nasik" as "a stain on the Brahmanical religion of mercy emphatically preached by Manu and other law-givers." After paying a warm tribute to Mr. Jackson's personal qualities and great learning, and quoting sacred texts to show that "such a murder is to be condemned the more when a Brahman commits it," and renders the murderer liable to the most awful penalties in the next world, the proclamation proceeded to declare that "his Holiness is pleased to excommunicate the wicked persons who have committed the present offence, and who shall commit similar offences against the State, and none of the disciples of this Petha shall have any dealings with such sinful men."

Amongst the majority of Brahmans in Kolhapur and elsewhere this proclamation, I fear, found no echo, for their hostility towards their own Maharajah had often assumed or encouraged criminal forms of violence. It had certainly not remained confined to the spiritual domain, and it became absolutely savage when, in 1902, his Highness declared that he would reserve at least half the posts in the State for qualified men of the non-Brahman communities. Under the constant inspiration of Poona, the Tilak Press waged relentless war against his Highness, preaching disaffection towards his Government, just as it preached disaffection towards the British *Raj*; and the agitation in Kolhapur itself was reinforced by the advent of a large number of Poona Brahmans who, in consequence of a recrudescence of plague, fled from that city to the Maharajah's capital. They flung themselves eagerly into the fray, and had the audacity even to start a mock "Parliament." But the Maharajah was determined to be master in his own State, and in Mr. Sabnis he had found a Prime Minister who loyally and courageously carried out his policy for the improvement of the administration and the spread of education amongst the non-Brahman castes. The Maharajah realizes that Brahman ascendency cannot be broken down permanently unless the non-Brahman castes are adequately equipped to compete with them in the public services. Amongst these there is plenty of loyalty to the ruling chief, for his Mahratta subjects have not wholly forgotten the tyranny of Chitpavan Brahman rule either under Shivaji IV.'s Prime Minister or in the less recent times of the Poona Peshwas. One of the most interesting institutions in Kolhapur is a hostel specially endowed for non-Brahman, Mahratta, Mahomedan, and Jain youths who are following the courses of the Rajaram College. The control of education plays in Kolhapur as conspicuous a part as at Poona in the struggle between the forces of order and disorder, and it is amongst the Kolhapur youth that the latter have made their most strenuous exertions and with the same lawless results.

The first organization started at Kolhapur in imitation of Poona was a Shivaji club, with which were associated bands of gymnasts, Ganpati choirs, an anti-cow-killing society, &c., all on the lines of those founded by Tilak. It was suppressed in 1900 as several of its members had been implicated in the disturbances at Bir, where a young "patriot" had proclaimed himself Rajah and collected a sufficient number of armed followers to require a military force to suppress the rebellion. The disturbances at Bir were, in fact, the starting point of that new form of political propagandism which takes the shape of dacoities or armed robberies for the benefit of the "patriotic" war-chest. After the suppression of the Kolhapur Shivaji Club, many of its leading members disappeared for a time, but only to carry on their operations in other parts of India, where they entered into relations with secret societies of a similar type. Three years later the club had been practically revived under the new name of "Belapur Swami Club," so called in honour of the late Swami of Belapur, to whose wooden slippers the members of the club were in the habit of doing worship, whilst his shrine was used as a sanctuary for sedition-mongers and a store-house for illicit weapons. "Political" dacoities were soon in vogue again, and in 1905 there was an epidemic of house-breaking in and around Kolhapur, which enriched the club with several thousands of rupees and a few arms. Seven members were finally arrested and some made full confessions. All of these except one were Brahmans and mostly quite well connected. But even those who were convicted got off with light sentences, and the campaign, which clearly had powerful aiders and abettors both inside Kolhapur and outside, was only temporarily checked.

Nor was it to stop at dacoities. A regular semi-military organization was introduced, and bands of young men used to go out into the country to carry out mimic manœuvres. It is of no slight significance that photographs have been discovered of groups of these young men—some of whom were subsequently convicted for serious offences—with Tilak himself in their midst. They were in constant communication with Poona, and when the Poona extremists began to specialize on bombs they were amongst the neophytes of the new cult. A conspiracy was hatched of which the admitted purpose was to murder Colonel Ferris, the Political Agent, at the wedding of the Maharajah's daughter on March 21, 1908, but, if it had been carried out successfully, the Maharajah himself and many of his other guests would almost inevitably have been killed at the same time. For, as was disclosed in the subsequent trial, a bomb was prepared and despatched from Poona which was to have been hurled into the wedding *pandal* or enclosure railed off in the courtyard of the Palace for the Maharajah and his family and the principal guests, including Colonel Ferris. Fortunately the bomb, which was subsequently discovered, did not reach Kolhapur in time. The conspirators had to fall back upon less potent weapons. Thanks to the Arms Act, which is one of the favourite grievances of Indian Nationalism, they had great difficulty in obtaining arms, but they secured a few, and on April 16, 1908, when Colonel Ferris, who was retiring, left Kolhapur, some of the conspirators followed him into the train, and, alighting at one of the stations, attempted to shoot him, but, again fortunately, their cartridges missed fire. A few weeks later placards giving formulæ for the making of bombs were actually posted up on the doors of schools and other buildings, and this was followed by a theft of dangerous chemicals from a Kolhapur private school. Finally ten youths, nine of whom were Brahmans, were committed for trial on these offences before a special Sessions Judge, lent by Government, and eight of them were convicted.

Quite as mueh as these convictions the downfall of Tilak helped to quell the forces of unrest in the State of Kolhapur as well as in the rest of the Deccan. For in Kolhapur, as in Poona, it was the Brahman Press controlled by Tilak that familiarized the rising generation with the idea of political murder. In the year which preceded the Kolhapur conspiracy, and just after the first dastardly bomb outrage at Muzafferpur to which Mrs. and Miss Kennedy fell victims, an article appeared in the *Vishvavritta*, a Kolhapur monthly magazine, for which its editor, Mr. Bijapurkar, a Brahman, who until 1905 had been Professor of Sanscrit at the Rajaram College, was subsequently prosecuted and convicted. The article, which was significantly headed "The potency of Vedic prayers," recalled various cases in which the Vedas lay down the duty of retaliation upon "alien" oppressors. "To kill such people involves no sin, and when Kshatryas and Vaidhyas do not come forward to kill them, Brahmans should take up arms and protect religion. When one is face to face with such people they should be slaughtered without hesitation. Not the slightest blame attaches to the slayer." Moreover, lest these exhortations should be construed merely as a philosophic treatise on Vedic teaching, the writer was careful to add that "these doctrines are not to be kept in books, but must be taught even to babes and sucklings."

Thus in a Native State of the Deccan, just as in British-administered Deccan, we find the same methods and the same doctrines adopted by the Brahmans, with the same demoralizing results, in pursuance of the same purpose, now under one guise and now under another, the maintenance or restoration of their own theocratic power, whether it be threatened by a Hindu ruler of their own race, or by "alien" rulers and the "alien" civilization for which they stand.

CHAPTER VI.

Bengal Before the Partition.

It is a far cry in every sense from the Deccan to Bengal. There is a greater diversity of races, languages, social customs, physical conditions, &c., between the different provinces of India than is often to be found between the different countries of Europe. Few differ more widely than the Deccan and Bengal—the Deccan, a great table-land raised on an average over 2,000ft. above sea level, broken by many deep-cut river valleys and throwing up lofty ridges of bare rock, entirely dependent for its rainfall upon the south-west monsoon, which alone and in varying degrees of abundancy relieves the thirst of a thin soil parched during the rest of the year by a fierce dry heat—Bengal, a vast alluvial plain, with a hot, damp climate, watered and fertilized by great rivers like the Ganges and the Brahmaputra, which drain the greater part of the Himalayas. The Deccan is thinly populated; it has no great waterways; there are few large cities and few natural facilities of communication between them, but the population, chiefly Mahratta Hindus, with a fair sprinkling of Mahomedans, survivors of the Moghul Empire, are a virile race, wiry rather than sturdy, with tenacious customs and traditions and a language —Marathi—which has a copious popular literature.

Maharashtra, moreover, has historical traditions, by no means inglorious, of its own. It has played, and is conscious of having played, a conspicuous part in the history of India down to relatively recent times; and the Brahmans of Maharashtra, who were once its rulers, have preserved to the present day the instincts and the aspirations of a ruling race, combined with great force and subtleness of intellect. In Bengal, on the other hand, there is a dense population, concentrated in part in large towns and cities along the great waterways, but also spread over the whole surface of the rich plains and deltas. The Bengalees are a quick-witted, imaginative, and warm-hearted people who have been the victims rather than the makers of history. The tide of conquest has swept over them again and again from times immemorial, but generally without leaving any lasting impression upon their elastic and rather timid temperament. With all his receptive qualities, his love of novelty and readiness to learn, his retentive memory, his luxuriant imagination, his gift of facile eloquence, the Bengalee has seldom shown himself to be a born ruler of men.

All these differences are reflected in the unrest in Bengal, though on the surface it presents a close resemblance to the unrest in the Deccan, and there have been constant contact and co-operation between the leaders. Except as a geographical expression, Bengal is practically a creation of British rule and of Western education. The claim of the modern Bengalees to be regarded as a "nation" has no historical basis. The inhabitants of Bengal are of mixed Dravidian, Mongolian, and Aryan origin, and in no other speech of India, writes Sir H. Risley, is the literary language cultivated by the educated classes more widely divorced, not only from the many popular dialects spoken in the province, but from that of ordinary conversation. Literary Bengalee is not even an altogether indigenous growth. It owes its birth mainly to the labours of English missionaries, like Carey, in the first half of the last century, assisted by the Pundits of Calcutta. Yet it is upon this community of language that the Bengalees mainly found their claim to recognition as a "nation"; or, to put it in another form, their claim rests upon education as they understand it—*i.e.*, upon the high proportion of literacy that exists in Bengal as compared with most parts of India. Education is unquestionably a power in Bengal. It has not superseded caste, which in all essentials is still unbroken, but it has to some extent overshadowed it.

The Brahmans of Bengal have never within historical times been a politically dominant force. They did not condescend to take office even in the remote days when there were Hindu Kings in Bengal, and still less under Mahomedan rule. They were content to be learned in Sanscrit and in the Hindu Scriptures, and they left secular knowledge to the Kayasthas, or writer caste, with whom they preserved, notwithstanding certain rigid barriers, much more intimate relations than usually exist between different Hindu castes. There is a tradition that the highest Brahman septs of Bengal are the descendants of five priests of special sanctity whom King Adisur of Eastern Bengal in the ninth century attracted to his Court from the holiest centres of Hinduism, and that the servants who accompanied them founded the septs to which precedence is still accorded amongst the Kayasthas of Bengal, and both have been at pains to preserve the purity of their descent by a most exclusive and complicated, and often unsavoury, system of matrimonial alliances known as Kulinism. Hence in Bengal the Brahmans share their social primacy to an extent unknown in other parts of India with the Kayasthas, and also with another high caste, the Vaidhyas, who formerly monopolized the practice of Hindu medicine. The *nexus* is education, and that *nexus* has been strengthened since the advent of British rule and of Western education. When the educational enterprise of the early British missionaries was followed up, under the impulse of Dr. Duff, the greatest figure in the missionary annals of India, and of Ram Mohun Roy, the most learned and earnest of all reforming Brahmans, by the famous Government Minute of March 7, 1835, many distinguished members of all these three castes responded to the call and began to qualify for employment under Government and for the liberal professions that were opening out in the new India we were making. They were first in the field, and, though other castes have followed suit, it is they who have practically monopolized the public offices, the Bar, the Press, and the teaching profession. It was they who were the moving spirits of the Brahmo Samaj and of Social Reform when progressive ideas seemed to be on the point of permeating Hinduism. But when the reaction came which first found public expression in the resistance provoked by the Age of Consent Act of 1891 for mitigating the evils of Hindu child marriage, and the spirit of reform was deflected from the social and religious into the political domain, it was they again who showed the most aptitude to clothe the new political movement in all the forms of Western political activities. It was Mr. W. C. Bonnerjee, an able Bengalee lawyer of moderate and enlightened views, who presided over the first Indian National Congress at Bombay and delivered an opening address of which the moderation has rarely been emulated, and though the Congress movement originated in Bombay rather than in Bengal, the fluent spokesmen of Bengal very soon had the satisfaction of feeling that for the first time in Indian history Bengal might claim to be marching in the van.

Owing to his greater plasticity and imagination, the Bengalee has certainly often assimilated English ideas as few other Indians have. None can question, for instance, the genuine Western culture and sound learning of men like Dr. Ashutosh Mookerjee, the Vice-Chancellor of the Calcutta University, or Dr. Rash Behari Ghose, than whom the English Bar itself has produced few greater lawyers; and it would be easy to quote many other names of scarcely less distinction amongst the many highly educated Bengalees who have served and are still serving the State with undoubted loyalty and ability. With the spread of English education, habits of tolerance have grown up, at any rate as to externals; and though on the crucial point of inter-marriage caste law has lost hardly anything of its rigidity, religion, in the ordinary intercourse of life, seems to sit almost as lightly upon educated Hindu society in Calcutta as upon English society in London. Another result of English education, combined with the absence of such traditions of Brahman supremacy as are still recent and powerful in the Deccan, has been to invest the political aspirations of the Bengalees with that democratic tinge which has won the sympathies of English Radicals; and, even if the tinge in most cases be very slight, the Bengalee's own adaptability enables him to clothe his opinions with extraordinary skill and verisimilitude in the form which he intuitively knows will best suit an English audience. Of any real democratic spirit amongst the educated classes of Bengal it is difficult to find a trace, for they are separated from the masses whom they profess to represent by a social gulf which only a few of the most enlightened amongst them have so far even recognized the necessity of making some attempt to bridge if they wish to give the slightest plausibility to their professions. It would be less far-fetched, though the analogy would still be very halting, to compare the position of the Bengalee "moderates" with that of the middle classes in England before the Reform Bill of 1832, who had no idea of emancipating the masses, but only of emancipating themselves to some extent from the control of a close oligarchy. From this point of view there are undoubtedly, and especially amongst the elder generation, many educated Bengalees who are convinced that in claiming by political agitation a larger share in the administration and government of the country they are merely carrying into practice the blameless theories of civic life and political activity which their reading of English history has taught them. Their influence, however, has been rapidly undermined by a new and essentially revolutionary school, who combine with a spirit of revolt against all Western authority a reversion to some of the most reactionary conceptions of authority that the East has ever produced, and, unfortunately, it is this new school which has now got hold of the younger educated classes.

Education, to which in its more primitive forms the Bengalees owed whatever influence they retained under Mahomedan rule, has given them under British rule far larger opportunities which they have turned to account with no mean measure of success. I must reserve the thorny question of education for separate treatment. All I need say for the present is that, had it grown less instead of more superficial, had it been less divorced from discipline and moral training as well as from the realities of Indian life, the results might have been very different. As it is, in the form given to it in our Indian schools and colleges, which have been allowed to drift more and more into native hands, English education has steadily deteriorated in quality as the output has increased in quantity. The sacrifices made by many Bengalees in humble circumstances to procure for their sons the advantages of what is called higher education are often pathetic, but the results of this mania for higher education, however laudable in itself, have been disastrous. Every year large batches of youths with a mere smattering of knowledge are turned out into a world that has little or no use for them. Soured on the one hand by their own failure, or by the failure of such examinations as they may have succeeded in passing to secure for them the employment to which they aspired, and scorning the sort of work to which they would otherwise have been trained, they are ripe for every revolt. That is the material upon which the leaders of unrest have most successfully worked, and it is only recently that some of the more sober-minded Bengalees of the older generation have begun to realize the dangers inherent in such a system. When in 1903 Lord Curzon brought in his Universities Bill to mitigate some of the most glaring evils of the system, there was a loud and unanimous outcry in Bengal that Government intended to throttle higher education because it was education that was making a "nation" of Bengal. Subsequent events have shown that that measure was not only urgently needed, but that it came too late to cure the mischief already done, and was, if anything, too circumscribed in its scope. The storm it raised was intensified shortly afterwards by Lord Curzon's famous Convocation speech, into which the sensitive and emotional Bengalee hastened to read a humiliating indictment of the "nation." Such a storm showed how heavily laden was the atmosphere with dangerous electricity.

For some years past the influence of Tilak and his irreconcilable school had been projected from the Deccan into Bengal, and nowhere did it make itself so rapidly felt as in the Press. The *Calcutta Review* has been publishing a very instructive history of the Indian Press by Mr. S. C. Sanial, a Hindu scholar who has had the advantage of consulting authentic and hitherto unpublished documents. His erudite work shows how the native Press of India first grew up in Bengal as the direct product of English education, and faithfully reflected all the fluctuations of educated Bengalee opinion, many of the most influential native newspapers continuing to be published in English, side by side with, and often under the same control as, more popular papers published in the vernacular. Among the "advanced" journalists of Bengal, none had fallen so entirely under the spell of Tilak's magnetic personality as Mr. Bepin Chandra Pal and Mr. Arabindo Ghose, and the former's *New India* and the latter's *Bande Mataram*, also published in English, soon outstripped the aggressiveness of Mr. Surendranath Banerjee's *Bengalee.* For though not immune from the reaction against Western influences and in favour of Hinduism as a religious and social system, the school represented by Mr. Banerjee confined itself at first mainly to political agitation and to criticism of British methods of administration. The new school represented, perhaps most conspicuously, by Mr. Arabindo Ghose scarcely disguised its hostility to British rule itself and to all that British ascendency stands for. Hinduism for the Hindus, or, as they preferred to put it, "Arya for the Aryans," was the war-cry of zealots, half fanatics, half patriots, whose mysticism found in the sacred story of the *Bhagvat Gita* not only the charter of Indian independence but the sanctification of the most violent means for the overthrow of an alien rule. With this "Aryan" reaction, having to a great extent the force of religious enthusiasm behind it, orthodoxy also recovered ground, and Brahmanism was not slow to show how potent it still is even in Bengal when it appeals to the superstitions of the masses. In one form or another this spirit had spread like wildfire not only among the students but among the teachers, and the schools of physical training to which young Bengal had taken, partly under the influence of our British love of sports and partly from a legitimate desire to remove from their "nation" the stigma of unmanliness, were rapidly transforming themselves into political societies modelled upon the bands of gymnasts which figured so prominently in Tilak's propaganda in the Deccan. Among the older men, some yielded to the new spirit from fear of being elbowed out by their youngers, some were genuinely impatient of the tardiness of the constitutional reforms for which they had looked to the agency of the Indian National Congress; a few perhaps welcomed the opportunity of venting the bitterness engendered by social slights, real or imaginary, or by disappointments in Government service.

Such appears to have been the *état d'âme* of Bengal when the Government of India promulgated the measure of administrative redistribution known as the Partition of Bengal.

CHAPTER VII.

THE STORM IN BENGAL.

The merits or demerits of the Partition of Bengal have already been discussed to satiety. As far as its purpose was to promote administrative efficiency it is no longer on its defence. Bengal proper is still the most populous province in India, but it has been brought within limits that at least make efficient administration practicable. The eastern districts, now included in the new province, which had been hitherto lamentably neglected, have already gained enormously by the change, which was at the same time only an act of justice to the large Mahomedan majority who received but scanty consideration from Calcutta. The only people who perhaps suffered inconvenience or material loss were absentee landlords, pleaders, and moneylenders, and some of the merchants of Calcutta, Anglo-Indian as well as native, who believed their interests to be affected by the transfer of the seat of provincial government for the Eastern Bengal districts to Dacca. Nevertheless the Partition was the signal for an agitation such as India had not hitherto witnessed. I say advisedly the signal rather than the cause. For if the Partition in itself had sufficed to rouse spontaneous popular feeling, it would have been unnecessary for the leaders of the agitation to resort in the rural districts to gross misrepresentations of the objects of that measure. What all the smouldering discontent, all the reactionary disaffection centred in

Calcutta read into the Partition was a direct attack upon the primacy of the educated classes that had made Calcutta the capital of the Bengalee "nation." The Universities Act of 1904, it was alleged, had been the first attempt on the part of a masterful Viceroy to reduce their influence by curtailing their control of higher education. Partition was a further attempt to hamper their activities by cutting half the "nation" adrift from its "intellectual" capital. This was a cry well calculated to appeal to many "moderates," whom the merely political aspects of the question would have left relatively unmoved and it certainly proved effective, for in Calcutta feeling ran very strong. Whilst "monster" demonstrations were organized in Calcutta and in the principal towns of the *mofussil,* the wildest reports were sedulously disseminated amongst the rural population. Partition was meant to pave the way for undoing the Permanent Settlement which governs the Land Revenue in Bengal, and, once the Permanent Settlement out of the way, Government would screw up the land tax. As for the creation of the new province, it was intended to facilitate the compulsory emigration of the people from the plains, who would be driven to work on the Englishmen's tea plantations in the far-off jungles of Assam. Reports of this kind were well calculated to alarm both the *Zemindars,* who had waxed fat on the Permanent Settlement, and the credulous *rayats,* whose labour is indispensable to the *zemindar* squirarchy. In the towns, on the other hand, the masses were told that Partition was an insult to the "terrible goddess" Kali, the most popular of all Hindu deities in Bengal, and, in order to popularize the protest amongst the small townsfolk, amongst artisans and petty traders, the cry of *Swadeshi* was coupled with that of *Bande Mataram.*

The spirit of revolt against Western political authority had been for some time past spreading to the domain of economics. *Swadeshi* in itself and so far as it means the intelligent encouragement of indigenous industries is perfectly legitimate, and in this sense the Government of India had practised *Swadeshi* long before it was taken up for purposes of political agitation by those who look upon it primarily as an economic weapon against their rulers. It was now to receive a formidable development. *Swadeshi* must strike at the flinty heart of the British people by cutting off the demand for British manufactured goods and substituting in their place the products of native labour. At the first great meeting held at the Calcutta Town Hall to protest against Partition, the building was to have been draped in black as a sign of "national" mourning, but the idea was ostentatiously renounced because the only materials available were of English manufacture. Not only did the painful circumstances of the hour forbid any self-respecting Bengalee from using foreign-made articles, but some means had to be found of compelling the lukewarm to take the same lofty view of their duties. So the cry of boycott was raised, and it is worth noting, as evidence of the close contact and co-operation between the forces of unrest in the Deccan and in Bengal, that at the same time as it was raised in Calcutta by Mr. Surendranath Banerjee it was raised also at Poona by Tilak who perhaps foresaw much more clearly the lawlessness to which it would lead. For, though the cry fell on deaf ears in Bombay, the boycott did not remain by any means an idle threat in Bengal. The movement was placed under the special patronage of Kali and vows were administered to large crowds in the forecourts of her great temple at Calcutta and in her various shrines all over Bengal. The religious character with which the leaders sought to invest the boycott propaganda showed how far removed was the *swadeshi* which they preached from a mere innocent economic propaganda for the furtherance of native industries. For a description of the Tantric rites connected with *Shakti* worship I must refer readers to M. Barth's learned work on "The religions of India," of which an English translation has been published by Messrs. Trübner in their Oriental series. In its extreme forms *Shakti* worship finds expression in licentious aberrations which, however lofty may be the speculative theories that gave birth to them, represent the most extravagant forms of delirious mysticism. Yet such men as Mr. Surendranath Banerjee [7], who in his relations with Englishmen claims to represent the fine flower of Western education and Hindu enlightenment, did not hesitate to call the popularity of *Shakti* worship in aid in order to stimulate the boycott of British goods. To prevent any blacksliding the agitators had ready to hand an organization which they did not hesitate to use. The gymnastic societies founded in Bengal for physical training and semi-military drill on the model of those established by Tilak in the Deccan were transformed into bands of *samitis* or "national volunteers," and students and schoolboys who had been encouraged from the first to take part in public meetings and to parade the streets in procession as a protest against Partition, were mobilized to picket the bazaars and enforce the boycott. Nor were their methods confined to moral suasion. Where it failed they were quite ready to use force. The Hindu leaders had made desperate attempts to enlist the support of the Mahomedans, and not without some success, until the latter began to realize the true meaning both of the Partition and of the agitation against it. Nothing was better calculated to enlighten them than another feature introduced also from the Deccan into the "national" propaganda. In the Deccan the cult of Shivaji, as the epic hero of Mahratta history, was intelligible enough. But in Bengal his name had been for generations a bogey with which mothers hushed their babies, and the Mahratta Ditch in Calcutta still bears witness to the terror produced by the daring raids of Mahratta horsemen. To set Shivaji up in Bengal on the pedestal of Nationalism in the face of such traditions was no slight feat, and all Mr. Surendranath Banerjee's popularity barely availed to perform it successfully. But to identify the cause of Nationalism with the cult of the Mahratta warrior-king who had first arrested the victorious career and humbled the pride of the Mahomedan conquerors of Hindustan was not the way to win over to it the Mahomedans of Bengal. In Eastern Bengal especially, with the exception of a few landlords and pleaders whose interests were largely bound up with those of the Hindus, the Mahomedans as a community had everything to gain and nothing to lose by the Partition. For those amongst them who were merchants the boycott spelt serious injury to their trade and led in some instances to reprisals in which the Hindus fared badly. Whenever it happened in this way that the biter was bit, the Bengalee Press accused the Government of encouraging the revival of sectarian strife, just as it denounced every measure for the maintenance of order which the Government was compelled to take in the discharge of one of its most elementary duties, as brutal repression and arbitrary vindictiveness, and any mistake of procedure made by some subordinate official under the stress of a very critical situation was distorted and magnified into a gross denial of justice. But it was out of the punishments very properly inflicted upon the misguided schoolboys and students whom the politicians had put in the forefront of the fray that the greatest capital was made. Whilst the politicians themselves prudently remained for the most part in Calcutta, making high-sounding speeches and writing inflammatory articles, or were careful in their own overt demonstrations not to overstep the extreme bounds of legality, they showered telegrams and letters of congratulation on the young "martyrs" who had been duly castigated.

The leaders of the movement had also another string to their bow which they used with considerable effect. Never before had there been such close contact between Indian politicians and certain groups of English politicians.

Lord Curzon's fall and the extremely injudicious references to Partition made by Mr. Brodrick, the then Secretary of State, in the correspondence published after the resignation of the Viceroy, had from the first given a great stimulus to the anti-Partition campaign. Mr. Brodrick's remarks led the Bengalees to form a very exaggerated estimate of the personal part played by Lord Curzon in the question of Partition, and they not unnaturally concluded that, if the Secretary of State had merely sanctioned the Partition in order to humour the Viceroy, he might easily be induced to reconsider the matter when once Lord Curzon had been got out of the way. Their hopes in that quarter were, it is true, very soon dashed, but only to be strung up again to the highest pitch of expectancy when the Conservative Government fell from power, and was replaced by a Liberal Administration, with Mr. John Morley at the India Office and an overwhelming majority in the House of Commons, in which the Radical element was very strongly represented. Several of the leading Radical organs in England had for a long time past joined hands with the Bengalee Press in denouncing Lord Curzon and all his works, and, most fiercely of all, the Partition of Bengal. The Bengalee politicians, moreover, not only had the active sympathy of a large section of Radical opinion at home, but they had in the House itself the constant co-operation of a small but energetic group of members, who constituted themselves into an "Indian party," and were ever ready to act as the spokesmen of Indian discontent. Some of them were of that earnest type of self-righteousness which loves to smell out unrighteousness in their fellow countrymen, especially in those who are serving their country abroad; some were hypnotized by the old shibboleths of freedom, even when freedom merely stands for licence; some were retired Anglo-Indians, whose experience in the public service in India would have carried greater weight had not the peculiar acerbity of their language seemed to betray the bitterness of personal disappointment. Every invention or exaggeration of the Bengalee Press found its way into the list of questions to be asked of the Secretary of State, who, with less knowledge than he has since acquired, doubtless considered himself bound to pass them on for inquiry to the Government of India A large proportion of these questions were aimed at Sir Bampfylde Fuller, who, as the first Lieutenant-Governor of the new province of Eastern Bengal, had been singled out for every form of vituperation and calumny, and no subject figured more prominently amongst them than the disciplinary treatment of turbulent schoolboys and students. It is so easy to appeal to the generous sentiments of the British public in favour of poor boys, supposed to be of tender years, dragged into police courts by harsh bureaucrats for some hasty action prompted by the generous, if foolish, exuberance of youth, especially when the British public is quite unaware that in India most students and many schoolboys are more or less full-grown and often already married. Every one of these questions was duly advertised in the columns of the Bengalee Press, and their cumulative effect was to produce the impression that the British Parliament was following events in Bengal with feverish interest and with overwhelming sympathy for the poor oppressed Bengalee.

Nevertheless, there came a moment when the first feverish excitement seemed to wane. Time had gone on, and though there was a new Viceroy in India and a new Secretary of State at Whitehall, the Partition had remained an accomplished fact. The visit of the Prince and Princess of Wales to Calcutta had temporarily exercised a restraining influence on the political leaders, and the presence of Royalty in a country where reverence for the Throne is still a powerful tradition seemed to hush even the forces of militant sedition. In Eastern Bengal, where the agitation had been much fiercer than in Bengal proper, the energy and devotion displayed by the Lieutenant-Governor in fighting a serious threat of famine had won for him the respect of many of his opponents, and the situation was beginning to lose some of its acuteness when it was suddenly announced that Sir Bampfylde Fuller had resigned. The effect was instantaneous. The points at issue between Sir Bampfylde Fuller and the Government of India have been fully and frequently debated, and it is needless to discuss here the reasons given for his resignation, or for its prompt acceptanee by the Viceroy. What I am concerned with is the effect produced by that incident. It was immediate and disastrous. The Bengalee leaders took heart. They claimed Sir Bampfylde's downfall as their triumph—theirs and their allies' at Westminster. Those, on the other hand, who imagined that it was Sir Bampfylde's methods that had intensified the agitation and that his removal would restore peace—even the sort of half peace which had been so far maintained in Bengal proper under the milder sway of Sir Andrew Fraser—were very soon undeceived. For if for a short time Sir Bampfylde Fuller's successor was spared, the Government of Eastern Bengal was compelled before long to take more vigorous measures than he had ever contemplated, and the agitation, which had hitherto refrained from exhibiting its more violent aspects in Bengal proper, not only ceased to show any discrimination, but everywhere broadened and deepened. The veteran leaders, who still posed as "moderates," ceased to lead or, swept away by the forces they had helped to raise, were compelled to quicken their pace like the Communist leader in Paris who rushed after his men exclaiming:—*Je suis leur chef, il faut bien que je les suive.* The question of Partition itself receded into the background, and the issue, until then successfully veiled and now openly raised, was not whether Bengal should be one unpartitioned province or two partitioned provinces under British rule, but whether British rule itself was to endure in Bengal or, for the matter of that, anywhere in India.

The first phase of unrest in Bengal, at any rate in its outward manifestations, had been mainly political, and on the whole free from any open exhibition of disloyalty to the British *Raj*. With the Partition of Bengal it passed into a second phase in which new eeonomic issues were superadded to the political issues, if they did not altogether overshadow them, and the *Swadeshi* movement and the boycott soon imported methods of violence and lawlessness which had hitherto been considered foreign to the Bengalee temperament. This phase did not last for much more than a year after the Partition, for, when once started on the inclined plane of lawlessness, the agitation rapidly developed into a much wider and deeper revolt, in which *Swadeshi* held its place, but only in a subordinate position. The revolt began rapidly to assume the revolutionary complexion, in the religious and social as well as in the political domain, which Tilak had for years past, as we have seen, laboured to impart to his propaganda in the Deccan, and, as far as his personal influence and counsels availed, in every part of India with which he was in contact. The ground had already been prepared for this transformation by spadework in the Bengalee Press conducted by two of Tilak's chief disciples in Bengal. One was Mr. Bepin Chandra Pal, the bold exponent of *Swaraj*, whose programme I have already quoted. The other was Mr. Arabindo Ghose, one of the most remarkable figures that Indian unrest has produced. Educated in England, and so thoroughly that when he returned to India he found it difficult to express himself in Bengali, he is not only a high-caste Hindu, but he is one of those Hindu mystics who believe that, by the practice of the most extreme forms of *Yoga* asceticism, man can transform himself into a super-man, and he has constituted himself the high priest of a religious revival which has taken a profound hold on the imagination of the emotional youth of Bengal. His ethical gospel is not devoid of grandeur. It is based mainly on the teachings of Krishna to Arjuna as revealed in the *Bhagvad Gita*, and I cannot hope to define its moral purpose better than by borrowing the following sentence from Mrs. Besant's introduction to her translation of "The Lord's Song":—

> It is meant to lift the aspirant from the lower levels of renunciation where objects are renounced, to the loftier heights where desires are dead and where the Yogi dwells in calm and ceaseless contemplation, while his body and mind are actively employed in discharging the duties that fall to his lot in life.

This reading of the *Bhagvad Gita* differentiates the newer Indian conception of renunciation, which does not exclude but rather prescribes the duty of service to society, from the older conception, which was concerned merely to procure the salvation of the individual by his complete detachment from all mundane affairs. With this gospel of active self-sacrifice none can assuredly quarrel, but it is the revolutionary form which Mr. Arabindo Ghose would see given to such activity that, unfortunately, chiefly fascinates the rising generation of Bengalees. For him British rule and the Western civilization for which it stands threaten the very life of Hinduism, and therefore British rule and all that it stands for must go, and in order that they may go every Hindu must be up and doing. That Mr. Arabindo Ghose himself holds violence and murder to be justifiable forms of activity for achieving that purpose cannot be properly alleged, for though he has several times been placed on his trial and in one instance for actual complicity in political crime—namely, in the Maniktolla bomb case—and though he is at present a fugitive from justice, the law has so far acquitted him. But that his followers have based upon his teachings a propaganda by deed of the most desperate character is beyond dispute. It has been openly expounded with fanatical fervour and pitiless logic in a newspaper edited by his brother, Barendra Ghose, of which the file constitutes one of the most valuable and curious of human documents.

Of the three Bengali newspapers that came into the field soon after Partition as the explicit champions of revolution—the *Sandhya*, the *Navasakti*, to which Mr. Arabindo Ghose was himself a frequent contributor, and the *Yugantar* —the last named achieved the greatest and most startling popularity. It was founded in 1906 by Barendra Kumar Ghose, a brother of Arabindo, and by Bhupendranath Dutt, only brother of the celebrated Swami Vivekananda, who visited Europe and America as the missionary of the Hindu revival and has been revered in India, since his premature death in 1905, as a modern *rishi* and a no less great one than those of ancient Vedic times. Barendra Ghose, who had studied history and political literature at Baroda, where Arabindo was a Professor in the Gaekwar's College, had originally intended to start a religious institution, and whilst he edited the *Yugantar* he founded a hostel for youths attending "National" schools. The *Yugantar* set itself to preach revolution as a religious even more than a political movement. Its profession of faith is to be found in an article headed "The Age of the Gita again in India":—

God (*i.e.*, Khrisna in the Gita) has said, "Oh, descendant of Bharata, whenever there be a decline of righteousness and the rise of unrighteousness, then I shall become incarnate again. I shall be born in every Yuga [era] to rescue the good, to destroy the wrongdoer, and to establish righteousness.

In the *Dwapara-Yuga* [the era which preceded the present *Kali-Yuga*, or era of darkness] when righteousness was on the wane and unrighteousness was springing up in the sacred land of India under the hands of Duryyodhana and other miscreants engaged in wickedness, then God, by becoming incarnate again and awakening his favourite disciple Arjuna to duty, re-established the kingdom of righteousness in India. At the present time righteousness is declining and unrighteousness is springing up in India. A handful of alien robbers is ruining the crores of the people of India by robbing the wealth of India. Through the hard grinding of their servitude, the ribs of this countless people are being broken to pieces. Endless endeavours are being made in order that this great nation by losing, as an inevitable result of this subjection, its moral, intellectual and physical power, its wealth, its self-reliance, and all other qualities, may be turned into the condition of the beasts of burden or be wholly extinguished. Why, oh Indians, are you losing heart, at the sight of many obstacles in your path, to make a stand against this unrighteousness? Fear not, oh Indians. God will not remain inactive at the sight of such unrighteousness in His kingdom. He will keep His word. Placing firm reliance on the promise of God, invoke His power, and He will descend in your midst to destroy unrighteousness. Do not be afraid. "When the lightning of heaven flashes in their hearts, men perform impossible deeds."

The article closes with a lyrical vision of the India of the future, with "the independent flag of righteousness" unfurled, her virtues restored, plague and famine banished, her industries brought to the highest pitch of scientific development, her armies and fleets going forth "to use the unlimited strength, knowledge, and righteousness of India for the benefit of the whole world."

The *Yugantar* at the same time set forth in a series of articles the scheme by which the enfranchisement of India was to be achieved—a scheme which was little more than a reasoned exposition of the methods already adopted in the previous decade by Tilak in the Deccan. These articles form a manual of directions for "the army of young men which is the *Nrisinha* and the *Varaha* and the *Kalki* incarnation of God, saving the good and destroying the wicked"—the *Kalki* incarnation being that in which Vishnu is to come and deliver India from the foreigner. To shake off slavery the first essential is that the educated classes shall learn to hate slavery. Then the lower classes will soon follow their lead. "It is easy to incite the lower classes to any particular work. But the incitement of the educated depends on a firm belief." Therefore the "poisonous" effects of slavery must be constantly brought home, and "we must always be trying to destroy the present unnatural liking for a state of servitude." The aspiration for freedom must be converted into a firm resolve, and to divert the Bengalee "from the unfailing attraction of a livelihood" to the cause of freedom "his mind must be excited and maddened by such an ideal as will present to him a picture of everlasting salvation." Public opinion must be built up by the newspapers, "which must be filled with the discussion of the necessity of independence and revolution," by soul-stirring musical and theatrical performances, glorifying the lives of Indian heroes and their great deeds in the cause of freedom, and by patriotic songs. "When in the Mahratta country the high-souled Shivaji stood up for independence the songs of the bards helped powerfully in his work." Above all, the materials for "a great sacrifice for liberty" must be prepared. "The stratagems known as resorting to eover in English military tactics are very necessary in all political endeavour," and "the enemy" must be kept constantly occupied by them. "A *Bande Mataram* procession to-day, a conference or congress to-morrow, a flourish of *Swadeshi* speeches the day after, and so on." A "great commotion may with advantage be made over small incidents," but "it must always be remembered that these do not constitute our real effort, and are very trifling accompaniments" which serve to keep the enemy busy and the country awake "whilst we are training," and the training consists in the organization, discreetly and silently, of bands of young men "with power to conceal secret counsel" and "to remain under complete obedience." Every band must "recognize the cultivation of physical strength as a principal means of attaining our object." Each band, working down from the chief town of the district, must be connected with other bands, and all must be initiated in the *Shakti mantra*—that *Shakti* worship which constitutes one of the most powerful and popular appeals to the sensuous side of Hindu mysticism. As for arming the bands, there are different ways of collecting arms, and in this business "there can be no considerations of right or wrong, for everything is laid at the feet of the goddess of independence." Bombs can be manufactured in secret places, and guns can be imported from foreign countries, for "the people of the West will sell their own Motherland for money," or they can be obtained from the native troops who, "though driven by hunger to accept service under Government, are men of our own flesh and blood," or, perhaps, even "secretly" from other Great Powers. Funds also can be collected in similar ways. Much money is required, and amongst other things for "secret preachers at home and abroad." It can be obtained "by voluntary donations," or "by the application of force," which is perfectly justifiable since the money is to be taken and used "for the good of society." Thefts and dacoities are, under normal conditions, crimes because they destroy the sense of social security, but "to destroy it for the highest good is no sin, but rather a work of religious merit." The taking of blood is, in the circumstances, equally praiseworthy. "The law of the English is established on brute force, and if to liberate ourselves we too must use brute force, it is right that we should do so." Nor is this doctrine merely stated in general terms:—

> Will the Bengali worshippers of *Shakti* shrink from the shedding of blood? The number of Englishmen in this country is not above one lakh and a half, and what is the number of English officials in each district? If you are firm in your resolution you can in a single day bring English rule to an end. Lay down your life, but first take a life. The worship of the goddess will not be consummated if you sacrifice your lives at the shrine of independence without shedding blood.

These are the doctrines of revolutionary Hinduism expounded day by day for nearly two years by a group of highly educated young Bengalees, the effectiveness of whose appeal to sacred traditions was enhanced by remarkable qualities of style. I have before me a letter from a Hindu scholar who certainly has no sympathy with the methods advocated by the *Yugantar*—"Nothing like these articles ever appeared before in Bengali literature." "Out of the abundance of the heart the mouth speaketh," and this was essentially true in the case of the *Yugantar*. The Government translator confessed in the High Court that he had never before read, in Bengali, language so lofty, so pathetic, and so stirring, that it was impossible to convey it in an English translation. Yet, the writers had never learnt to write Bengali in their school-days, and the organ tone of Milton, which was distinctly audible in the Bengali, betrayed their English education. The sale was unbounded. The circulation of the *Yugantar* rose to over 50,000, a figure never attained before by any Indian newspaper, and sometimes when there was a special run upon a number the Calcutta newsboys would get a rupee for a single copy before the issue was exhausted. So great indeed was the demand that the principal articles, forming a complete gospel of revolution, were republished in a small volume, entitled *Mukti con pathe*: "Which way does salvation lie?" Not only were these appeals to racial and religious passion reflected in many other papers all over Bengal, but the most lamentable fact of all was that scarcely any native paper, even amongst those of an avowedly moderate complexion, attempted to counteract, or ventured to protest against, either the matter or the tone of these publications. Their success, on the other hand, induced not a few to follow suit. What is forgotten in England by the uncompromising champions of the freedom of the Press is that in a country like ours, with its party system fully represented in the public Press, even the newspapers which either party may consider most mischievous find their corrective in the newspapers of the other party. In India that is not the case. There is no healthy play of public opinion. The classes whose confidence in the British *Raj* is still unshaken are practically unrepresented in the Press, which is mostly in the hands of the intellectuals, of whom the majority are drifting into increasing estrangement, while the minority are generally too timid to try to stem the flowing tide. Nor, if the "moderates" in Bengal were overawed by the violence of the new creed, can the whole blame be laid upon their shoulders when one remembers how little was being done by Government, and how ineffective that little was to check this incendiarism. Though there were many Press prosecutions, and action was repeatedly taken against the *Yugantar* in respect of particular articles, the limited powers possessed by Government were totally inadequate, and it was not till the Indian Newspapers (Incitement to Offences) Act was passed in June, 1908, that the *Yugantar* was suppressed. In the meantime it had left an indelible mark on Indian history, and many innocent victims paid with their lives for the extraordinary supineness displayed during those first disastrous two years of Lord Minto's administration.

The list of outrages and deeds of violence which had begun in Bengal in 1907 grew heavier and heavier as 1908 wore on, but none perhaps created such a sensation there as the murder of Mrs. and Miss Kennedy, who were killed at Muzafferpur on April 30, 1908, by a bomb intended for the Magistrate, Mr. Kingsford. The bomb had been thrown by a young Bengalee, Khudiram Bose, and it was the first occasion on which an Indian had used this product of modern science with murderous effect. The excitement was intense. The majority of the Bengalee papers, it is true, were fain to reprobate or at least to deprecate this particular form of propaganda, but such comments were perfunctory, whilst they generally agreed to cast the whole responsibility upon an alien Government whose resistance to their "national" aspirations goaded impatient patriotism to these extremes. Even amongst many who did not actually sympathize with the murderer there seems to have been a lurking sense of pride that it was a Bengalee who had had the courage to lay down his life in the striking of such a blow. Khudiram Bose at any rate was not "lily-livered." Khudiram Bose at any rate had shown that "determination" with the lack of which the writers in the *Yugantar* had so often taunted their fellow-countrymen. So for the Nationalists of Bengal he became a martyr and a hero. Students and many others put on mourning for him and schools were closed for two or three days as a tribute to his memory. His photographs had an immense sale, and by-and-by the young Bengalee bloods took to wearing *dhotis* with Khudiram Bose's name woven into the border of the garment.

Bomb explosions followed in quick succession in Calcutta itself, and a secret manufacture of explosives was discovered in a suburban garden. Norendranath Gosain, who had turned approver in this last case, was shot dead in Alipur Gaol, and a Hindu police-inspector in the streets of Calcutta. Four attempts made upon the life of the Lieutenant-Governor of Bengal, Sir Andrew Fraser, showed how little effect leniency had upon the growing fierceness of the revolutionists. Scarcely a month and often not a week passed without adding to the tale of outrages. I need not recite them in detail. Perhaps the most significant feature was the double purpose many of them indicated of defeating the detection and punishment of crime and of striking terror into Indians who ventured to serve the British *Raj*[8]. Thus, on February 10, 1909, Mr. Ashutosh Biswas, the Public Prosecutor and a Hindu of high character and position, was shot dead outside the Alipur Police Court, and, in like manner, nearly a year later, Mr. Shams-ul-Alam, a Mahomedan Inspector of the Criminal Investigation Department in the High Court itself of Calcutta.[4] Sedition was seething over the greater part of both Bengals, and though the agricultural population remained for the most part untouched or indifferent, there were few even of the smaller towns and larger villages that were not visited by the missionaries of revolution. *Swadeshi* and the boycott were now merely an accompaniment to the deeper and more menacing trumpet-call of open revolt, but they helped "to keep the country awake" even where the true spirit of *Swaraj* had not yet been kindled. The *mofussil* was honeycombed with secret societies, whose daring dacoities served not only to collect the sinews of war, but to impress the timid and recalcitrant with the powerlessness of the State to protect them against the midnight raider. Truly the teachings of the *Yugantar* were bearing fruit, even to the laying down of life and the taking of life. Unlike the majority of Bengalee agitators, the writers in the *Yugantar*, it must be admitted, did not flinch from the danger of practising what they taught. Most of them came ultimately within the grasp of the Criminal Code, and Barendra Ghose, who was arrested in connexion with the manufacture of bombs in the Maniktolla garden, was sentenced to death, though subsequently reprieved. His brother, Arabindo, on the other hand, though arrested at the same time, had the good fortune to be acquitted. The work done by the *Yugantar* lived, nevertheless, after it, and is still living.

A very heavy responsibility must at the same time attach to those responsible both at home and in India for the extraordinary tolerance too long extended to this criminal propaganda. For two whole years it was carried on with relative impunity under the very eyes of the Government of India in Calcutta. Month after month they must have seen its audacity grow in direct proportion to official apathy. They must have seen a reign of lawlessness and intimidation spread steadily over a great part of the Metropolitan province. The failure of the ordinary machinery of justice to check these crying evils was repeatedly brought home to them. Yet it was not until 1908 that the necessity of exceptional measures to cope with an exceptional situation was tardily and very reluctantly realized. The Indian Explosive Substances Act and Summary Justice Act of 1908, together with the Press Act of the same year and the more drastic one enacted last February, have at last to some extent checked the saturnalia of lawlessness that continued, though with signs of abatement, into the beginning of this year. The Press Act of 1910, especially, seems to have really arrested the poisonous flow of printer's ink and with it the worst forms of crime to which it maddened the feverish blood of Bengal. But some of those who are most intimately acquainted with the inner workings of the revolutionary movement hold strongly that none of these enactments had such an immediately sobering effect as the deportation of the nine prominent Bengalees who were arrested at the end of 1908. Such a measure is, I know, very repugnant to British traditions and British sentiment, and in this particular instance it unfortunately included two men whose criminal guilt was subsequently believed not to be altogether beyond doubt, though it may well have been argued that by financing and administering a dangerous organization such as the *Anusilan Samiti* they made themselves responsible for the deeds of its members. Nevertheless, the deportation struck just at that type of agitator whose influence is most pernicious because it is most subtle, and whose responsibility is greatest because of his more experienced years and greater social position. Such a measure, however, is only warranted in extreme circumstances and cannot be transformed into indefinite detention. The grounds on which Government announced the release of these deportees last winter were even more unhappily chosen than the moment for the announcement, but the event seems so far to have justified Lord Minto's confidence, though one of the deported agitators, Pulin Bahari Das, of Dacca, has had to be rearrested and is now under trial at Dacca for conspiracy of a most serious character.

There is still much lawlessness in both Bengals[9]. The continued prevalence of political dacoities, and especially the difficulty experienced in securing legal evidence against them, are distinctly unfavourable symptoms. There are many peaceful citizens who will give private information as to the outrages committed by these armed bands, consisting mainly of youths of respectable connexions, but that so few have the courage to face terrorism by going into the witness-box shows that the secret societies which inspire such terror have not yet been broken up. The extent to which disaffection is rampant in the native Bar also hampers the administration of justice, for whilst there is an eager competition for earning political notoriety by an eloquent defence of political prisoners, it is sometimes difficult to find pleaders who will undertake to conduct prosecutions. On the other hand, it is all to the good that many of those who were ready to coquet with sedition in its earlier stages or who had not the moral courage to speak out against it seem now to be taking heart, and in this respect the reforms embodied in the Indian Councils Act have usefully supplemented the sobering effect of repressive legislation. For one of the stock arguments of "advanced" politicians has been the failure of the "moderates" to obtain any recognition from Government, and the enlargement of the Legislative Councils took the sting out of that taunt. Independently, however, of the reforms, the extreme violence of language and of methods which had come into vogue was bound to produce some reaction. Amongst the educated classes, many respectable fathers of families, whatever their political opinions may be, have taken fright at the growth of turbulence and insubordination in schools and colleges, which were often carried into the home circle; for when once the principle of authority has been undermined the parent's authority cannot remain unshaken. In the same way some even of the "advanced" leaders have been alarmed by the development of secret societies which often attract young men of very good connexions, and they have proposed to use for the detection and suppression of dacoities the local bands of "national volunteers" whom they formerly helped to organize for the purpose of enforcing the boycott and stimulating unrest. How far, even if unreservedly exercised, the influence of such men as

Mr. Surendranath Banerjee will be as potent for checking the mischief as it was for promoting it remains to be seen. For the present also the boycott is being discountenanced in the same quarters, though Mr. Banerjee, presumably to "save his face," professes to have agreed only to a suspension pending the revision of Partition. But his paper, the *Bengalee*, is almost the only one that pretends to regard the Partition as still an open question. It has been eclipsed by far graver issues of which the further development cannot yet be foreseen.

The return to more sober counsels seems to be confined unhappily to the older generation, and the older generation, even if we include in it the middle-aged, must before long pass away. What we have to reckon with, especially in Bengal, is the revolt of the younger generation, and this revolt draws its inspiration from religious and philosophical sources which no measures merely political, either of repression or of conciliation, can reach. It often represents a perversion of the finest qualities, as, apparently, in the case of Birendranath Gupta, who murdered Shams-ul-Alam in the Calcutta High Court last January. An English missionary who knew him well assured me that in his large experience of Indian youths he had never met one of more exemplary character or higher ideals, nor one who seemed more incapable of committing such a crime. The oaths and vows administered on initiation to secret societies are not directed only to political ends. They impose on the initiates in the most explicit terms a life of self-denial, and sometimes celibacy; and though these vows do not always avail against some of the worst forms of sensuality, it would be foolish and wrong to generalize from unworthy exceptions. In its moral aspects the revolt of young Bengal represents very frequently a healthy reaction against sloth and self-indulgence and the premature exhaustion of manhood which is such a common feature in a society that has for centuries been taught to disregard physiological laws in the enforcement of child marriage. To this extent it is a revolt, though in the name of Hinduism, against some of the worst results of the Hindu social system, and that it has spread so largely amongst the Brahmans of Bengal shows that it has affected even the rigidity of Brahmanism. Thus, whereas we have seen in Kolhapur the Brahmans of the Deccan assert that in this "age of darkness" there can be no Kshatriyas, their fellow-castemen in Bengal are quite willing to invest Kayasthas with the sacred thread, on the ground that they are really of Kshatriya descent, in order to stimulate martial virtues amongst the Bengalees by reviving for their benefit the old Vedic caste of warriors. Equally significant is the propaganda that has been carried on by Brahmans amongst the Namasudras, a large and mainly agricultural caste, chiefly located in the Jessor district of Bengal and the Faridpur district of Eastern Bengal. The purpose of the propaganda was political, but the inducement offered to the Namasudras in order to stimulate their Nationalism was that the Brahmans would relax the rigour of caste in favour of those who took the *Swadeshi* vow, and it is stated that, in several villages where they succeeded in making a large number of converts, the Brahman agitators marked their approval by condescending to have their "twice-born" heads shaved by the village barber—an act which, however trivial it may seem to us, constituted an absolutely revolutionary breach with a 3,000-years-old past.

On the other hand, the constant invocation of the "terrible goddess," whether as Kali or as Durga, against the alien oppressors, shows that Brahmanism in Bengal is equally ready to appeal to the grossest and most cruel superstitions of the masses. In another of her forms she is represented holding in her hand her head, which has been severed from her body, whilst the blood gushing from her trunk flows into her open mouth. A very popular picture of the goddess in this form has been published with a text to the effect that the great goddess as seen therein symbolizes "the Motherland" decapitated by the English, but nevertheless preserving her vitality unimpaired by drinking her own blood. It is not surprising that amongst extremists one of the favourite euphemisms[10] applied to the killing of an Englishman is "sacrificing a white goat to Kali." In 1906 I was visiting one of the Hindu temples at Benares and found in the courtyard a number of young students who had come on an excursion from Bengal. I got into conversation with them, and they soon began to air, for my benefit, their political views, which were decidedly "advanced." They were, however, quite civil and friendly, and they invited me to come up to the temple door and see them sacrifice to Kali a poor bleating kid that they had brought with them. When I declined, one of them who had already assumed a rather more truculent tone came forward and pressed me, saying that if I would accompany them they would not mind even sacrificing a white goat. There was a general shout of laughter at what was evidently regarded by the others as a huge joke. I turned away, though I did not then understand its grim humour, as I do now.

The blind hatred of everything English with which the younger generation is so largely saturated can only, in most cases, be the result of the teachings that have impressed upon them the existence of a fundamental antagonism between Hindu ideals and ours. Like the wretched Kanhère at Nasik, they would have to admit that they never suffered injustice themselves nor knew of any one who had. A great many have never come into contact with a single Englishman, and their ignorance even of the system of government under which they live is profound. Not the least ominous symptom is that this spirit of revolt seems to have obtained a firm hold of the zenana; and the Hindu woman behind the *purdah* often exercises a greater influence upon her husband and her sons than the Englishwoman who moves freely about the world. Absolute evidence in such matters is difficult to obtain, but there was a very significant and quite authentic case last year, which I may as well quote here, though it occurred in the Bombay Presidency. Two Brahman ladies of good position from Bombay were discovered at Kolhapur wearing the garb of *sanyasis, i.e.*, mendicant ascetics. They confessed that they had left their homes, to which the police wisely restored them, to invoke the assistance of a great ruling chief of Southern India in a plot to exterminate the hated foreigner, and their main object in starting upon this insane venture had been to regain their hold upon their husbands' affections by a great "patriotic" achievement. That real *sanyasis* are frequently the missionaries of sedition is certain, and their reputed sanctity gives them access to the zenana. In Bengal even small boys of so tender an age as still to have the run of zenanas have, I am told, been taught the whole patter of sedition, and go about from house to house dressed up as little *sanyasis* in little yellow robes preaching hatred of the English.

The question is, can we extricate the better elements from this tangle of passion and prejudice? There are many foul spots in the Hindu revival in Bengal, apart even from tendencies which we cannot but regard as politically criminal. At the same time there runs through it a strain of idealism which probably constitutes its real force, and also our danger. For strangely emotional and often a creature of his senses, the Bengalee is accessible to spiritual influences with which the worldly-ambitious Brahmanism of the Deccan, for instance, is rarely informed. He is always apt to rush to extremes, and just as amongst the best representatives of the educated classes there was in the last century a revolt against the Hindu social and religious creed of their ancestors which tended first towards Christianity or at least the ethics of Christianity and then towards Western agnosticism, so the present revolt may be regarded in some of its aspects as a reaction against these earlier tendencies, and in spite of its extreme violence it may not be any more permanent. The problem is still full of unknown quantities, but the known quantities are at any rate sufficient to make us appreciate its gravity.

CHAPTER VIII.

The Punjab and the Arya Samaj.

The Punjab, the Land of the Five Rivers, differs as widely both from the Deccan and from Bengal as these two differ the one from the other. It has been more than any other part of India the battlefield of warring races and creeds and the seat of power of mighty dynasties. Among its cities it includes Imperial Delhi and Runjit Singh's Lahore. It is a country of many peoples and of many dialects. It is the home of the Sikhs, but the Mahomedans, ever since the days of the Moghul Empire, form the majority of the population, and the proportion of Hindus is smaller than in any other province of India, except Eastern Bengal. Owing to the very small rainfall, its climate is intensely dry—fiercely hot during the greater part of the year, and cold even to freezing during the short winter months. Nowhere in India has British rule done so much to bring peace and security and to induce prosperity. The alluvial lands are rich but thirsty, and irrigation works on a scale of unparalleled magnitude were required to compel the soil to yield beneficent harvests. At the most critical moment in the history of British India it was against the steadfastness of the Punjab, then under the firm but patriarchal sway of Sir John Lawrence, that the Mutiny spent itself, and until a few years ago there seemed to be no reason whatever for questioning the loyalty of a province which the forethought of Government and the skill of Anglo-Indian engineers were gradually transforming into a land of plenty. Least of all did any one question the loyalty of the Sikhs. Many of them believed that British rule was the fulfilment of a prophecy of one of their martyred *gurus*, and the Sikh regiments were regarded as the flower of the Native Army.

Yet it was in the Punjab, at Lahore and at Rawal Pindi, that the first serious disturbances occurred in 1907 which aroused public opinion at home to the reality of Indian unrest, and stirred the Government of India to such strong repressive measures as the deportation of two prominent agitators under an ancient Ordinance of 1818 never before applied in such connexion. Local and temporary causes may to some extent have accounted for those disturbances. An increase in the land revenue demanded in the Rawal Pindi district was very strongly resented. The regulations issued with regard to the tenure of land in some of the new irrigation colonies were probably unwise and carried out with some harshness. Famine in the unirrigated tracts, and especially the plague, which had desolated parts of the province, had created much misery and bitterness. Other and more remote causes of a social and economic character had also been at work. Nowhere had Anglo-Indian legislation and the introduction of elaborate forms of legal procedure produced results more unfortunate and less foreseen by their authors than in the Punjab. The conversion of the occupants of the land into full proprietors was intended to give greater stability and security to the peasant ownership of land, but the result was to improve the position of the moneylender, who, owing to the thriftlessness of the Indian *rayat* and the extravagant expenditure to which he is from time to time driven by traditional custom in regard to marriages, funerals, and other family ceremonies, has always played a disastrously important part in village life. As M. Chailley remarks in his admirable study of these problems, "the agricultural debtor had now two securities to offer." He had always been able to pledge his harvest, and now he could pledge also his land. On the other hand, "a strict system of law and procedure afforded the moneylender the means of rapidly realizing his dues," and the pleader, who is himself a creation of that system, was ever at the elbow of both parties to encourage ruinous litigation to his own professional advantage. Special laws were successively enacted by Government to check these new evils, but they failed to arrest altogether a process which was bringing about a veritable revolution in the tenure of land, and mainly to the detriment of an essentially peaceful and law-abiding class that furnished a large and excellent contingent to the Native Army. The wretched landowner who found himself deprived of his land by legal process held our methods rather than his own extravagance responsible for his ruin, and on the other hand, the pleaders and their clients, the moneylenders, who were generally Hindus, resented equally our legislative attempts to hamper a process so beneficial to themselves.

But all these were only contributory causes. There were still deeper influences at work which have operated in the Punjab in the same direction as the forces of unrest in the Deccan and in Bengal, but differ from them nevertheless in their origin and in some of their manifestations. In the Punjab too the keynote of unrest is a spirit of revolt not merely against British administrative control, but, in theory at least, against Western influence generally, though in some respects it bears very strongly the impress of the Western influence which it repudiates. The motive force is not conservative Brahmanism as in the Deccan, nor does it betray the impetuous emotionalism of Bengal. It is less rigid and purely reactionary than the former, and better disciplined than the latter.

Orthodox Hinduism ceased to be a dominant factor in the Punjab when the flood of Mahomedan conquest swept over the land of the Five Rivers. Even Islam did not break the power of caste, and very distinct traces of caste still survive amongst the Mahomedan community itself. But nowhere has caste been so much shaken as in the Punjab, for the infinity of sub-castes into which each caste has resolved itself gives the measure of its disintegration. Sikhism still represents the most successful revolt against its tyranny in the later history of Hinduism. Hence the relatively slight ascendency enjoyed by the Brahmans in the Punjab amongst the Hindus themselves, even the Brahmans having split up into so many sub-castes and sub-sub-castes that many a non-Brahman Hindu will hardly accept food cooked by the lower order of Brahmans—and, next to inter-marriage, food is the great test of caste. Nevertheless it is amongst the Hindus of the Punjab that one of the earliest apostles of reaction against the West has found the largest and most enthusiastic body of followers. Swami Dayanand Saraswati, the founder of the Arya Samaj, was a Brahman of Kathiawar; he was not born in the Punjab, and it was not in the Punjab but in Bombay, where, however, it struck no roots, that he founded the Arya Samaj. Only in the later years of his life did the Punjab become the chief centre of his activities. The doctrines he taught were embodied by him in his *Satyarath Prakash*, which has become the Bible of his disciples, and in his *Veda Bashya Basmika*, a commentary on the Vedas. He had at an early age lost faith in the Hindu Pantheon, and to this extent he was a genuine religious reformer, for he waged relentless war against the worship of idols, and whether his claims to Vedantic learning be or be not conceded, his creed was "Back to the Vedas." His ethical code, on the other hand, was vague, and he pandered strangely in some directions to the weaknesses of the flesh, and in others to popular prejudices. Nothing in the Vedas, for instance, prohibits either the killing of cattle or the eating of bovine flesh. But, in deference to one of the most universal of Hindu superstitions,

Dayanand did not hesitate to include cow-killing amongst the deadliest sins. Here we have in fact the keynote of his doctrines. The sanctity of the cow is the touchstone of Hindu hostility to both Christian and Mahomedan, and the whole drift of Dayanand's teachings is far less to reform Hinduism than to rouse it into active resistance to the alien influences which threatened, in his opinion, to denationalize it. Hence the outrageously aggressive tone of his writings wherever he alludes either to Christianity or to Mahomedanism. It is the advent of " meat-eating and wine-drinking foreigners, the slaughterers of kine and other animals," that has brought " trouble and suffering " upon " the Aryas " — he discards the word Hindu on account of its Persian origin—whilst before they came into the country India enjoyed " golden days," and her people were " free from disease and prosperous and contented." In fact, " Arya for the Aryans " was the cry that frequently predominated in Dayanand's teachings over that of " Back to the Vedas," and Lajpat Rai, one of his most zealous disciples, has stated emphatically that " the scheme of Swami Dayanand has its foundation on the firm rock of *Swadeshi* and *Swajati*."

Since Dayanand's death the Arya Samaj has split up into two sections—the " vegetarians " who with regard to religious doctrine may be described as the orthodox, and the " meat-eaters," as the latitudinarians. It is difficult to differentiate between the precise tendencies of these two sections, whose feuds seem to be waning. In both are to be found not a few progressive and enlightened Aryas who, whatever their political activities may be, have undoubtedly applied themselves with no small success to the carrying out of that part of Dayanand's gospel which was directed to the reforming of Hinduism. Their influence has been constantly exerted to check the marriages between mere boys and almost infant girls which have done so much physical as well as moral mischief to Hindu society, and also to improve the wretched lot of Hindu widows whose widowhood with all that it entails of menial degradation often begins before they have ever really been wives. To this end the Aryas have not hesitated to encourage female education, and the Girls' Orphanage at Jalandhar, where there is also a widows' home, has shown what excellent social results can be achieved in that direction. Again in the treatment of the "untouchable" low-castes, the Arya Samaj may claim to have been the first native body to break new ground and to attempt something akin to the work of social reclamation of which Christianity and, in a lesser degree, Islam had hitherto had the monopoly. Schools and especially industrial classes have been established in various districts which cannot fail to raise the *status* of the younger generation and gradually to emancipate the lower castes from the bondage in which they have been hitherto held. These and many other new departures conceived in the same liberal spirit at first provoked the vehement hostility of the orthodox Hindus, who at one time stopped all social intercourse with the Arya reformers. But whereas in other parts of India the idea of social reform came to be associated with that of Western ascendency and therefore weakened and gave way before the rising tide of reaction against that ascendency, it has been associated in the Punjab with the cry of "Arya for the Aryans," and the political activities of the Arya Samaj, or at least of a number of its most prominent members who have figured conspicuously in the anti-British agitation of the last few years, have secured for it from Hindu orthodoxy a measure of tolerance and even of good will which its social activities would certainly not otherwise have received. That the Arya Samaj, which shows the impress of Western influence in so much of its social work, should at the same time have associated itself so intimately with a political movement directed against British rule is one of the many anomalies presented by the problem of Indian unrest.

Many Aryas, indeed, deny strenuously that the Samaj is disaffected, or even that it concerns itself with politics, and the president of the Lahore branch, Mr. Roshan

Lal, assured me that it devotes itself solely to moral and religious reform. I do not question that assurance, as far as Mr. Roshan Lal is himself personally concerned, and it may be true that the Samaj has never committed itself as a body to any political programme, and that many individual members hold aloof from politics; but the evidence that many others, and not the least influential, have played a conspicuous part in the seditious agitation of the last few years, both in the Punjab and in the neighbouring United Provinces, is overwhelming. In the Rawal Pindi riots in 1907 the ringleaders were Aryas, and in the violent propaganda which for about two years preceded the actual outbreak of violence none figured more prominently than Lala Lajpat Rai and Ajit Singh, both prominent Aryas. The immediate effect produced by their deportation in restoring order is in itself corroborative evidence of the share they were believed to have taken in producing lawlessness. Ajit Singh himself is at the present moment a fugitive from justice, against whom proceedings *in absentia* were instituted this winter in Lahore for translating and publishing seditious books that dealt with the making of bombs, the taking of life, the destruction of buildings, &c. In the course of these proceedings letters from Lajpat Rai were produced in Court showing that just about the time of the disturbances he had been in communication with Shyamji Krishnavarma, of *Indian Sociologist* fame, for a supply of books, "containing true ideas on politics" for the students of Lahore, as well as for assistance towards defraying the cost of "political missionaries." In one of these letters also Lajpat Rai, after remarking that "the people are in a sullen mood" and that "the agricultural classes have begun to agitate," adds significantly that his "only fear is that the bursting out may not be premature." Lajpat Rai's correspondent was another prominent Arya, Bhai Parmanand, who, whilst he was Professor at the Dayanand Anglo-Vedic College, was found in possession of various formulæ for the manufacture of bombs, including the same manual that was discovered in the Maniktola Garden at Calcutta.

In Patiala, one of the Sikh native States of the Punjab, Aryas constituted the great majority of defendants, 76 in number, and many of them officials and persons of position, who were put on their trial last December for seditious practices. So seriously were the charges felt to reflect upon the Arya Samaj as a whole that one of its leading legal members was briefed on its behalf for the defence. From the speech made by counsel for the prosecution in opening the case it appears that some of the defendants were schoolmasters, who were charged with preaching revolutionary doctrines in their schools and carrying on correspondence of the same character with old pupils; others were charged with circulating papers of the *Yugantar* and *Swarajiya* type; others with holding secret meetings and delivering inflammatory lectures; others again with distributing pictures and photographs of well-known revolutionists, including Khudiram Bose, the Muzafferpur murderer. Not only were most of these defendants Aryas, but they were very prominent Aryas, who had founded local branches of the Samaj or been members of committees in the State of Patiala. How far the evidence outlined by counsel would have borne out these charges it is impossible to say, though one may properly assume it to have been of a very formidable character, for after the case had been opened against them the defendants hastened to send in a petition invoking the clemency of the Maharajah. They expressed therein their deep sorrow for any conduct open to misconstruction, tendered their unqualified apology for any indiscreet acts they might have committed, and testified their "great abhorrence and absolute detestation" of anarchists and seditionists and their diabolical methods. His Highness thereupon ordered the prosecution to be abandoned, but at the same time banished the defendants from his State and declared their posts to be forfeited by such as had been in his service, and only in a few cases were these punishments subsequently remitted.

The large number of Aryas who have unquestionably taken part in the political agitation of the last few years certainly tends to corroborate the very compromising certificate given only two years ago to the Samaj by Krishnavarma himself in his murder-preaching organ. He not only stated that "of all movements in India for the political regeneration of the country none is so potent as the Arya Samaj," but he added that "the ideal of that society as proclaimed by its founder is an absolutely free and independent form of national Government," and Krishnavarma, it must be remembered, had been appointed by Dayanand to be a member of the first governing body in the lifetime of the founder and, after his death, one of the trustees of his will.

What makes the question of the real tendencies of the Arya Samaj one of very grave importance for the future is that it has embarked upon an educational experiment of a peculiar character which may have an immense effect upon the rising generation. One of its best features is the attention it has devoted to education, and to that of girls as well as of boys. But it was not till 1898 that the governing body of the Samaj in the Punjab decided to carry into execution a scheme for restoring the Vedic system of education which Dayanand had conceived but had never been able to carry out. Under this system the child is committed at an early age to the exclusive care of a spiritual teacher or *guru*, who stands to him *in loco parentis* and even more, for Manu says that "of him who gives natural birth, and of him who gives knowledge of the Vedas, the giver of sacred knowledge is the more venerable father, since second or divine birth ensures life to the twice-born, both in this world and eternally." In the *gurukuls* or seminaries founded by the Arya Samaj pupils or *chelas* are admitted between the ages of six and ten. From that moment they are practically cut off from the outer world during the whole course of their studies, which cover a period of 16 years altogether—*i.e.*, ten years in the lower school and six years in the upper, to which they pass up as *Brahmacharis*. During the whole of that period no student is allowed to visit his family, except in cases of grave emergency, and his parents can only see him with the permission of the head of the *gurukul* and not more than once a month. There are at present three *gurukuls* in the Punjab, but the most important one, with over 250 students, is at Kangri, in the United Provinces, five miles from the sacred city of Hardwar, where the Ganges flows out of a gorge into the great plain. A large and very popular *mela* or fair is held annually at Kangri, and it is attended by the *Brahmacharis*, who act as volunteers for the maintenance of order and collect funds for the support of their *gurukul*. The enthusiasm is said to be very great, and donations last year are credibly reported to have exceeded 300,000 rupees.

Life in the *gurukuls* is simple and even austere, the discipline rigorous, the diet of the plainest, and a great deal of time is given to physical training. As the *chelas* after 16 years of this monastic training at the hands of their *gurus* are to be sent out as missionaries to propagate the Arya doctrines throughout India, the influence of these institutions in the moulding of Indian character and Indian opinion in the future cannot fail to be considerable. Some five years more must elapse before we shall be able to judge the result by the first batch of *chelas* who will then be going forth into the world. For the present one can only echo the hope tersely expressed a few months ago by Sir Louis Dane, the Lieutenant-Governor of the Punjab, in reply to assurances of loyalty from the President of the Arya Samaj, that "what purports to be a society for religious and social reform and advancement may not be twisted from its proper aims" and "degenerate into a political organization with objects which are not consonant with due loyalty to the Government as established." But neither the spirit of Dayanand's own teachings nor the record of many of his disciples, including some of those actually connected with the *gurukuls*, is in this respect encouraging.

There has been, however, no recurrence of serious disturbances in the Punjab since 1907, and if the native Press lost little of its virulence until the new Press Act of this year, and numerous prosecutions bore witness to the continued prevalence of sedition, the province has been free from the murderous outrages and dacoities which have been so lamentable a feature of the unrest in Bengal and in the Deccan. None the less there is still a very strong undercurrent of anti-British feeling. It has partly been fostered in the large cities by Bengalee immigrants who have come into the Punjab in considerable numbers, and thanks to their higher education have acquired great influence at the Bar and in the Press, but it is rife wherever the Arya Samaj is known to be most active, and the Arya Samaj has already proved a very powerful proselytizing agency. Its meeting houses serve not only for religious ceremonies, but also as social clubs for the educated classes in all the larger towns where they congregate. Access to them is readily given to Hindus and Sikhs who have not actually joined the Samaj. They are attracted by the political discussions which are carried on there with great freedom, and having no such resorts of their own, they are soon tempted to obtain the fuller privileges of membership. In this way the Samaj has made many converts among the educated classes and even among native officials. But its influence is by no means confined to them. It makes many converts among the Sikhs, and not a few among *Nau-Muslims* or Mahomedans who have embraced Islam in relatively recent times and mainly for the purpose of escaping from the tyranny of caste. For the same reason it attracts low-caste Hindus, for though it does not ostentatiously denounce or defy caste, it has the courage to ignore it. Though the Arya leaders are generally men of education and sometimes of great culture, they know how to present their creed in a popular form that appeals to the lower classes and especially to the agricultural population. One of the most unpleasant features has been the propaganda carried on by them among the Sepoys of the Native Army, and especially among the Jats and the Sikhs, with whom they have many points of affinity. The efforts of the Aryas seem to be chiefly directed to checking enlistment, but they have at times actually tampered with the loyalty of certain regiments, and their emissaries have been found within the lines of the native troops. Sikhism itself is at the present day undergoing a fresh process of transformation. Whilst it tends generally to be reabsorbed into Hinduism, the very remarkable movement for sinking the old class distinctions—themselves a survival of caste—and recognizing the equality of all Sikhs, is clearly due to the influence of the Arya Samaj. The evolution of the Arya Samaj recalls very forcibly that of Sikhism, which originally, when founded by Nanak in the early part of the 16th century, was merely a religious and moral reform movement, and nevertheless within 50 years developed under Har Govind into a formidable political and military organization, It is not, therefore, surprising that some of those who know the Punjab best and the sterner stuff of which its martial races are made look upon it as a potentially more dangerous centre of trouble than either the Deccan or Bengal. One of the most mischievous results of the Aryan propaganda, and one which may well cause the most immediate anxiety, is the growing antagonism which it has bred between Hindus and Mahomedans, for the Mahomedans are convinced that the Arya Samaj is animated with no less bitter hostility towards Islam than towards British rule.

CHAPTER IX.

THE POSITION OF THE MAHOMEDANS.

Whilst I was at Delhi one of the leading Mahomedans of the old Moghul capital drove me out one afternoon to the great Mosque which still bears witness, in the splendour of its surviving fragments quite as much as in the name it bears, *Kuwwat ul Islam*, or Power of Islam, to the ancient glories of Mahomedan rule in India. Two or three other Mahomedan gentlemen had come out to meet us, and there, under the shadow of the Kutub Minar, the loftiest and noblest minaret from which the Musulman call to prayer has ever gone forth, we sat in the Alai Darwazah, the great porch of red sandstone and white marble which formed the south entrance to the outer enclosure of the Mosque, and still presents in the stately grandeur of its proportions and the infinite variety and delicacy of its marble lattice work, one of the most perfect monuments of early Mahomedan art, and discussed for upwards of two hours the future that lies before the Mahomedan community of India. It is a scene I shall never forget, so startling was the contrast between the racial and religious pride of power which those walls had for centuries reflected and the note of deep and almost gloomy apprehension to which they now rang. For if the burden of my friends' story was reasoned loyalty to the British *Raj*, it was weighted with profound anxiety as to the future that awaited the Mahomedans of India, either should 'our *Raj* disappear or should it gradually lose its potency and be merged in a virtual ascendency of Hinduism under the specious mantle of Indian self-government. They spoke without bitterness or resentment. They acknowledged freely the shortcomings of their own community, its intellectual backwardness, its reluctance to depart from the ancient ways and to realize the necessity of equipping itself for successful competition under new conditions, its lack of organization, due to an inadequate sense of the duty of social service, and the selfishness and jealousy often displayed by different sections and classes. They were beginning to awaken to the dangerous consequences of their shortcomings, but would time be given to them to repair them? The British *Raj* had always claimed that its mission in India was to hold the balance evenly between the different races and creeds and classes, and to exercise its paternal authority equally to the detriment of none and for the benefit of all. That the Hindus had from the beginning secured a considerably larger share in Government employment of all kinds was, no doubt, inevitable, as they had shown much greater alacrity to qualify themselves by education on Western lines than the Mahomedans, unfortunately, had until much more recently begun to show. But so long as Government *employés* were merely the servants of Government, and Hindus had no more influence than the Mahomedans in shaping the policy of the Government, the Mahomedans had no serious grievance, or, at any rate, none for which they had not themselves very largely to blame. But of late years they had seen the policy of the British Government itself gradually yielding to the pressure of Hindu agitation and the British *Raj* actually divesting itself of some of the powers which it had hitherto retained undiminished for the benefit, in fact if not in theory, of certain classes which, however loudly they might claim to be the representatives of the Indian people, represented with few exceptions nothing but the political ambitions of aggressive Hinduism. The Mahomedans, they assured me, recognized quite as fully as, and perhaps more sincerely than, the Hindus the generous spirit which had inspired the British Government to grant the reforms embodied in the Indian Councils Act, but they also realized what it was far more difficult for Englishmen to realize, that those reforms must inevitably tend to give the Hindus a predominant share, as compared with the Mahomedans, in the counsels of Government. In its original shape the scheme of reforms had indeed threatened the Mahomedans with gross unfairness and the wrath which its subsequent modification in deference to Mahomedan representations had roused among the Hindu politicians was in itself enough to betray to all who had eyes to see and ears to hear the purpose to which they had hoped to turn the excessive predominance they had claimed and expected. That purpose was to advance the political ascendency of Hinduism which was the goal of Hindu aspirations, whether under the British *Raj* or without it.

The whole tendency of the Hindu revival, social, religious, and political, during the last 20 years had been as consistently anti-Mahomedan as anti-British, and even more so. Some of the more liberal and moderate Hindu leaders no doubt honestly contemplated the evolution of an Indian "nation" in which Mahomedan and Hindu might sink their racial and religious differences, but these were leaders with a constantly diminishing body of followers. Even among the Extremists not a few would gladly have purchased by pious professions of good will a temporary alliance with the Mahomedans against the British *Raj*, subject to an ulterior settlement of accounts for their own benefit. But the Mahomedans, with their many close points of contact with the Hindus, knew, as Englishmen could not know, what were the real sentiments and hopes of the advanced leaders into whose hands had passed the control of militant Hinduism. They had noted the constant exhortation of the Hindu Nationalist Press that the youth of India must prepare for the coming Lalki incarnation of Vishnu when the *mlencchas*—*i.e.*, the infidels, Moslem as well as British—should be driven out of India. The attitude of the Hindus towards the Mahomedans of E .stern Bengal, after the Partition, had shown how they resented the position that the creation of the new province gave to the Moslem element. Nor had the Mahomedans in the Punjab been left without a foretaste of what was to come. In every Government office, in every profession, the Hindus were banding themselves closer and closer together against their few Mahomedan colleagues. The Mahomedans had refused to join in the boycott of British goods, and in Delhi, in Lahore, and in many other cities the word had been passed round among the Hindus not to deal with Mahomedan shops, not to trade with Mahomedan merchants. Some of the more violent spirits were even prepared to challenge the Mahomedans in places where the Mahomedan element is strong and excitable, in order that the inevitable intervention of the British troops for the restoration of order should lead to the shedding of Mahomedan blood, and thus perhaps drive the Mahomedans themselves into disaffection. What educated Mahomedans, they told me, chiefly feared, and the Hindus themselves chiefly hoped—for few of them probably believed in any speedy overthrow of British rule—was that the British Government and the British people would be wearied by an agitation of which it was difficult for Englishmen to grasp the real inwardness into making successive concessions to the Hindus which would gradually give them such a controlling voice in the government of the country that they would actually be in a position to achieve their policy of ascendency under the aegis of the British *Raj*. Such fears might seem exaggerated, but the Mahomedans could not but take note of the extent to which the Hindu politicians had already secured the ear of an important section of the British Press and of not a few members of the British Parliament, whilst in those same quarters the Mahomedan case never even obtained a hearing, and when the Mahomedans at last realized the necessity of creating an organization for the defence of their legitimate interests they were denounced for reviving racial and religious hatred. For 20 years and more the educated Mahomedans had strictly followed the advice of their revered leader, Sir Syed Ahmed, and had put their trust in the sense of justice of the British Government and the fair-mindedness of the British people instead of plunging into political agitation. They had not lost their faith in the British Government or in the British people if their case was properly put before them, but they felt that if they were not to become the victims of organized misrepresentation they must have an organization of their own which should speak for them with authority. Moreover, it was impossible for the Mahomedans to stand any longer completely aloof from politics, since the general trend of events in India and the enlargement of the Indian Councils had thrust new responsibilities upon the leaders of their community. Of those responsibilities none was more fully realized than that of showing their loyalty to the British *Raj*—a loyalty all the more unalterable in that it was based upon their growing conviction that the maintenance of the British *Raj* was essential to the welfare, and even to the existence, of the Mahomedans of India.

As I write I have before me a letter from another Mahomedan friend, a man both of European education and very wide knowledge of his Indian co-religionists, with whom he enjoys exceptional credit. I was so much impressed with the prevalence of this form of fatalism that I wrote and asked him for his opinion. This is his answer :—

Moslems feel that while at present the Government in India is British in spirit as well as in name, there are already indications that it might gradually become Hindu in fact, though the British form might remain. The whole object of the advanced Congress Party and of the leaders of the Nationalist movement is not the overthrow of British rule in name, but in fact. You may say that this is a wild apprehension, and that the Government is not foolish enough or weak enough to degenerate into a mere form. That may be the attitude of an Englishman who is in India only as a bird of passage (and all Englishmen are there as birds of passage, for only those whose children belong to the country are permanently bound up with it). For us who live here, and whose children are to live here, the distant as well as the immediate future is of essential importance. Now what is the tendency of Government? Can any one deny that, taken as a whole, it is towards Hindu predominance in the long run? English observers must not forget that there is throughout India amongst Hindus a strong tendency towards imitating the National movements that have proved successful in European history. Now, while *vis-à-vis* the British the Hindu irreconcilables assume the attitude of the Italian patriots towards the hated Austrian, *vis-à-vis* the Moslems there is a very different European model for them to follow. Not only Tilak and his school in Poona, but throughout the Punjab and Bengal the constant talk of the Nationalists is that the Moslems must be driven out of India as they were driven out of Spain.

This is no invention of ours. Nor is it quite so wild as it appears at first sight. I have gone into the matter carefully and I can certainly conceive circumstances—50 or 100 years hence—that would make India intolerable for our upper middle classes; and once you get rid of the intelligent and wealthy Moslems the masses could be reduced to absolute subjection in the hands of Hindu rulers. Far be it from me to say that all Hindus are of this purpose or that the school of "liberal Nationalism" to which Gokhale belongs has ceased to exist. But the other school predominates, and as our very existence is at stake we Moslems do not want to take any risks or to see even the very first steps taken towards transforming the British into a Hindu *raj*. Yet those steps are now being taken, though not quite so fast as we at one time feared and Hindus expected. That the sad and terrible fate which our people had in Spain may still be ours in India is a proposition that sounds extravagant at first, but I for my part (and most thoughtful Moslems agree with me) consider it quite possible, and in a matter of such moment we must take possibilities as well at probabilities into consideration.

The Imperial problem in India is not to get this or that law changed, or so and so many troops increased, or such and such measures of repression or concession adopted. It is to bring about a new mental and spiritual attitude, and to replace the narrow "Nationalism" of the present day by a broad and truly liberal Imperialism in the practical sense of securing general recognition for India's difficulties and divisions, and for the natural and necessary maintenance of the British connexion and of British rule. The statesman who can suggest practical means for carrying out this intellectual conversion will certainly have saved England and India much unhappiness and disaster.

On the other hand, I am bound to say that there are also many Mahomedans who, though professing similar apprehensions, show no disposition towards fatalistic resignation. For they believe that, whatever may be the fate of the British *raj*, the future must belong to the more virile peoples of India, and certainly those who do not merely put their trust in the fighting traditions of a conquering race may find a good deal of encouragement for the faith within them from the vital statistics of Hindus and Mahomedans respectively in India.

Whilst it is most important that nothing should be done to give colour to the idea sedulously promoted by the Hindu politician that Government intend to favour, or, as he generally puts it, to "pamper," the Mahomedans at the expense of the Hindus, it is equally important that Government should do nothing to strengthen the apprehensions entertained by so many intelligent and educated Mahomedans. Those apprehensions are no doubt exaggerated, and may even be quite unfounded; but they correspond exactly with what I have been told were Tilak's hopes and anticipations, and if we will only take the trouble to try to see things as they may well strike an Indian Mahomedan we can hardly dismiss them as wholly unreasonable.

The antagonism between the two communities is not the creation or the result of British rule. It is the legacy of centuries of conflict before British rule was ever heard of in India. It has been and must be one of the chief objects of British statesmanship to compose this conflict, and the Mahomedans do not deny that their British rulers have always desired to deal as fairly with them as with the Hindus. They hold, however, that, as a matter of fact, British rule has in many ways worked out to the relative detriment of Mahomedan influence and to the greater advantage of the Hindus. Nor is that fact rendered any more palatable to the Mahomedans because it is mainly duc to the greater adaptability and suppleness displayed by the Hindus ever since India has been brought into contact with Western education and Western methods. The establishment of English as the official language of the Law Courts and of all public Departments necessarily favoured the Hindus by displacing Persian and the vernaculars in which the Mahomedans were most proficient. At the present day the vast majority of Indians employed in every branch of the Government service are Hindus, and this majority is entirely out of proportion to the numerical preponderancy of the Hindu community at large[11]. According to the last Census Report the Hindus of Bengal (which was then unpartitioned), though only twice as numerous as the Mahomedans, held 1,235 higher appointments under Government in Bengal, as against only 141 held by Mahomedans. In the Bombay Presidency the Hindus held 266 such appointments, as against 23 held by Mahomedans ; and in the Central Provinces 339, as against 75. Of the provinces in reference to which the report furnishes detailed statistics the United Provinces alone failed to show the same disparity, the number of posts held by the Mahomedans, 453, against 711 held by Hindus, being actually and very largely in excess of their proportion to population. The Mahomedans, moreover, complain that where Mahomedans are employed as clerks in Government Departments the head clerks, who are almost always Hindus and alone have direct access to the English superior officers, use their influence with the latter to prejudice them against their Mahomedan subordinates. Education has passed very largely from our own hands into those of Hindu teachers. In all the liberal professions, at the Bar, in the Press, the preponderance of Hindus is greatly out of proportion even to the numerical preponderance of the Hindu population as a whole. Intelligent Mahomedans are conscious that all this is to a great extent the result of the backwardness of their community, but hardships are none the less hardships because they are largely of one's own making. Again, the principal seat of the Government of India and those of the two great Presidency Governments are in centres of Hindu life where the voice of the Mahomedan element does not make itself easily heard.

Then Mahomedans who watch public opinion in England note that one of the two great parties in the State has for many years past professed to recognize in the views of Hindu politicians a commendable affinity to its own political principles, whilst the memory of its greatest leader, Mr. Gladstone, is chiefly associated in India with a violent hostility to Turkey, which, at any rate amongst many of his followers, degenerated into violent denunciations of Islam in general. By his personal qualities Lord Ripon, the most pronounced Liberal ever sent out in our time as Viceroy, endeared himself to many Mahomedans as well as to the Hindus, but he never made any secret of his political sympathies with Hindu aspirations. Whilst Unionist Governments were in office, with only one short break during a period of nearly 20 years, and especially whilst Lord Curzon was Viceroy, the alliance between the Hindu leaders and Radical politicians at home became more and more intimate. The Hindu National Congress, which the Mahomedans had come to regard as little more than a Hindu political organization, was not only generally acclaimed by English newspapers of an advanced complexion as the exponent of a new-born Indian democracy, but it had founded [12] in London an organ of its own, *India*, subsidized out of its funds, and edited and managed by Englishmen, which may not have a very large circulation at home, but is the chief purveyor of

Indian news to a large part of the Liberal Press. When Radical members of Parliament visited India the views they chiefly cared to make themselves acquainted with or reproduced when they went home were the views of Hindu politicians, and when the latter visited England they could always depend upon the demonstrative hospitality not only of Radical clubs and associations but also of the Radical Press for their political propaganda.

When the Liberal Party returned to power at the end of 1905 the majority in the new House of Commons included a very active group that identified itself whole-heartedly with a campaign which, in Bengal, soon assumed a character of scarcely less hostility to the Mahomedans than to the British Administration, and the new Government announced their intention of preparing a scheme of reforms which, whatever its merits, was greeted in India as a concession to Hindu rather than to Mahomedan sentiment. For the Mahomedan has always been a believer in personal rule, and one of the objects of the reforms scheme was to diminish to some extent that element in the Indian Administration. Moreover, when it was first outlined by the Secretary of State, the scheme contained provisions which seemed to the Mahomedans to be at variance both with principles of fair and equal treatment for all races and creeds and classes upon which British rule had hitherto been based, and with the specific pledges given by the Viceroy to the Mahomedan deputation that waited upon him four years ago at Simla when the reforms were first contemplated. The new representation in the enlarged Indian Councils was based proportionally upon a rough estimate of the populations of India which credited the Hindus with millions that are either altogether outside the pale of Hinduism or belong to those castes which the majority of educated Hindus of the higher castes still regard as "untouchable." The effect would have been to give the Hindus what the Mahomedans regarded as an unfairly excessive representation. Happily, though the question trembled for a long time in the balance, Lord Morley listened to the remonstrances of the Mahomedans, and in its final shape the Indian Councils Act made very adequate provision for the representation of Mahomedan interests. But the Mahomedans saw in the angry disappointment of the Hindu politicians when the scheme was thus modified ample justification for the fears they had entertained. Even as it is—and the Mahomedans recognize both the many good points of the scheme and Lord Morley's desire to deal fairly with them—these new reforms may well seem to the Mahomedans to have enured mainly to the benefit of the Hindus. The Mahomedans appreciate as warmly as the Hindus the appointment of an Indian member to the Viceroy's Executive Council, and if the first Indian member was to be a Hindu they admit that Mr. Sinha had exceptional qualifications for the high post to which he was called. The Indian members added under the new Act to the Executive Councils of Bombay and Madras are also both Hindus, and another Hindu will almost certainly be nominated in like manner to the Executive Council of Bengal. None of these appointments may be open to objection, but the fact nevertheless remains that it is the Hindus and not the Mahomedans who will have had the immediate benefit of this new departure to which Indian opinion attaches the greatest importance.

The fact is that the more we delegate of our authority in India to the natives of India on the principles which we associate with self-government, the more we must necessarily in practice delegate it to the Hindus, who form the majority, however much we may try to protect the rights and interests of the Mahomedan minority. This is what the Mahomedans know and fear. This is what explains their insistence upon separate electorates wherever the elective principle comes into play in the composition of representative bodies. It is not merely that they have yet to learn the elementary business of electoral organization, in which the Hindus, on the contrary, have shown great proficiency, and that they have consequently fared badly even in local bodies where their numbers ought to have secured them more adequate representation. Many Mahomedans realize the disadvantage of locking up their community in a watertight compartment, but they regard it as the lesser evil. It is, they contend, an essential safeguard not only against an excessive Hindu predominance in elective or partly elective bodies, but also against the growing disposition which they note amongst those who claim to be the spokesmen of the rising British democracy to accelerate the rate at which political concessions should be made to Hindu opinion, and also to disregard the claim of the Mahomedan minority to be protected against any abuse by the Hindus of the power which a majority must necessarily wield.

My object is to explain the views actually held by the leaders of the Indian Mahomedan community, rather than to endorse or to controvert them. Even if the construction they place upon the attitude of their Hindu fellow-countrymen and of an influential section of British public opinion be wholly unreasonable, the fact that that attitude is liable to such a construction is one which we ought to bear in mind. Nor can it be disputed that, however generous the sentiments that prompt us to delegate some part of our authority to elective or partly elective assemblies, it must to some extent diminish the power of the Executive to ensure that equality of treatment for all races and creeds and classes by which we have hitherto justified our rule in India. Our sense of equity should make us, therefore, all the more scrupulously careful to adjust the balance as evenly as possible under the new conditions which we are ourselves creating, and to err, if at all, in favour of the protection of minorities. Elementary considerations of statesmanship impose the same obligation upon us.

The Mahomedans of India form more than a fifth of the whole population. They are not racially any more homogeneous than the Hindus, and except towards the north-western frontier, where they are to be found chiefly amongst the half-tamed tribes of the Indian borderland, and in the Punjab and United Provinces, where there are many descendants of the Moslem conquerors, they consist chiefly of converted Hindus who accepted Islam as a consequence of Mahomedan rule. But whatever racial differences there may be amongst them, they are now bound together by a creed which has an extraordinary welding power. That there are also explosive potentialities in their creed the Wahabi rising in Bengal little more than 30 years ago and the chronic turbulence of the tribes and frequent exploits of *ghazis* on the north-western frontier are there to show. But amongst the large body of Mahomedans scattered through India, and especially amongst the higher classes, Islam has in a great measure lost its aggressive character. Surrounded on all sides by an overwhelming majority of Hindus, whose religion he regards as detestably idolatrous, the Indian Moslem is inclined to sink his hostility to Christianity and to regard us less as "infidels" than as fellow-believers in the central article of his monotheistic faith, the unity of God. We, too, in his eyes are "People of the Book," though our Book is not the Koran, but the Bible, of which he does not altogether deny the sacred character. Other things also often draw him towards the Englishman. The Englishman to him represents a ruling race, and to such an one he feels that he who also represents a once ruling race can yield a more willing allegiance than to any one of a race which he himself ruled over. Equally his fighting and his sporting instincts also appeal to many Englishmen. Hence both Englishmen and Mahomedans in India frequently feel that they have more in common than either of them has with the Hindu. The Mahomedans, moreover, consisting very largely of the most virile races in India, have always furnished some of the best contingents of the British Indian Army. Their loyalty has never wavered except during the Mutiny, and modern Indian writers of the Nationalist school are themselves at pains to show that, though the mutineers rallied round the feeble descendant of the Moghul Emperors as the only available figurehead, and many Mahomedans proved themselves good "patriots," it was Hindus like Nana Sahib and Tantia Tope and the Ranee of Jhansi who were the real heroes and moving spirits of that "War of Indian Independence."

In our day the British connexion has had no stouter and more convinced supporter than the late Sir Syed Ahmad, than whom no Mahomedan has deserved or enjoyed greater influence over his Indian co-religionists. Not only does his educational work, based on the English public school system, live after him in the college which he founded at Aligarh, but also his political faith which taught the vast majority of educated Mahomedans to regard their future as bound up with the preservation of British rule. The revival of Hinduism has only served to strengthen that faith by bringing home to the Mahomedans the value of British rule as a bulwark against the Hindu ascendency which in the more or less remote future they have unquestionably begun to dread. The creation of a political organization like the All-India Moslem League, which is an outcome of the new apprehensions evoked by Hindu aspirations, may appear on the surface to be a departure from the teachings of Sir Syed Ahmad, who, when the Indian National Congress was appealing in its early days for Mahomedan support, urged his people to hold altogether aloof from politics and to rely implicitly upon the good will and good faith of Government. But things have moved rapidly since Sir Syed Ahmad's time, and when the British Government themselves create fresh opportunities for every Indian community to make its voice heard in political counsel, the Mahomedans hold that none can afford to stand back.

The Moslem League founded by the Aga Khan, one of the most broad-minded and highly-educated of Indians, with the full approval of the late Nawab Mohsin-ul-Mulk, the confidant and successor of Sir Syed Ahmad, is moreover not merely or even chiefly a political organization. It is intended to serve as a centre for the maintenance and consolidation of the communal interests of the Mahomedans all over India in their social, educational, and economic as well as political aspects. Its programme was unfolded at the annual meeting of the League held in January last at Delhi both in an address read on behalf of Mr. Ameer Ali, who was detained in England by his duties on the Judicial Committee of the Privy Council, and in a speech delivered by the Aga Khan, the recognized leader of the whole community. The programme of the Moslem League puts forward no such ambitious demands as self-government for India. All it asks for is "the ordered development of the country under the Imperial Crown." It accepts the reforms with much more gratitude and enthusiasm than were displayed by the spokesman of the Indian National Congress at Lahore, and it accepts them in no narrow or sectarian spirit. The Aga Khan was in fact at special pains to indicate the various directions in which Mahomedans and Hindus might and ought to act in harmonious co-operation. The functions of the Mahomedan representatives on the new Councils would, the Aga Khan said, be threefold.

> In the first place they must co-operate as representative Indian citizens with other Indians in advancing the well-being of the country by working wholeheartedly for the spread of education, for the establishment of free and universal primary education, for the promotion of commerce and industry, for the improvement of agriculture by the establishment of co-operative credit and distribution societies, and for the development of the natural resources of India. Here, indeed, is a wide field of work for Hindus and Mahomedans acting together. In the second place our representatives

must be ready to co-operate with the Hindus and all other sections of society in securing for them all those advantages that serve their peculiar conditions and help their social welfare, for although the two sister communities have developed on different lines, each suffers from some peculiar weakness in addition to the misfortunes common to general economic and educational backwardness. And then our representatives must watch and promote social measures required exclusively for the benefit of their Moslem co-religionists, with the co-operation, we hope, of the Hindu members, for we too have needs that are not known to them and which we alone can fully understand.

No language could be more generous or more statesmanlike. The Aga Khan doubtless realizes that, whatever the more or less remote future may have in store for the two communities, their increasing antagonism in consequence of the aggressive tendencies displayed by Hindu "nationalism" during the last few years is pregnant with immediate danger, and nowhere more so than in the Punjab where he was speaking. Not only have the preachers of the Arya Samaj, taking their cue from the writings of their apostle Dayanand, frequently indulged, both in the Press and on the platform, in outrageous attacks upon the Mahomedans' religion, but the militant Hindus have visited upon the Mahomedans their refusal to join in an anti-British agitation by enforcing against them a commercial and social boycott, none the less oppressive and damaging because it is not openly proclaimed. The bitterness thus engendered found vent in serious riots this year at Peshawar, just as it did in Eastern Bengal, when the boycott campaign there was at its height. Even in Hyderabad, the capital of the Nizam's dominions, where, under the wise administration of a great Mahomedan ruler whose Prime Minister is a Hindu, the relations between Moslem and Hindu have hitherto been quite harmonious, a change is gradually making itself felt under the inspiration of a small group of Bengali Hindus who have brought with them the Nationalist cry of "Arya for the Aryan." The animosity which has always existed between the Mahomedans and the Hindus, especially amongst the lower orders, has been a constant source of anxiety to Anglo-Indian administrators. As far as it springs from the clash of religious beliefs, social customs, and historical traditions, it can only be eradicated by the slow process of education. The most trivial incident, the meeting of rival processions, the maltreatment of a cow, so sacred to the Hindus, some purely personal quarrel suddenly leads to violent affrays in which the whole populace on both sides joins in without knowing even what it is all about. The danger must be enormously heightened if one community begins to believe that the other community is compassing deep-laid schemes for the promotion of its own ultimate ascendency. The political agitation conducted by the Hindus has for some time past tended to create such a belief amongst the Mahomedans. As far back as 1893, at the time of the Bombay riots and of Tilak's "anti-cow-killing" propaganda in the Deccan, which spread sporadically to other parts of India, the Bombay Government reported "an uneasy feeling among Mahomedans that they and their faith were suffering at the hands of the Hindus, that they were being gradually but surely edged out of the position they have hitherto held, and that their religion needed some special protection." That uneasy feeling has gradually ripened since then into a widespread and deep-rooted conviction—not the least of the many deplorable results of a movement that claims to be called "national."

It would be an evil day for the internal peace of India if a people still so proud of their history, so jealous of their religion, and so conscious of their virile superiority as the Mahomedans came to believe that they could only trust to their own right hand, and no longer to the authority and sense of justice of the British *Raj*, to avert the dangers which they foresee in the future from the establishment of an overt or covert Hindu ascendency. Some may say that it would be an equally evil day for the British *Raj* if the Mahomedans came to believe in the futility of unrequited loyalty and joined hands with its enemies in the confident anticipation that, whatever welter might follow the collapse of British rule, they could not fail sooner or later to fight their way once more to the front. Certainly at no time since we have ruled India has greater circumspection been needed in holding the balance between the two communities. It would be as impolitic to forget that the Mahomedans have held steadfastly aloof from the anti-British movement of the last few years and represent on the whole a great conservative force, as to create the impression amongst the Hindus at large, of whom the vast majority are still our friends, that we are disposed to visit upon them the disloyalty of what is after all a small section of their community by unduly favouring the Mahomedans at their expense.

CHAPTER X.

SOUTHERN INDIA.

Unrest in its most dangerous forms has hitherto been almost entirely confined to the Deccan, Bengal, and the Punjab. It has spread to some extent from the Bombay Presidency into the Central Provinces, which, indeed, include part of the Deccan, and it has overflowed both from Bengal and from the Punjab into some of the neighbouring districts of the United Provinces. But thanks very largely to the firm and experienced hands in which the administration of the Central Provinces under their Commissioner, Mr. Craddock, and that of the United Provinces under their Lieutenant-Governor, Sir John Hewett, have rested during these troublous years, the situation there has never got seriously out of hand. Except in Peshawar, where the political propaganda of a somewhat militant colony of Bengalees has stimulated the latent antagonism between Hindus and Mahomedans, our difficulties in the new Frontier Province, as well as along the whole North-West frontier, are of quite a different order, and though the turbulence of Pathan tribes and the occasional outbreaks of Moslem fanaticism amongst them are a cause of constantly recurring anxiety to the Government of India, it is not amongst those hardy and only half-tamed hillsmen that the cry of *Swadeshi* and *Swaraj* from Bengal or of "Arya for the Aryans" from the Punjab is likely to elicit any response. Such echoes of far away sedition as may reach their mountain fastnesses provoke only vague wonder at the forbearance and leniency of British rulers, and if ever the British *Raj* were in jeopardy, Pathan and Baluch would be the first to sharpen their swords and shoulder their rifles either in response to our call or in order to descend on their own account, as their forbears have done before, into the fair plains of Hindustan and carve out kingdoms for themselves from the chaos that would follow the collapse of British power. Along the North-East frontier British India marches with semi-independent States that have little or nothing in common with the rest of India. Nepal, Bhutan, and Sikkim are Himalayan highlands inhabited chiefly by Mongolian Buddhists, who have far more affinity with Tibetans and Chinese than with their Indian neighbours to the south. Assam is little more than an administrative dependency of Eastern Bengal, whilst Burma has been even more accurately described as a mere appendage of India, attached for purposes of administrative convenience to our Indian Empire, but otherwise as effectively divided from it by race, religion, customs, and tradition as by the waters of the Bay of Bengal and the dense jungles of the Patkai Mountains.

In none of these borderlands has Hinduism ever struck root, and in none of them, therefore, is Indian Nationalism, which is so largely bound up with Hinduism, likely to find a congenial soil. But that Southern India where Hinduism is supreme should have remained hitherto so little affected by the political agitation which has swept across India further north from the Deccan to Bengal may at first sight cause some surprise. Yet the explanation is not far to seek, if one bears in mind the profound differences which nature itself has imposed upon this vast sub-continent. Southern India, which may be defined as including the whole of the Madras Presidency and the three native States of Mysore, Cochin, and Travancore, differs, indeed, almost immeasurably from Central and Northern India. South of the high, sun-scorched plateau of the Deccan, from the mouth of the Kistna to the Indian Ocean, the great Indian peninsula rapidly narrows. Tempered by more frequent rains and the moist breezes which sweep across it from both the Malabar and the Coromandel coasts, the climate is more equable and the heat, though more continuous, is less fierce. The whole character of the country is luxuriantly tropical, and though the lowlands are not more fertile than the matchless delta of the Ganges, the more varied prodigality of nature shows itself alike in the waving forests of cocoanut, which are common all along the coast, in the rich tobacco-fields of Madura and Coimbatore, in the plantations of cinchona, pepper, cardamoms, and other spices on the slopes of the Nilgiri highlands, and in the splendid growths of teak, ebony, and sandalwood that clothe the Western Ghats. The population, which in some parts attains extraordinary density and lives almost exclusively on the fruits of the soil, is of the old Dravidian stock, industrious and frugal as in other parts of India,and of a placid and gentle temper. Nowhere else in India does one come into such close contact with its original non-Aryan peoples ; and nowhere else has the earliest type of religious and social institutions evolved by the superior civilization of the Aryans been so completely preserved from the disturbing influences of later ages. And yet—such are the curious contrasts which abound in this strange country—nowhere else does one find so many living survivals of the intercourse which occurred from time to time between India and the West, many centuries before Europe turned her eyes towards that Terra Incognita. Nowhere, for instance, has Christianity made more converts of recent years, perhaps because in Southern India there may still be found indigenous Christian communities which trace their origin back to the first centuries of the Christian era. Even if there be no historical foundation for the tradition that it was St. Thomas the Apostle who himself first evangelized Southern India, and was ultimately martyred at St. Thomas's Mount near Madras, there is good authority for believing that Christianity was imported not many centuries later into Southern India by the Nestorian or Chaldæan missionaries from Persia and Mesopotamia, whose apostolic zeal ranged all over Asia, even into Tibet and Tartary. According to the Saxon chronicle, our own King Alfred sent alms to India in 883 for St. Thomas and St. Bartholomew, and at that date there certainly existed, besides some small Christian communities on the Coromandel coast, two flourishing communities on the Malabar coast, where the so-called Syrian Church has maintained itself to the present day. Another curious and perhaps equally ancient link with the West may still be seen to survive to-day in the small community of white Jews at Cochin, which, according to their own tradition, was founded when their forefathers were driven out of Palestine after the destruction of the second Temple. To the charter which they still have in their possession, inscribed, like most west coast title deeds, on copper plates, the date assigned by the best authorities is about 700 A.D., and the powers and privileges which were specifically conferred upon their ancestors show that at that period already they had acquired in a remarkable degree the confidence and friendship of the Hindu Kings of Malabar. The decline of both Christian and Jewish communities seems to have begun, indeed, with the appearance of the first Portuguese invaders from Europe, whose incursions destroyed the peace and tolerance which Christian and Jew had enjoyed in the days of undisturbed Hindu rule.

To what period the subjection of the old Dravidian stock to the superior civilization of the Aryans dates back, or in what manner it was continued, there is little as yet to show. All that is actually known is that at some very remote period Aryan Hinduism was imported into Southern India by Brahmans from the north, who established it in the first place probably by force, and whose descendants have ever since maintained the claims of their sacred caste to a position of religious and social pre-eminence even greater than that which any other Brahmans of the present day have succeeded in retaining. Nowhere else in India does the Brahman, as such, wield the power and assert the prerogatives which the Namputri Brahman enjoys on the Malabar coast. Even the Maharajahs of Travancore, who by birth belong to the Kshatrya or warrior caste, have to be "born again" by a peculiar and costly ceremony into the superior caste before they ascend the throne, and one sept of the Namputri Brahmans successfully exacts in the person of the head of the Azhvancheri family recognition of its spiritual overlordship by personal homage from the Maharajah once in every six years. Nothing, perhaps, conveys more graphically the extraordinary sanctity which attaches to the Brahman caste than the uncompromising manner in which all along the Malabar coast they have enforced and maintained the laws of ceremonial "pollution." Nowhere else have such stringent rules been enacted to fix the precise distance at which the bodily presence of a member of the lower castes is held to defile the sacred person of the Brahman. A Bazar may approach, but must not touch him; a Chogan may not approach him within 24 feet, nor a Kanisan within 36, nor a Pulayan within 64, nor a Nayadi within 72 feet. Equally definite and elaborate are the manifold restrictions on marriage, commensality, occupation, food, ceremonial observances and personal conduct which affect the mutual relations not only between the different castes but also between the innumerable sub-castes into which the higher castes especially have in turns split up. The laws which govern marriage, descent, and inheritance amongst the more important castes throw a peculiarly interesting light on the archaic type of society which has survived in Southern India. Under the matriarchal system of *Manumakkathayam*, which on the Malabar coast obtains to the present day, descent is traced only through the female line. The male member of the family inherits, but he does so only as the son of a female member of the family through whom he may justly claim kinship, or, to put it in another form, a man's natural heir is not his son, or his brother's son, or the descendant of a common male ancestor, but his sister's, or his sister's daughter's son, or the descendant of a common female ancestress. In the event of failure of heirs through the female line, adoption is permissible, but the adoption must be of females, through whose subsequent offspring the line of natural descent may be carried on. With this ancient system are bound up forms of matrimonial union and tenure of property into the complicated and peculiar nature of which I need not enter here.

In the wild hill countries weird remnants of the most primitive races still survive that have not yet been brought within the pale of Hinduism, and here and there a sprinkling of Mahomedans remains as a reminder of the shortlived incursions of Moslem conquerors from the north. But ninety per cent. of the population consists of Hindus, and the social and religious supremacy of Hinduism has never been seriously assailed. Nowhere has Hindu architecture taken such majestic shape, the massive pylons of Madura and Tanjore recalling the imperishable grandeur of the noblest Egyptian temples on the Nile. Southern India is in fact a land of stately shrines which dominate the whole country just as our own great cathedrals dominated England in the Middle Ages. Yet in Southern India, Hinduism has not assumed the aggressive character which it has developed in other regions. Perhaps it feels too secure of the unchallenged supremacy which it has enjoyed through the ages as a social and religious force without ever aspiring to direct political ascendancy. Perhaps the admixture of Dravidian blood has imparted to it a more serene tolerance. Perhaps it appreciates more fully the relief from the turmoil, strife, and bloodshed which was brought to Southern India by the advent of British rule. Compare the legend of a pre-British "golden age" propagated by Tilak and his disciples in the Deccan and in Bengal with the remarkable picture of the condition of Southern India at the time when the British power first appeared on the scene which was drawn by a Madras Brahman, the late Mr. Srinivasaraghava Iyangar :—

Southern India had been devastated by wars, famines, and bands of plunderers ; the cultivating classes were ground down by oppressive taxation, by the illegal exactions of the officers of Government, of the renters employed to collect the Government dues, and of the sowkars without whose assistance the ryots could not subsist and carry on their calling, and who kept them in a state little removed from perpetual bondage ; trade was hampered by insecurity of property, defective communications, and onerous transit duties ; the vast majority of the population suffered extreme hardships when there was even a partial failure of crops in small tracts, owing to the great difficulty and cost of obtaining supplies of grain from more favoured regions ; the peasantry and even possessors of considerable landed property, when not holding office under Government themselves, were cowering before the pettiest Government officer and submitting to tortures and degrading personal ill-treatment inflicted on the slightest pretext ; persons who had chanced to acquire wealth, if they belonged to the lower classes, dared not openly use it for purposes of enjoyment or display for fear of being plundered by the classes above them ; the agricultural classes as a whole had few wants beyond those imposed by the necessity for bare subsistence, no ambition or enterprise to try untrodden ways, and no example to stimulate them to endeavour to better their condition, while the rigid usages of castes and communities in which society was organized repressed all freedom of action and restricted the scope for individual initiative. To understand the full significance of the change which has come over the country one has to contrast what he sees at present, unsatisfactory as it may appear from some points of view, with the state of things described above. . . . Remembering that methods of progress calculated to evoke national feeling and religious enthusiasm are unavailable under the conditions of the case, the progress that has been made . . . is little short of marvellous.

It was from Madras that the British power set

forth on its unpremeditated course of conquest which was destined ultimately to reach from Tuticorin to the Himalayas. Since the beginning of the nineteenth century the Madras Presidency has been in the fortunate position of having no history. Its northern rivals call it despitefully the "benighted" Presidency. No epithet, however, could be more undeserved, for if its annals for the last hundred years have been unsensational, its record in respect of education, intelligent administration, material prosperity, and all that goes with peaceful continuous progress would entitle it rather to be called the "Model" Presidency. The Native States of Southern India, and above all Mysore, which was for many years under direct British administration, will equally bear favourable comparison with any of the Native States of Central or Northern India. From the standpoint of education, Southern India has long held and probably still holds the lead, thanks in a great measure to the large Christian communities which comprise more than two-thirds of the whole Christian population of India. But in the statistics of literacy based on the last census, the Brahmans figure at the head of all the Hindu castes with the very creditable proportion of 578 males and 40 females per mille. The Western-educated classes in Southern India, whilst as progressive as in any other part, show greater mental balance than in Bengal, and less reactionary tendencies than in the Deccan. Western education has been a steady and perhaps on the whole a more solid growth in Southern India. It has produced a large number of able and distinguished public servants of unimpeachable loyalty to the British *raj*. The harvest yielded by the ingermination of Western ideas has produced fewer tares. Educated Hindus of the higher castes have played an important part in social reform, and many of them have been associated with the moderate section of the Indian National Congress. The enthusiastic reception given to Mr. Bepin Chandra Pal, during his short crusade at Madras three years ago on behalf of *Swaraj*, showed that, especially amongst the younger generation, there is at least an appreciable minority who are ready to listen to the doctrines of advanced Nationalism, and the existence of inflammable materials was revealed in the riots which occurred not long afterwards at Tinnevelly and Tuticorin, and again a year later at Guntur. But these appear to have been merely sporadic outbreaks which were promptly quelled, and the undisturbed peace which has prevailed since then throughout Southern India, at a time when whole provinces in other parts have been honeycombed with sedition, is one of the most encouraging features of the situation. There is in the Hinduism of Southern India a peculiar element of conservative quietism to which lawlessness in any form seems to be repugnant. Probably also the racial cry of "Arya for the Aryans" raised in the North of India as the watchword of an anti-British movement is not calculated to rouse the blood of a purely Dravidian population, however powerful the ties created by a common social and religious system.

CHAPTER XI.

REVOLUTIONARY ORGANIZATIONS OUTSIDE INDIA.

It required nothing less than the shock of a murder perpetrated in the heart of London to open the eyes of those in authority at home to the nature of the revolutionary propaganda which has been, and is still being, carried on outside India in sympathy, and often in connivance, with the more violent leaders of the anti-British agitation in India itself. Even now it may be doubted whether they fully realize the importance of the support which the extremists receive from outside India. I am not alluding to the moral countenance which the Hindu reaction has received from eccentric Americans and Europeans on the look out for any novel religious sensation, or which "advanced" politicians have derived from sympathetic members of Parliament and journalists in England [13], but to the secret organizations established in Europe and in America by the Indian extremists themselves as a base for hostile operations against the British *Raj*. However loudly the extremists protest against the importation of Western influences into India they have certainly not been too proud to borrow the methods of Western revolutionists. They have of all Indians been the most slavish imitators of the West, as represented, at any rate, by the Irish Fenian and the Russian anarchist. Their literature is replete with references to both. Tilak took his "No-rent" campaign in the Deccan from Ireland, and the Bengalees were taught to believe in the power of the boycott by illustrations taken from contemporary Irish history. When the informer Gosain was shot dead in Alipur gaol the Nationalists gloried in the deed, which had far excelled that of Patrick O'Donnell, who shot dead James Carey, the approver in the Phœnix Park murders, inasmuch as Gosain had been murdered before he could complete his "treachery," whereas the murder of Carey had been only a tardy "retribution" which could not undo the past. The use of the bomb has become the common property of revolutionists all over the world, but the employment of amateur dacoits, or armed bands of robbers, for replenishing the revolutionary war-chest has been directly taken from the revolutionary movement in Russia a few years ago. The annals of the Italian *risorgimento* have also been put under contribution, and whilst there is no Indian life of Cavour, Lajpat Rai's Life of Mazzini and Vinayak Savarkar's translation of Mazzini's Autobiography are favourite Nationalist text-books of the milder order. European works on various periods of revolutionary history figure almost invariably amongst seizures of a far more compromising character whenever the Indian police raids some centre of Nationalist activity. Hence in the literature of unrest one frequently comes across the strangest juxtaposition of names, Hindu deities, and Cromwell and Washington, and celebrated anarchists all being invoked in the same breath.

Equally foreign in its origin has been the establishment of various centres of revolutionary activity outside of India. In America there appear to be two distinct organizations both having their headquarters in

California, and branches in Chicago, New York, and other important cities. The Indo-American Association runs an English periodical, *Free Hindustan,* which was originally started in Canada and thence transferred to Seattle when it began to attract the attention of the Canadian authorities. The moving spirits are students, chiefly from Bengal, who have found ready helpers amongst the Irish-American Fenians. They have also been able to make not a few converts amongst the unfortunate British Indian immigrants who suffered heavily from the anti-Asiatic campaign along the Pacific slope, and some of these converts, being Sikhs and old soldiers, were of special value, as through them direct contact could be established with the regiments to which they had belonged, or, at any rate, with the classes from which an important section of the native army is recruited. Large quantities of seditious leaflets, circulated broadcast three years ago amongst Sepoys, were printed in America. The other organization, called the Young Indian Association, with "head centres" and "inner" and "outer circles" that have a genuine Fenian ring, is even more "extreme," and is connected with the "Indian Red Flag" in India, to which Khudiram Bose, who murdered Mrs. and Miss Kennedy at Muzafferpur, and other young fanatics of the same type belonged. The Young Indian Association seems to devote itself chiefly to the study of explosives and to smuggling arms into India. In Anglo-Indian official circles extreme reticence is naturally observed in these matters, but from other sources I have seen evidence to show that both these associations were in frequent communication with the seditious Press all over India, in the Deccan as well as in Bengal and in the Punjab.

The emergence of Japan has created so powerful an impression in India that one is not surprised to find the Indian revolutionaries, who live for the most part in the dreamland of their own ignorance, looking in that quarter for guidance and even, perhaps, for assistance. But they have been sorely disappointed. Indian students are well received in Japan, but they are in nowise specially petted or pampered, and when they begin to air their political opinions and to declaim against British rule they are very speedily put in their place. Crossing the Pacific from Japan to America last year I met one who had spent two or three years at Tokyo and was going on to continue his technical studies in the United States. He was a pleasant and intelligent young fellow, and confessed to me that what he had seen in Japan had very much modified the views he had held when he left Bengal as to the ripeness of his fellow-countrymen for independence or self-government. He had received a great deal of kindness from his Japanese professors, but the general attitude of the Japanese was by no means friendly, and there was no trace of sympathy with the political agitation in India. There is an Indo-Japanese Society in Tokyo, but it has no connexion with politics, and the Indians complain that it is run for the benefit of the Japanese rather than for theirs. Those who have joined it in the hope of using it as a base for anti-British operations have certainly got very little for their pains. They occasionally write articles for the very few Socialist papers of Japan, but their effective contribution to the cause is of trifling account.

The most dangerous organization outside India was unquestionably that which had its headquarters at the "India House" at Highgate. It was there that Dinghra appears to have concocted the plot which resulted in the murder of Sir W. Curzon Wyllie and Dr. Lalcaca, and though the London correspondent of the *Kal*, Vinayak Savarkar, who was arrested this year in London to take his trial on the gravest charges at Bombay, magnified the success of the plot by describing its chief victim as "the eyes of the Secretary of State through which he saw all Indian affairs." there is some reason to believe that Dinghra expected to find at the reception another Anglo-Indian official whom the "extremists" were particularly anxious to "remove," and only in his absence struck at Sir W. Curzon Wyllie. There is reason, too, to believe that it was from this "India House" also that came both the idea of murdering Mr. Jackson and the weapons used by the murderer. Though students from all parts of India were enticed into the "India House," the organization seems to have been controlled by Deccan Brahmans, and in the first instance by Shyamji Krishnavarma, who founded scholarships in connexion with it to honour the Indian "martyrs" executed for murderous outrages in India. When the authorities in London very tardily awoke after the murder of Sir W. Curzon Wyllie to the dangerous nature of this organization, to which *The Times* first drew attention in the spring of 1908, it was still controlled from the Continent by Krishnavarma, who had retreated to Paris long before, leaving his lieutenants to carry on his campaign amongst the young Indian students. The *Indian Sociologist* itself continued to be openly published in London and to advocate assassination until the tragedy at the Imperial Institute led the authorities to take wofully-belated action in prosecuting successively two printers of the sheet, which was then transferred to Paris.

That altogether considerable quantities of incendiary literature have been produced abroad and imported into India through these various organizations is beyond doubt. Sometimes books like Savarkar's "War of Indian Independence of 1857"—in its way a very remarkable history of the Mutiny, combining considerable research with the grossest perversions of facts and great literary power with the most savage hatred—were bound in false covers as "Pickwick Papers," or other equally innocuous works. Other seditious leaflets besides those for the incitement of mutiny in the native army appear to have come from America, whilst newspapers like the *Talvar* and the *Bande Mataram*, which preach the same gospel of murder as Krishnavarma's *Indian Sociologist*, are printed on the Continent of Europe. These papers are either smuggled into India in large parcels or sent through the post in envelopes addressed by name to students in schools and colleges, as well as to schoolmasters, pleaders, Government *employés*—in fact, to all sorts and conditions of people who, for some reason or other, are supposed to be suitable recipients. They naturally fall sometimes into quite the wrong hands.

The importance which the "extremists" attach to the maintenance of these channels of communication with India appears from the following extract from the March issue of the *Bande Mataram*, which purports to be published in Geneva, and calls itself "a monthly organ of Indian independence":—

We must recognize at present that the importation of revolutionary literature into India is the sheet-anchor of the party. It keeps up the spirit of all young men, and assures them that the party is living. We must therefore try to strengthen all groups of workers outside India. The centre of gravity of political work has been shifted from Calcutta, Poona, and Lahore to Paris, Geneva, Berlin, London, and New York. The Wahabi conspiracy of 1862 was completely crushed because there was no centre in foreign countries where the work could be carried on during the period of persecution. We must take this lesson to heart, that if we desire to hear more of the murder of British officials as a token of the progress and vitality of the party we must strengthen and establish centres of work in many foreign countries. The circulation of revolutionary leaflets, journals, and manifestoes should be looked upon as a sacred duty by all patriots. We are not exaggerating the importance of this work when we use that expression. Let us look upon every leaf of revolutionary literature with almost superstitious veneration and try to make it reach India by all means in our power. For it is the seed of life of our people, &c.

As to the importation of arms into India, the murder of Mr. Jackson, "another Nationalist fête celebrated at Nasik amidst the rejoicings of all true patriots," furnishes an occasion for similar exultation:—

We know that the hero possessed Browning pistols. Now these pistols are not manufactured in India, but in Europe.

How have they been imported by the revolutionaries? It is clear that this fact is a testimony to the efficiency of our organization and the secrecy of our activity. Besides, the imported arms are not the only weapons on which we have to rely. Daggers can be manufactured in India out of sharp nails to stab all vile agents of the British Government, English or Indian.

Increased vigilance in this country as well as in the Indian Customs and Post Offices is, however, beginning to check these importations, and only two months later the *Bande Mataram* was already compelled to strike a less exuberant note. It declares, of course, that "our movement cannot be repressed so long as there are patriotic Indians living under other flags than the Union Jack," but it recognizes that the situation "gives rise to anxious thought," and it winds up in a somewhat depressed tone :—

> We admit that for the present all active propaganda among the young men of India with a view to the acquisition of new workers is exceedingly difficult. But there are hundreds of patriotic Indian students in America and Japan who can be inspired with apostolic fervour if only some capable workers are sent among them. The harvest is plenteous, but the labourers are few. We should now realize that, even if the Government succeeds in checkmating us in India at every step, there is ample scope for work for several years among Indians living abroad. We should reflect that steady work is its own reward. We must not imagine that the Idea is not making progress because our particular journal cannot be circulated, or because those workers whom we know personally have been lost. Again, we must not fancy that if heroic exploits of political assassination do not occur every week the movement will die out.

It is not only in regard to the introduction of poisonous literature or of weapons into India that the activity of these organizations deserves to be closely and continuously watched. One of their main objects, as the *Bande Mataram* points out, is to gain over young Indians who go abroad, especially those who go abroad for purposes of study. The India Office has recognized the necessity of establishing some organization in London to keep in touch with them and to rescue them from unwholesome influences, political and other. This is a step in the right direction, but much more will require to be done, and not only in London. Committees should be formed in other centres, and public-spirited Englishmen abroad could not do more useful work than by social service of this kind. If we want to do any real and permanent good we must spread our nets as wide as the revolutionists have spread theirs. In Paris, for instance, Krishnavarma has set up, since he migrated to the other side of the Channel, an organization for waylaying and indoctrinating young Indians on their way to England, so as to induce them to hold aloof from those who would wish to be their friends when they arrive in London. The number of Indian students abroad is bound to go on increasing, especially with the growing demand for scientific and technical edueation for which the provision hitherto made in India is regarded as inadequate. Indian parents and Indian associations that ought to know better are apt to think that, if they can only provide for a youth's travelling expenses, he will somehow be able afterwards to shift for himself. It is not infrequently the misery and distress to which he thus finds himself reduced abroad that drive the young Indian into pol tical recklessness, or, at least, render him peculiarly liable to temptation. British manufacturers might a'so render valuable assistanee. Indian parents complain that, owing to the resentment which crimes like the murder of Sir W. Curzon Wyllie have provoked there is great reluetance now on the part of British firms to admit Indians as apprentices to their works, and that in consequence they are compelled to go to other countries where they are treated with less suspicion. This reluctance is perhaps in reality more often due to the fear lest young Indians should afterwards turn their knowledge to too good an account, as the Japanese have often done, in the promotion of compet ng industries in their own country. However that may be, the results are certainly regrettable. For, if there is one thing that has impressed itself on me during my last visit to India, it is that, if we want to retain our hold, not only upon the country, but upon the people, we must neglect no opportunity of arresting the estrangement which is growing up between us and the younger generation of Indians. It is upon this estrangement that the revolutionary organizations outside of India chiefly rely for the success of their propaganda, and nothing helps them more than the bitterness with which young Indians who come abroad often return to India ready for any desperate adventure [14].

CHAPTER XII.

THE INDIAN NATIONAL CONGRESS.

It is impossible to acquit the Congress of having contributed to the growth of active and violent unrest, though the result may have lain far both from the purpose of its chief originators and from the desire of the majority of its members. Western education has largely failed in India because the Indian, not unnaturally, fails to bring an education based upon conceptions entirely alien to the world in which he moves into any sort of practical relation with his own life. So with the Indian politician, who, even with the best intentions, fails to bring the political education which he has borrowed from the West into any sort of practical relation with the political conditions of India.

The Indian National Congress assumed unto itself almost from the beginning the functions of a Parliament. There was and is no room for a Parliament in India, because, so long as British rule remains a reality, the Government of India, as Lord Morley has plainly stated, must be an autocracy—benevolent and full of sympathy with Indian ideas, but still an autocracy. Nor would the Congress have been in any way qualified to discharge the functions of a Parliament had there been room for one. For it represents only one class, or rather a section of one class—the Western educated middle, and mainly professional, class, consisting chiefly of lawyers, doctors, schoolmasters, newspaper men; an important and influential class, no doubt, but one which itself only represents an infinitesimal fraction—barely, perhaps, one-hundredth part—of the whole population. To what extent it is really representative even of that small section it is impossible to say, as the members are not returned by any clearly defined body of constituents or by any formal process of election. Originally it attracted the support of not a few non-Hindus, though the Hindu element always largely preponderated, and a small group of distinguished Parsees, headed by Mr. Dadhabai Naoroji, together with a sprinkling of Mahomedans, helped to justify its claim to be called National, in so far as that appellation connoted the representation of the different creeds and races of India. But gradually most of the Mahomedans dropped out, as it became more and more an exponent of purely Hindu opinion, and the Parsees retained little more than the semblance of the authority they had at one time enjoyed.

On broader grounds still the Congress could never be called National in the Western democratic sense of the term, for whatever exceptions it may have been willing to make in favour of individuals, there can be no question of popular representation in India so long as the Hindu caste system prevails, under which whole classes numbering millions and millions are regarded and treated as beyond the pale and actually "untouchable." From time to time a few enlightened Hindus recognize the absurdity of posturing as the champions of democratic ideals so long as this monstrous anomaly subsists, but, whilst professing in theory to repudiate it, the Indian National Congress has during the whole course of its existence taken no effective step towards removing it. Nor is the Congress any more representative of the toiling masses that are not "unclean." No measures have been more bitterly assailed in the Congress than those which, like the Punjab Land Alienation Act of 1900, were framed and have operated for the benefit of the agricultural and other humbler classes—*i.e.*, of the real "people of India," in whose name the Congress speaks so loudly and with so little title.

An earlier generation of Hindus had fully recognized the urgency of social problems, like that of the "depressed" castes, and had realized that, until Indians had brought their own customs and beliefs to some extent into line with the social customs and beliefs of the West, they could not hope to raise their political life on to the Western plane. The Indian National Congress, unfortunately, succumbed to the specious plea put forward in an evil hour many years ago by a distinguished Hindu, afterwards a Judge of the Bombay High Court, Mr. K. T. Telang, who was himself unquestionably an enlightened social reformer, that the "line of least resistance" was to press for political concessions from England where they had "friends amongst the garrison," instead of fighting an uphill battle for social reforms against the dead-weight of popular ignorance and prejudice amongst their own people. That many members of the Congress take part also in social reform conferences and are fully alive to the importance of social reform cannot alter the fact that, by turning its corporate back upon the cause they have at heart, the Indian National Congress has arrested instead of promoting one of the most promising movements to which Western education had given birth.

Do not, however, let us throw the blame wholly upon the Congress. For, like Mr. Telang, it has been induced to put its trust in "the friends amongst the garrison"—Englishmen often of widely different types and characters, like Bradlaugh and Hume and Webb and Sir William Wedderburn, and in more recent days Sir Henry Cotton and Mr. Mackarness—and upon them must rest no small responsibility for the diversion of many of the best talents and energies of educated India from the thorny path of social reform into the more popular field of political agitation.

What has been the result? A self-constituted body of Indian gentlemen who have no title to represent the people and a very slender title to represent the upper classes of Indian society, but who, as I have already said, doubtless represent to some extent a considerable and influential section of Western educated opinion, might have given very useful assistance to Anglo-Indian legislators and administrators had they devoted themselves to the study of those social problems in the solution of which it is peculiarly difficult and dangerous for an alien Government to take any initiative. Instead of that, they set before themselves a task that was impossible because they had no *status* to perform it. They were fighting all the time in the air, and their proceedings therefore lacked reality. The Congress was not only an irresponsible body, but it was never steadied by a healthy divergency of opinions and the presentation of conflicting arguments. It was not even a debating society, for all represented practically the same interests, held the same views, made the same speeches, which there was no one to question or to refute. Hence the monotony of the proceedings, the sameness of the speeches, sometimes marked with great ability, and generally delivered with much eloquence and fervour, at the short annual sessions. The proceedings were usually controlled by a small caucus who drew up long-winded resolutions, often embodying half a score of resolutions carried in previous sessions. Some one delivered a soul-stirring oration, and then the "omnibus" resolution, which was not even always read out, was put to the vote and passed unanimously. Every one knew beforehand that every speaker would attack the policy of Government, whether he dealt with the ancient stock grievances or with some new question raised by the legislative and administrative measures of the current year; and every one knew also that all the others would applaud. There was no other way of bidding for popularity and making a mark than by achieving pre-eminence in the arts of pungent criticism and exuberant rhetoric. Behind the scenes there were, doubtless, often fierce fights and jealousies, and the struggles *in camera* are reported to have been sometimes very violent and bitter. But an unbroken front was maintained to the outside world, and the divisions which ultimately almost shipwrecked the Congress very rarely showed themselves on the surface of its proceedings till nearly 20 years after its birth.

The attitude of Government who had accepted the Congress's assurances of loyalty, and recognized its aims, as defined by it, to be "perfectly legitimate in themselves," was laid down for the first time officially in 1890, under Lord Lansdowne's Viceroyalty, in terms that were certainly not hostile :—

> The Government of India recognize that the Congress movement is regarded as representing in India what in Europe would be called the more advanced Liberal Party as distinguished from the great body of Conservative opinion which exists side by side with it. They desire themselves to maintain an attitude of neutrality in their relations with both parties, so long as these act strictly within constitutional limits.

To the principles of that declaration the Government of India has strictly adhered ever since, even when, as in 1905, the Congress might have been deemed to have overstepped those constitutional limits by endorsing the Bengalee doctrine of boycott.

Though the majority of the Congress probably glided unconsciously or without any deliberate purpose from its earlier attitude of remonstrance and entreaty into violent denunciation of Government and all its works, there had always been a smal group determined to drive or to manœuvre their colleagues as a body into an attitude of open and irreconcilable hostility. That group was headed by Tilak, the strongest personality in Indian politics, who was gradually making recruits among the more ardent spirits all over India. On one occasion, as far back as 1895, when the Congress held its annual session in his own city of Poona, he had attempted to commit it to the aggressive doctrines which he was already preaching in the Deccan, but he soon discovered that the temper of the majority was against him. He was, however, far too tenacious ever to accept defeat. He bided his time. He knew he had to reckon with powerful personal jealousies, and he remained in the background. His opportunity did not come till ten years later when he pulled the strings at the two successive sessions held in 1905 at Benares and in 1906 at Calcutta. It was then that the Congress passed from mere negative antagonism into almost direct defiance of Government. It must have been a proud moment for Tilak when the very man who had often fought so courageously against his inflammatory methods and reactionary tendencies in the Deccan, Mr. Gokhale, played into his hands, and from the presidential chair at Benares got up to commend the boycott as a political weapon used for a definite political purpose. A year later, it is true, Mr. Gokhale and the "moderate" party in the Congress, who had seen in the meantime to what lawlessness the boycott was leading, were anxious to undo or to mitigate at the Calcutta session what they had helped to do at Benares. But again, by dint of lobbying and even more by threatening to break up the Congress, Tilak carried the day, and a resolution was passed in the form upon which he insisted to the effect that the boycott movement was legitimate. It was not till the following year at Surat, after the preaching of lawlessness had begun to yield its inevitable harvest of crime, that the "moderates" recoiled at last from the quicksands into which the "extremists" were leading them. Tilak, however, carried out his threat, and he and his friends wrecked that session of the Congress amidst scenes of disgraceful riot and confusion.

Yet even after this the "moderates" lacked the courage

of their convictions. The breach has never been altogether repaired, but there have been frequent negotiations and exchanges of courtesies. In the very next year at Madras a man as incapable of promoting or approv ng criminal forms of agitation as Dr. Rash Behari Ghose was holding out the olive branch to "the wayward wanderers" who had treated him so despitefully at Surat; and last year at Lahore, when Pandit Mohan Malavya was expounding from the chair the latest formula adopted by Congress as a definition of its aims, his chief anxiety seemed to be to prove that it offered no obstacle to the return of the Surat insurgents to the fold. This formula, it may be mentioned, lays down that "the objects of the Indian National Congress are the attainment by the people of India of a system of Government similar to that enjoyed by the self-governing members of the British Empire and a participation by them in the rights and responsibilities of the Empire on equal terms." This is a formula which many "moderates" no doubt construe in a spirit of genuine loyalty, but it does not exclude the construction which more "advanced" politicians like Mr. Pal place upon *Swaraj*.

The last session of the Congress at Lahore, in December last, is generally admitted to have aroused very little enthusiasm, and there are many who believe that, weakened as it has been by recent dissensions, it will scarcely survive the creation of the new enlarged Councils. These Councils have been so constituted that they will be able to discharge usefully the functions which the Congress arrogated to itself without any title or authority. Perhaps it was the consciousness that the Congress would at any rate be henceforth overshadowed by the new Councils that led Pandit Malavya to inveigh so bitterly in his presidential address at Lahore against the shape ultimately given to the reforms. What one may hope above all is that the Councils will help to give the Indian "moderates" a little more self-reliance than they have hitherto shown. The Indian National Congress has at all times contained many men of high character and ability, devoted to what they conceived to be the best interests of their country, and at first, at any rate, quite ready to acknowledge the benefits of British rule and to testify to their conviction that the maintenance of British rule is essential to the welfare and safety of India. Many of them must have seen that the constant denunciation of Government by men who claimed to represent the intelligence of the country must tend to stimulate a spirit of disaffection and revolt amongst their more ignorant and inexperienced fellow-countrymen. Yet not one of them had the courage to face the risk of temporary unpopularity by pointing out the danger of the inclined plane down which they were sliding, until they actually saw themselves being swept hopelessly off their feet at Surat. It was then too late to avert the consequences of pusillanimity or to shake off their share of responsibility for the evils which the tolerance they had too long extended to the methods of their more violent colleagues had helped to produce. One of the main purposes of the Indian National Congress has avowedly been to set up a claim for the introduction of representative government in India. Yet it has itself seldom escaped the control of a handful of masterful leaders who have ruled it in the most irresponsible and despotic fashion. The Congress has, in fact, displayed exactly the same feature which has been so markedly manifested in the case of municipalities, namely, the tendency of "representative" institutions in India to resolve themselves into machines operated by, and for the benefit of, an extremely limited and domineering oligarchy.

CHAPTER XIII.

Constitutional Reforms.

When Lord Minto closed at the end of March the first Session of the Imperial Council, as the Viceroy's Legislative Council, enlarged under the Indian Councils Act of 1909, is now officially designated, n contradistinction to the enlarged Provincial Councils of Provincial Governments, his Excellency very properly described it as "a memorable Session." It was, indeed, far more than that. Even to the outward eye the old Council Chamber at Government House presented a very significant spectacle, to which the portrait of Warren Hastings over the Viceregal Chair always seemed to add a strange note of admiration. The round table at which the members of the Viceroy's Legislative Council used to gather, with far less of formality, had disappeared, and the 59 members of the enlarged Council had their appointed seats disposed in a double hemicycle facing the Chair. They sat for the most part according to provinces, and the features as well as, in some cases, the dresses, of the Indian members showed at a glance how representative this new Council really was.

The tall burly frame of the Kuvar Sahib of Patiala was only more conspicuous than that of the Maharajah of Burdwan, because the former wore the many-folded turban and brocaded dress of his Sikh ancestry, whereas the latter, like most Bengalees of the upper classes, has adopted the much more commonplace broadcloth of the West. The bold, hawk-like features of Malik Umar Hyat Khan of Tiwana in the Punjab were as characteristic of the fighting Pathan from the North as were the Rajah of Mahmudabad's more delicate features of the Mahomedan aristocracy of the erstwhile kingdom of Oudh. The white *swadeshi* garments affected by Pandit Madan Mohan Malaviya, from the United Provinces—who opened the last meeting of the Indian National Congress at Lahore with a presidential address which lasted for two hours and a quarter, and wound up with an apology for its brevity on the ground that he had had no time to prepare it—testified, at any rate more loudly, to the sternness of his patriotic convictions than the equally *swadeshi* homespun, cut at least in European fashion, of another "advanced" politician, Mr. Bhupendranath Bose, of Bengal. More worthy of attention was the keen, refined, and intellectual face of Mr. G. K. Gokhale, the Deccanee Brahman with the Mahratta cap, who, by education, belongs to the West quite as much as to the East, and, by birth, to the ruling caste of the last dominant race before the advent of the British *Raj*. The red fez worn by the majority of Mahomedan members showed that their community had certainly not failed in this instance to secure the generous measure of representation which Lord Minto spontaneously promised to them three years ago at Simla. The peculiar glazed black headdress of the Parsee and the silk kerchief of the Burman in turn indicated the racial catholicity of the assembly in which Sir Sassoon David, of Bombay, worthily represents, by his authority as a financier, the small Jewish community of India.

Nor were the different interests and classes, with two important exceptions, less adequately represented than the different races and creeds. Besides the great territorial magnates, of whom I have already mentioned two or three by name, there were not a few other well-known representatives of the landed interests which, in a country like India where agriculture is still the greatest of all national industries, have a special claim to respectful hearing, even though they have hitherto for the most part held aloof from the fashionable methods of political agitation. There was indeed a good deal of disappointment among the urban professional classes, in whose eyes a Western education—or rather education on what are, often quite erroneously, conceived to be Western lines—should apparently constitute the one indispensable qualification for public life. But they too had secured no inconsiderable number of seats, and if the voice of the Indian National Congress did not predominate it had certainly not been reduced to silence.

Doubts were freely expressed among Englishmen before the meetings of the new Councils as to the competence of the Anglo-Indian officials for the novel duties allotted to them in these assemblies. It was argued, not unreasonably, that men who had never been trained or accustomed to take part in public discussions might find themselves at a disadvantage in controversial encounters with the quick-witted Hindu politician. It is generally admitted now that the first Session at any rate of the Imperial Council by no means justified any such apprehensions. Not a few official members, it is true, were inclined at first to rely exclusively upon their written notes, and there was indeed, from beginning to end, but little room for the rapid thrust and skilled parry of debate to which we are accustomed at Westminster. Most of the Indian members themselves had carefully prepared their speeches beforehand, and read them out from typed or even printed drafts before them. In many cases the speeches had been communicated two or three days ahead to the Press, and sometimes a speech was printed and commented upon in the favoured organ of some honourable member, though he had ultimately changed his mind and preserved silence, without, however, informing the editor of the fact. In other cases a speech was published without the interruptions and calls to order which had compelled the orator to drop out some of his most cherished periods. As it was the custom for Indian members to communicate also to the departments immediately concerned the gist of the remarks which they proposed to make, the official members were tempted at first to frame their replies on similar lines and to read out elaborate statements bristling with figures, which would have been much more suitable for circulation as printed minutes. But gradually many of them took courage and showed that they could speak easily and simply, and quite as effectively as most of the Indian members.

Indeed one of the best speeches of this kind was that delivered on the last day but one of the Session by Mr. P. C. Lyon, a nominated member for Eastern Bengal, in reply to the fervid oration of Mr. Bupendranath Bose on the threadbare topic of Partition. On this, as on other occasions, the florid style of eloquence cultivated by the leaders of the Indian National Congress fell distinctly flat in the calmer atmosphere of the Council-room, as indeed Mr. Gokhale warned some of his friends it was bound to do. During the last two days discussion was allowed, somewhat needlessly under the new rules, to roam at large over all manner of irrelevant subjects, but on this occasion it served at least one useful purpose. If it were not that the Bengalee politician has no other grievance to substitute for it, the question of the Partition of Bengal should, one would think, have received its *quietus*, for two excellent speeches, delivered with much simple force by Maulvi Syed Shams ul Huda, Mahomedan member for Eastern Bengal, and by Mr. Mazhar-ul-Haq, another Mahomedan who sits for Bengal, completed the discomfiture which poor Mr. Bose had already experienced at Mr. Lyon's hands.

Needless to say that amongst the Indian members it was the politician, and especially the more "advanced" politician, who figured most prominently in the discussions. The more conservative Indians were usually content to listen, with more or less visible signs of weariness, to the facile and sometimes painfully long-winded eloquence of their colleagues. When they did intervene, however, their speeches were usually short and none the less effective. In most of the divisions that were taken they supported the Government, and in no single instance was the Government majority hard pressed. The minority in support of any resolution resisted by Government never reached 20, and generally fluctuated somewhere between 16 and 20. The only resolution which would have certainly combined all the native members in support of it was Mr. Gokhale's resolution with regard to the position of British Indians in South Africa, but, as it was accepted by Government, it was passed *nem. con.* without a division.

That in these circumstances the official members who are at the same time heads of the most important administrative and executive departments should be kept in constant attendance during debates in which many of them are not in any way directly concerned, and that they should thus be detained in Calcutta at a season when their presence would be far more useful elsewhere, constitutes one of the most serious of the many practical drawbacks of the new system for which a remedy will have to be found. It is as if not only the Parliamentary representatives but the permanent officials of our own great public departments were expected to sit through the debates in the House of Commons, without even the facilities which the private rooms of Ministers, the library, and the smoking rooms at Westminster afford for quiet intervals of work between the division bells. Nor is that all. The Council sat during the very months of the short "cold weather," when it is customary and alone practicable for heads of departments to undertake their annual tours of inspection. The *reductio ad absurdum* is surely reached in the case of the Commander-in-Chief and the Chief of the Staff. Though the Imperial Council is itself debarred from dealing with Army questions, they could be seen any day sitting through the debates merely because their votes might conceivably be required to maintain the official majority, and, except for one or two short excursions in the intervals between the meetings of Council, they were tied to Calcutta when they ought to have been travelling about the country and inspecting the troops. Yet it is generally admitted that at no period since the Mutiny has it been more important for the Commander-in-Chief to maintain the closest possible contact with the native army—especially when the Commander-in-Chief is as popular with the Indian soldier as Sir O'Moore Creagh.

Another obvious drawback of the present arrangements is the inconvenience to which members of Council from the provinces were subjected by the irregular intervals at which the Council held its actual sittings. Either they had to waste their time at Calcutta during the intervals, to the detriment of their interests at home, or they had to spend days in railway carriages rushing backwards and forwards from their homes to the capital, for in a country of such magnificent distances there are few journeys that take less than 24 hours, and from Calcutta, for instance, either to Madras or to Bombay takes the best part of 48 hours. Unless arrangements are remodelled so as to enable the Council to transact its business, whether *in pleno* or in committee, either in one session or in two short sessions, but in any case continuously, many of its most valuable members, who have important business of their own which they cannot afford to neglect, will cease to attend, and the Council will not only lose much of the representative character, which is one of its best features at present, but will fall inevitably under the preponderating influence of the professional politician. In his closing speech Lord Minto outlined a scheme which would in some measure meet this difficulty, but it is doubtful whether it will prove by any means adequate. Another point which requires consideration is whether it is desirable for the Viceroy to preside himself over the deliberations of the Council. Even if he could properly afford the time for it, it seems hardly expedient that the immediate representative of the King-Emperor should be drawn into the arena of public controversies. Proceedings are bound to grow more and more contentious, and delicate questions of procedure will arise and have to be settled from the chair. These are all matters in which the Viceroy should not be committed to the premature exercise, on the spur of the moment, of his supreme authority.

One of the chief purposes which the creation of the new Councils is intended to achieve is that of enlightening Indian opinion throughout the country by means of the enlarged opportunities given for the discussion of public affairs. But that purpose will be defeated unless the discussions receive adequate publicity. They certainly did not do so this winter. Not only is the art of gallery reporting still in its infancy, but many of the Indian newspapers have still to learn that "it is not cricket" to report only the speeches of their political friends and to omit or compress into a few lines the speeches of their adversaries. A glaring instance of this shortcoming was afforded by the *Bengalee.* The Nationalist organ published Mr. Bupendra Nath Bose's speech on the partition of Bengal *in extenso,* as he had intended to deliver it, without taking the slightest notice of the fact that he was repeatedly called to order by the Viceroy and had in consequence to drop out whole passages of his oration, and it published practically nothing else—though perhaps no other indictment of the Government during the whole session was more successfully refuted, both by the official spokesman, Mr. Lyon, and by other Indian members. Apart, however, from any such deliberate unfairness, the communication of speeches in advance to the Press should be strenuously discountenanced. Many official members showed that they could perfectly well dispense with the doubtful advantage of knowing beforehand exactly what their critics were going to say, and, if once this practice is stopped, newspapers, relieved from the temptation of giving undue preference to easy "copy," will learn to cultivate and to rely upon more legitimate methods of reporting. It is to be hoped also that the *Gazette of India*, which publishes the official verbatim reports, will not in future lag so far behind the actual proceedings.

All these are minor points. The dominant feature of the Session was that in spite of wide divergences of views, the proceedings were generally dignified, sometimes even to the verge of dulness, and with one or two exceptions they were marked by good feeling on all sides. It would be unfair not to give to Mr. Gokhale his full share of credit for this happy result. Though often an unrelenting critic of the Administration, he struck from the first a note of studied moderation and restraint to which most of his political friends attuned their utterances. He naturally assumed the functions of the leader of his Majesty's Opposition, and he discharged them, not only with the ability which every one expected of him, but with the urbanity and self-restraint of a man conscious of his responsibilities as well as of his powers. His was, amongst the Indian members, not only the master mind, but the dominant personality. The European members, on the other hand, showed themselves invariably courteous and good-tempered, and not a few awkward corners were turned by a little good-humoured banter. Nor was it unusual to see the Englishman come and sit down by the side of the Indian member to whose indictment he had just been replying, and in friendly conversation take all personal sting out of the controversy. As Lord Minto aptly put it, the Council-room "has brought people together. Official and non-official members have met each other. The official wall which of necessity to some extent separated them has been broken down. They have talked over many things together." From this point of view, if future sessions fulfil the promise of the first one, the Imperial Council may grow into a potent instrument for good.

Of the deeper significance which underlay the meeting of this remarkable assembly it is still perhaps premature to speak. But cautious and tentative as was the attitude of all partics concerned, and frec as, from bcginning to end, the proceedings were from any startling incidents, no one can have watchcd them without being conscious of the presence of new forces of vast potentiality which must tend to modify very profoundly the relations between the governors and the governed in India itself, and possibly even between India and the Mother Country. They are the forces, largely still unknown, which have been brought into play by Lord Morley's Constitutional reforms, and though they made themselves naturally more conspicuously felt in the Imperial Council at Calcutta, they were present in every one of the enlarged Legislative Councils of the Provincial Governments.

It is no part of my purpose to recount in detail the long, though generally dispassionate, controversy to which these reforms gave rise. We may not all be agreed as to the necessity or wisdom of some of the changes embodied in them, and some may think that we are inclined to travel too fast and too far on a road which Indians have not up to the present shown themselves qualified to tread without danger. But there are few Englishmen either at home or in India who do not recognize the statesmanlike spirit in which Lord Morley, loyally seconded throughout by Lord Minto, has approached the very diffieult problem of giving to the people of India a larger consultative voice in administration as well as in legislation without jeopardizing the stability or impairing the supremacy of British control. The future alone can show how far these far-reaching changes will justify the generous expectations of their author, but taken as a whole they undoubtedly represent a constructive work which is fully worthy of the fine record of British rule in India.

How very far-reaching they are the merest indication of their most salient features will suffice to indicate. For the sake of convenience, though they form a homogeneous whole, they may be divided roughly into two categories—those that affect the Executive Councils and those that have remodelled the Legislative Councils. To the former category belong :—

(1) The appointment of an Indian member to the Viceroy's Executive Council. Mr. S. P. Sinha, a Bengalee barrister in large practice, was appointed to be legal member, and the ability and distinction with which he discharged the duties of his high office have gone far to remove the misgivings of many of those who were at first opposed to this new departure. It is the more to be regretted that his services will be lost to the new Viceroy, as he has announced his intention of retiring, for personal reasons, at the end of Lord Minto's Viceroyalty [15].

(2) The appointment of one Indian member to the Executive Councils of the Governors of Madras and Bombay. The Rajah of Bobbili has been appointed in Madras and Mr. M. B. Chaubal in Bombay. An Indian will also be appointed to the Executive Council of the Lieutenant-Governor of Bengal as soon as that body has been finally constituted [16], and similar appointments will be made to the Executive Councils of the chief Indian provinces when the powers taken to create those bodies shall be put into operation.

(3) The appointment of two Indians, one a Hindu and the other a Mahomedan, to be members of the Council of the Secretary of State, generally known as the India Council, in Whitehall. Mr. K. G. Gupta and Mr. Husain Bilgrami were appointed by Lord Morley in 1907. Mr. Bilgrami retired early in 1910 owing to ill-health, and his place has been taken by Mr. M. A. Ali Baig.

In principle, the introduction of natives of India into these inner lines of the British Executive power undoubtedly constitutes, as Lord Lansdowne has said, a "tremendous innovation," but it may be doubted whether in practice the consequences will be as considerable as those of the changes effected by the India Councils Act of 1909 in the composition and attributions of the Imperial and Provincial Legislative Councils. These changes are of a twofold character. In the first place the total number of members has been very materially increased—*e.g.*, in the Imperial Legislative Council from 21 to a *maximum* of 60; in the Madras and Bombay Legislative Councils from 24 to a *maximum* of 50; in the Bengal Legislative Council from 20 to 50, &c. Room has thus been made for the introduction of a much larger number of elected members, of whom there will be in future not less than 135 altogether in the different Legislative Councils, as against only 39 under the old statutes. Still more important than the mere increase in the number of elected members is the radical change in the proportion they will bear to official members. Except in the Imperial Council, where, at the instance of Lord Morley, a small official majority has been retained which Lord Minto himself was willing to dispense with, there will no longer be any official majority. The regulations determining the electorates and the mode of election have been framed with praiseworthy elasticity in accordance with local requirements, and care has been taken to provide as far as possible for an adequate representation of all the most important communities and interests. In view of the manifold and profound lines of cleavage which exist in Indian society, it is extremely improbable that all the elected members will ever combine against the official minority except in such rare and improbable cases as might produce an absolute consensus of Indian opinion, and in such cases it is even more improbable that Government would ignore so striking a manifestation. Nevertheless, as a safeguard against the possibility of factious opposition, the right of veto has been reserved to the Provincial Executives and in the last resort to the Governor-General in Council.

Thus the Indian Councils Act of 1909 cannot be said to have actually modified the position of the Indian Legislatures. With regard to the most important of them—viz., the Imperial Council—Lord Morley was careful to make this perfectly clear in his despatch of November 27, 1908, in which he reviewed the proposals put forward in the Government of India despatch of October 1. " It is an essential condition of the reform policy," the Secretary of State wrote, " that the Imperial supremacy should in no degree be compromised. I must therefore regard it as essential that your Excellency's Council, in its legislative as well as in its executive character, should continue to be so constituted as to ensure its constant and uninterrupted power to fulfil the constitutional obligation that it owes, and must always owe, to his Majesty's Government and to the Imperial Parliament." The Indian Executive therefore remains, as hitherto, responsible only to the Imperial Government at home, and the Imperial Council can exercise over it no directly controlling power. The same holds good, *mutatis mutandis*, of the Provincial Executives and their Councils.

Indirectly, however, the Indian Councils Act of 1909 materially modifies the relations between the Legislative Councils and the Executive by giving to elected and non-official members opportunities which they have never enjoyed before of discussing public policy and making their voices heard and their influence felt on both administrative and legislative matters. The revised rules of procedure, under which supplementary questions may be grafted on to interpellations, and resolutions can be moved not only in connexion with the financial statements of Government, but, with certain specified reservations, on most matters of general public interest, are undoubtedly calculated to afford a vastly larger scope than in the past to the activities of Indian Legislatures, and it will depend very much upon the ability and resourcefulness of members themselves to what extent they may utilize these facilities for the purpose of ultimately creating real powers of control. In an extremely interesting and dispassionate study of the Indian Constitution, and of the effects which the new reforms may have upon it, Mr. Rangaswami Iyengar, a Hindu journalist of Madras, comes to the conclusion that "if the powers now entrusted to the Councils are used with care, wisdom, and discrimination, precedents and procedure analogous to those of the House of Commons might gradually grow up, and might serve as a useful means if not of directly controlling the Executive—a power which under the present constitutional arrangement of the Government of India it is impossible that the Council should possess—at least of directing the Executive into correct and proper channels in regard to administrative policy and administrative action." Not the least important of the changes are those made in regard to Budget procedure. Indian Legislatures will no more than in the past have power to vote or to veto the Budget, but they will have henceforth an opportunity of setting forth their views before the Budget has assumed its final shape. Members will be able to discuss beforehand any changes in taxation, as well as any new loans or additional grants to local governments, and they will be taken into the confidence of Government with regard to the determination of public expenditure. No doubt important heads of revenue are still excluded from the purview of the Councils, but members will have the right of placing on record their views in the form of resolutions on all items not specifically excluded from their cognisance, and the Finance Member will be bound to explain the reasons why Government declines to accept any resolution that may have been passed in the first two stages of the Budget. Much will depend upon the reasonable and practical use which members make of these novel opportunities, for, to quote

Mr. Iyengar again, "the progress of constitutional government is not dependent so much upon what is expressly declared to be constitutional rights as upon what is silently built up in the form of constitutional conventions."

In the great speech in which Lord Morley gave the House of Lords the first outline of his Indian reforms scheme there was one singularly pregnant passage. "We at any rate," he said, "have no choice or option. As an illustrious member of this House once said, we are watching a great and stupendous process, the reconstruction of a decomposed society. What we found was described as a parallel to Europe in the fifth century, and we have now, as it were, before us in that vast congeries of people we call India, a long, slow march in uneven stages through all the centuries from the fifth to the twentieth. Stupendous indeed, and to guide that transition with sympathy, political wisdom, and courage, with a sense of humanity, duty, and national honour, may well be called a glorious mission." Whether we succeed in that mission must depend largely upon the loyal assistance we receive from those Indians who claim, in virtue of their superior education, to represent this twentieth century. Lord Morley has fulfilled in no niggardly spirit his pledge to associate the people of India with the Government far more closely than has hitherto been the case in the work of actual day-to-day administration as well as in the more complex problems of legislation. It rests now with the Indian representatives both in the Executive and Legislative Councils to justify Lord Morley's expectations by using the new machinery which he has placed in their hands not for purposes of mere destructive criticism and malevolent obstruction, but for intelligent and constructive co-operation with the British rulers of India, to whom alone, whatever may be their shortcomings, India owes it that the spirit of the twentieth century has spread to her shores.

CHAPTER XIV.

THE DEPRESSED CASTES.

The only classes in British India for whom no real representation has been devised in the enlarged Indian Councils are the millions of humble toilers who constitute what are known as the " depressed castes." Under present social conditions in India, this was probably inevitable. Though, rather unreasonably, the vast majority of them go to swell the numbers of the Hindu population in the census upon which Hindu representation ought, according to Hindu politicians, to be based, those politicians have certainly not as yet shown any title to speak on their behalf. For there is no more striking contrast to the liberal and democratic professions of a body which claims, as does the Indian National Congress, to represent an enlightened, progressive, and national Hinduism than the fact that in the course of its 25 years' existence it has scarcely done anything to give practical effect to its theoretical repudiation of a social system that condemns some 50 millions out of the 300 millions of the Hindu population of India to a life of unspeakable degradation. For a long time to come, the depressed castes will probably find, as in the past, their truest friends and best qualified representatives among the European members of Council, who, just because they are aliens, are free from all the influences, whether of interest or of prejudice, which tend to divide Hindu society into so many water-tight compartments. Let any one who has any doubts on this point read some of the documents published in the Blue-books on the reforms—petitions from low-caste communities imploring Government not to commit the defence of their interests to the Hindu Brahman, but to continue to them the direct and unselfish protection which they have hitherto enjoyed at the hands of British administrators.

The " depressed classes " of whom we generally speak as Pariahs, though the name properly belongs only to one particular caste, the Pareiyas in Southern India, include all Hindus who do not belong to the four highest or " clean " castes of Hinduism, and they are therefore now officially and euphemistically designated as the Panchamas—*i.e.*, the fifth caste. Many of the Panchamas, especially in Southern India, are little better than bonded serfs; others are condemned to this form of ostracism by the trades they ply. Such are not only the scavengers and sweepers, but also the workers in leather, the Chamars and Muchis of Northern and Central India, and the Chakilians and Madigas of Southern India, who with their families number 14 or 15 million souls; the washermen, the *tadi*-drawers and vendors of spirituous liquors, the pressers of oil, and, in many parts of the country, the cowherd and shepherd castes, &c. They are generally regarded as descendants of the aboriginal tribes overwhelmed centuries ago by the tide of Aryan conquest. Some of those tribes, grouped together in the Indian Census under the denominational rubric of " Animists " and numbering about 8½ millions, have survived to the present day in remote hills and jungles without being absorbed into the Hindu social system, and have preserved their primitive beliefs, in which fetish worship and magic are the dominant elements. Low as is their social *status*, it is but little lower than that of the Panchamas, who have obtained a footing on the nethermost rung of the social ladder of Hinduism without being admitted to any sort of contact with its higher civilization or even to the threshold of its temples.

Hinduism with all its rigidity is, it is true, sufficiently elastic to sanction, at least tacitly, a slow process of evolution by which the Panchama castes—for there are many castes even amongst the "untouchables"—gradually shake off to some extent the slough of "uncleanness" and establish some sort of ill-defined relations even with Brahmanism. For whilst there is on the one hand a slowly ascending scale by which the Panchamas may ultimately hope to smuggle themselves in amongst the inferior Sudras, the lowest of the four "clean" castes, so there is a descending scale by which Brahmans, under the pressure of poverty or disrepute, sink to so low a place in Brahmanism that they are willing to lend their ministrations, at a price, to the more prosperous of the Panchamas and help them on their way to a higher *status*. Thus probably half the Sudras of the present day were at some more or less remote period Panchamas, Again, during periods of great civil commotion, as in the 18th century, when brute force was supreme, not a few Panchamas, especially low-caste Mahrattas, made their way to the front as soldiers of fortune, and even carved out kingdoms to themselves at the point of the sword. Orthodox Hinduism bowed in such cases to the accomplished fact, just as it has acquiesced in later years when education and the equality of treatment brought by British rule have enabled a small number of Panchamas to qualify for employment under Government.

But these exceptions are so rare and the evolutionary process is so infinitely slow and laborious that they do not visibly affect the yawning gulf between the "clean" higher-caste Hindu and the "unclean" Panchama. The latter may have learned to do *puja* to Shiva or Kali or other members of the Hindu Pantheon, but he is not allowed within the precincts of their sanctuaries and has to worship from afar. Nor are the disabilities of the Panchama merely spiritual. In many villages he has to live entirely apart. He is not even allowed to draw water from the village well, lest he should "pollute" it by his touch, and where there is no second well for the "untouchables," the hardship is cruel, especially in seasons of drought when casual water dries up. In every circumstance of his life the vileness of his lot is brought home to the wretched pariah by an elaborate and relentless system of social oppression. I will only quote one or two instances which have come within my own observation. The respective distances beyond which Panchamas must not approach a Brahman lest they "pollute" him differ according to their degree of uncleanness. Though they have been laid down with great precision, it is growing more and more difficult to enforce them with the increasing promiscuity of railway and street-car intercourse, but in more remote parts of India, and especially in the south, the old rules are still often observed. In Cochin a few years ago I was crossing a bridge, and just in front of me walked a respectable-looking native. He suddenly turned tail, and running back to the end of the bridge from which we had both come, plunged out of sight into the jungle on the side of the road. He had seen a Brahman entering on to the bridge from the other end, and he had fled incontinently rather than incur the resentment of that high-caste gentleman by inflicting upon him the "pollution" of forbidden proximity, as the bridge, though a fairly broad one, was not wide enough for them to pass each other at the prescribed distance. In the native State of Travancore it is not uncommon to see a Panchama witness in a lawsuit standing about a hundred yards from the Court so as not to defile the Brahman Judge and pleaders, whilst a row of *peons*, or messengers, stationed between him and the Court, hand on its questions to him and pass back his replies.

No doubt the abject ignorance and squalor and the repulsive habits of many of these unfortunate castes help to explain and to perpetuate their ostracism, but they do not exculpate a social system which prescribes or tolerates such a state of things. That if a kindly hand is extended to them, even the lowest of these depressed can be speedily raised to a higher plane has been abundantly shown by the efforts of Christian missionaries. They are only now beginning to extend their activities to the depressed castes of Northern India, but in Southern India important results have already been achieved. The Bishop of Madras claims that within the last 40 years, in the Telugu country alone, some 250,000 Panchamas have become Christians, and in Travancore another 100,000. During the last two decades especially the philanthropic work done by the missionaries in plague and famine time has borne a rich harvest, for the Panchamas have naturally turned a ready ear to the spiritual ministrations of those who stretched out their hands to help them in the hour of extreme need. Bishop Whitehead, who has devoted himself particularly to this question, assures me that, in Southern India at least, the rate at which the elevation of the depressed castes can be achieved depends mainly upon the amount of effort which the Christian missions can put forth. If their organizations can be adequately strengthened and extended so as to deal with the increasing numbers of inquirers and converts, and, above all, to train native teachers, he is convinced that we may be within measurable distance of the reclamation of the whole Panchama population. What the effect would be from the social as well as the religious point of view may be gathered from a recent report of the Telugu Mission, which most lay witnesses would, I believe, readily confirm :—

If we look at the signs of moral and spiritual progress during the last 40 years, the results of the mission work have been most encouraging. It is quite true that naturally the Panchamas are poor, dirty, ignorant, and, as a consequence of many centuries of oppression, peculiarly addicted to the more mean and servile vices. But the most hopeful element in their case is that they are conscious of their degradation and eager to escape from it. As a consequence, when formed into congregations under the care of earnest and capable teachers, they make marked progress materially, intellectually, and morally. Their gross ignorance disappears ; they become cleaner and more decent in their persons and homes ; they give up cattle poisoning and grain stealing, two crimes particularly associated with their class ; they abstain from the practice of infant marriage and concubinage, to which almost all classes of Hindu society are addicted ; they lose much of the old servile spirit which led them to grovel at the feet of their social superiors, and they acquire more sense of the rights and dignity which belong to them as men. Where they are able to escape their surroundings they prove themselves in no way inferior, either in mental or in moral character, to the best of their fellow-countrymen. Especially is this the case in the Mission Boarding Schools, where the change wrought is a moral miracle. In many schools and colleges Christian lads of Panchama origin are holding their own with, and in not a few cases are actually outstripping, their Brahman competitors. . . . In one district the Hindus themselves bore striking testimony to the effect of Christian teaching on the pariahs. "Before they became Christians," one of them said, "we had always to lock up our storehouses, and were always having things stolen. But now all that is changed. We can leave our houses open and never lose anything."

In the heyday of the Hindu Social Reform Movement, before it was checked by the inrush of political agitation, the question of the elevation of the depressed castes was often and earnestly discussed by progressive Hindus themselves, but it is only recently that it has again been taken up seriously by some of the Hindu leaders, and notably by Mr. Gokhale. One of the utterances that has produced the greatest impression in Hindu circles is a speech made last year by the Gaekwar of Baroda, a Hindu Prince who not only professes advanced Liberal views, but whose heart naturally goes out to the depressed castes, as the fortunes of his own house were made in the turmoil of the eighteenth century by a Mahratta of humble extraction, if not actually of low-caste origin.

His Highness does not attempt to minimize the evils of the system.

> The same principles which impel us to ask for political justice for ourselves should actuate us to show social justice to each other. . . . By the sincerity of our efforts to uplift the depressed classes we shall be judged fit to achieve the objects of our national desire. . . . The system which divides us into innumerable castes claiming to rise by minutely graduated steps from the pariah to the Brahman is a whole tissue of injustice, splitting men equal by nature into divisions high and low, based not on the natural standard of personal qualities but on accidents of birth. The eternal struggle between caste and caste for social superiority has become a constant source of ill-feeling. . . . Want of education is practically universal amongst the depressed classes, but this cannot have been the cause of their fall, for many of the so-called higher classes in India share in the general ignorance. Unlike them, however, they are unable to attend the ordinary schools owing to the idea that it is pollution to touch them. To do so is to commit a sin offensive alike to religion and to conventional morality. Of professions as a means of livelihood these depressed classes have a very small choice. Here, too, the supposed pollution of their touch comes in their way. On every hand we find that the peculiar difficulty from which they suffer, in addition to others that they share with other classes, is their "untouchableness."

After a powerful argument against the theory of "untouchableness" and against priestly intolerance, the Gaekwar urges not only upon Hindus but upon Government the duty of attacking in all earnestness this formidable problem.

> A Government within easy reach of the latest thought, with unlimited moral and material resources, such as there is in India, should not remain content with simply asserting the equality of men under the common law and maintaining order, but must sympathetically see from time to time that the different sections of its subjects are provided with ample means of progress. Many of the Indian States where they are at all alive to the true functions of government, owing to less elevating surroundings or out of nervousness, fear to strike out a new path and find it less troublesome to follow

the policy of *laisser faire* and to walk in the footsteps of the highest Government in India, whose declared policy is to let the social and religious matters of the people alone except where questions of grave importance are involved. When one-sixth of the people are in a chronically depressed and ignorant condition, no Government can afford to ignore the urgent necessity of doing what it can for their elevation.

Can the Government of India afford to disregard so remarkable an appeal? The question is not merely a social and moral question, but also a political one. Whilst some high-caste Hindus are beginning to recognize its urgency, the more prosperous of the socially depressed castes themselves are showing signs of restlessness under the ostracism to which they are subjected. From almost all of these castes a few individuals have always emerged, who acquired wealth and the relative recognition that wealth brings with it, and the numbers of such individuals are increasing. In some cases a whole caste has seen its circumstances improve under new economic conditions entirely beyond its own control—like the Namasudras of Bengal, who, as agriculturists, have had their share of the growing agricultural prosperity of that region. They are materially better off than they used to be, and so they are no longer content with their old social *status* of inferiority. Not only Christian but Mahomedan missionaries have been at work amongst them, and though the vast majority remain Hindus, they note, like the Panchamas all over India must note, the immediate rise in the social scale of their fellow-castemen who embrace either Christianity or Islam. For it is one of the anomalies of this peculiar conception that the most untouchable Hindu ceases to be quite as untouchable when he becomes a Christian or a Mahomedan. The Bengalee politician was quick to see the danger of losing hold altogether of the Namasudras, and he set up a propaganda of his own, which I have already described, with the object of winning them over to his side and to his methods of agitation by promising them in return a relaxation of caste stringency. The question with which we are confronted is whether we shall ourselves take a hand in the elevation of the depressed castes or whether we shall leave it to others, many of whom would exploit them for their own purposes. Is not this an opportunity for the Government of India to respond to the Gaekwar's invitation and depart for once from their traditional policy of *laisser faire*? In the Christian Missions they have an admirable organization ready to hand which merely requires encouragement and support. Though there are manifold dangers in giving official countenance to proselytizing work amongst the higher classes of Indian society, none of those objections can reasonably lie to co-operating in the reclamation of whole classes which the orthodox Hindu regards as beyond the pale of human intercourse. From the religious point of view, this is a matter which should engage the earnest attention of the great missionary societies of this country. The hour seems to be at hand when a great and combined effort is required of them. From the moral and social point of view they may well claim in this connexion the sympathy and support of all denominations and no-denominations that are interested in the welfare and progress of backward races. From the political point of view the conversion of so many millions of the population of India to the faith of their rulers would open up prospects of such moment that I need not expatiate upon them.

CHAPTER XV.

The Native States.

One of the chief features of the original scheme of constitutional reforms submitted to the Secretary of State by the Government of India was the creation of an Imperial Advisory Council composed of ruling chiefs and territorial magnates. The proposal gave rise to a variety of objections, the most serious one being the difficulty of adjusting the relations to the Government of India of a Council in which the most conspicuous members could have had no definite *locus standi* in regard to the internal affairs of British India—*i.e.*, of the larger part of our Indian dependency under direct British administration. The difficulty was evaded by dropping the proposal. But to evade a difficulty is only to postpone it. Though the constitutional reforms are confined, in their immediate application, to British India, measures of such far-reaching importance must react more or less directly upon the whole of our Indian Empire. Is it therefore politic, or, indeed, possible, to leave out of account the Native States, which occupy altogether about one-third of the total area of India and have an aggregate population of over 68 millions, or to ignore the rulers charged with their administration ?

The Native States of India vary in size and importance from powerful principalities like the Nizam's State of Hyderabad, with an area of 82,000 miles—nearly equal to that of England and Wales and Scotland—and a population of over 11 millions, down to diminutive chiefships, smaller than the holdings of a great English landlord. Distributed throughout the whole length and breadth of the peninsula, they display the same extraordinary variety of races and creeds and castes and languages and customs and traditions as the provinces under the immediate governance of the Viceroy, and their rulers themselves represent almost every phase and aspect of Indian history. The Princes of Rajputana, headed by the Maharana of Udaipur, with genealogies reaching back into the mythical ages, have handed down to the present day the traditions of Hindu chivalry. In the south of India, the rulers of Mysore and Cochin and Travancore, who also claim Rajput blood, still personify the subjection of the older Dravidian races to the Aryan invaders from the north. Mahratta chiefs like Scindia and the Gaekwar date from the great uplifting of the Mahratta power in the eighteenth century, whilst the Maharajah of Kolhapur is a descendant of Shivaji, the first Mahratta chieftain to stem the tide of Mahomedan conquest more than a century earlier. The great majority of the ruling princes and chiefs are Hindus, but besides the Nizam, the most powerful of all, there are not a few Mahomedan rulers who have survived the downfall of Moslem supremacy, just as the Sikh chiefs of Patiala, Nabha, and Kapurthala, in the Punjab, still recall the great days of Ranjit Singh and the Sikh confederacy. In some of the Native States the ruling families are neither of the same race nor of the same creed as the majority of their subjects. The Nizam is a Sunni Mahomedan, but most of his subjects are Hindus, and of the Mahomedans some of the most influential are Shias. The Maharajah of Kashmir, a Hindu Rajput, rules over many Mongolian Buddhists, whilst there are but few Mahrattas in Gwalior or Indore, though both Holkar and Scindia are Mahratta Princes.

In all the Native States the system of government is more or less of the old patriarchal or personal type which has always obtained in the East, but in its application it exhibits many variations which reflect sometimes the idiosyncrasies of the ruler and sometimes the dominant forces of inherited social traditions. In Cochin and Travancore, for instance, the ancient ascendency of the Northern Brahmans over the Dravidian subject races survives in some of its most archaic forms. Udaipur and Jaipur have perhaps preserved more than any other States of Rajputana the aristocratic conservatism of olden days, whilst some of the younger Rajput chiefs have moved more freely with the times and with their own Western education. The Gaekwar has gone further than any other ruling chief in introducing into his State of Baroda the outward forms of what we call Western progress, though his will is probably in all essentials as absolute as that of Scindia, another Mahratta chief, whose interest in every form of Western activity is displayed almost as much in his physical energy as in his intellectual alertness. Some no doubt abandon the conduct of public affairs almost entirely to their Ministers and prefer a life of easy self-indulgence. Others, on the contrary, are keen administrators, and insist upon doing everything themselves. As masterful a ruler as any in the whole of India is a lady, the Begum of Bhopal, a Mahomedan Princess of rare attainments and character. The Nizam, on the other hand, though an absolute ruler, has recently placed it on record that he attributes the peaceful content and law-abiding character of his subjections to the liberal traditions he has inherited from his ancestors. "They were singularly free from all religious and racial prejudices. Their wisdom and foresight induced them to employ Hindus and Mahomedans, Europeans, and Parsees alike, in carrying on the administration, and they reposed entire confidence in their officers whatever religion and race they belonged to." To those principles his Highness rightly claims to have himself adhered.

Again, though the relationship of the Supreme Government to all these rulers is one of suzerainty, it is governed in each particular case by special and different treaties which vary the extent and nature of the control exercised over them. In some of its aspects, the principles of our policy towards them were admirably set forth in a speech delivered in November, 1909, by Lord Minto at Udaipur. "In guaranteeing their internal independence and in undertaking their protection against external aggression, it naturally follows that the Imperial Government has assumed a certain degree of responsibility for the general soundness of their administration, and would not consent to incur the reproach of being an indirect instrument of misrule. There are also certain matters in which it is necessary for the Government of India to safeguard the interests of the community as a whole, as well as those of the Paramount Power, such as railways, telegraphs, and other services of an Imperial character." At the same time the Viceroy wisely laid great stress on the fact that, in pursuance of the pledges given by the British Crown to the rulers of the Native States," our policy is with rare exceptions one of non-interference in their internal affairs," and he pointed out that, as owing to the varying conditions of different States "any attempt at complete uniformity and subservience to precedent" must be dangerous, he had endeavoured "to deal with questions as they arose with reference to existing treaties, the merits of each case, local conditions, antecedent circumstances, and the particular stage of development, feudal and constitutional, of individual principalities." It is obviously impossible to enforce a more rigid control over the feudatory States at the same time as we are delegating larger powers to the natives of India under direct British administration. This is a point which Lord Minto might indeed have emphasized with advantage. For there seems to be a growing tendency, probably at home rather than in India, to ignore our responsibilities towards the ruling chiefs, and to regard them as more or less negligible quantities in the constitutional experiments we are making in our Indian Empire. When an emergency arises such as a frontier war or a military expedition in the Sudan or in China, we appeal unhesitatingly to the loyalty of the Princes of India, and so far they have cheerfully borne their share in these Imperial enterprises though they were never drawn into consultation beforehand, and their own material interests were not directly involved. On the other hand, questions which do involve their material interests, questions which necessarily affect the well-being of their States quite as much as that of British India, questions of tariff and of currency that react upon the economic prosperity of the whole of India are settled between Whitehall and Government House at Calcutta without their opinion being even invited. Sometimes even decisions are taken without their knowledge on matters that directly affect their own exchequers, as in the matter of the opium trade with China. Some of the native States are the largest producers of the Indian poppy, and in order to satisfy the susceptibilities, very meritorious in themselves, of our national conscience, we lightheartedly impose upon them, without consultation or prospect of compensation, the sacrifice, which costs us nothing, of one of the most valuable products of their soil and chief sources of revenue. Can they do otherwise than draw unfavourable comparisons between the harsh measure meted out to them in this matter and the generous treatment of the West Indies by the Mother Country when £20,000,000 were voted out of the Imperial Exchequer towards compensation for the material losses arising out of the abolition of slavery?

How important it is to associate the Princes of India with the purposes of our Indian policy has seldom been more clearly shown than during these last troublous years when the forces of disaffection have revealed themselves as a serious public danger. The principle of authority cannot be attacked in British India without suffering diminution in the Native States. They are not shut up in watertight compartments and sedition cannot be preached on one side of a border, which in most cases is merely an administrative boundary line, without finding an echo on the other side. The prestige of an Indian Prince in his own land is great. It is rooted in most cases in ancient traditions to which no alien rulers can appeal. Nevertheless some of the most experienced and enlightened of the ruling chiefs showed a much earlier and livelier appreciation of the subversive tendencies of Indian unrest than those responsible for the governance of British India. Some of them, like the Maharajahs of Kolhapur and of Patiala, have been brought face to face with the same violent, and even with the same criminal, methods of agitation as the Government of India has had to deal with in provinces under British administration. The Maharajah of Jaipur and Maharajah Scindia felt themselves constrained just about a year ago to enact vigorous measures on their own account against sedition and against the importation into their States of seditious literature which was still allowed to circulate with impunity in British India, whilst the State of Bikanir was the first to introduce an Explosive Substances Act immediately after the epidemic of bomb-throwing had broken out in Bengal. Other States have also taken strong preventive measures, but many have fortunately been spared so far any serious trouble within their own borders, and their rulers have been able to study the problem merely as interested observers and from the point of view of the general welfare of the country.

On August 6, 1909, the Viceroy took the unusual step of communicating direct with all the principal ruling Princes and Chiefs of India on the subject of the active unrest prevalent in many parts of the country, and invited an exchange of opinions "with a view to mutual co-operation against a common danger." Some doubts were then expressed as to the wisdom of such a course, on the ground that it might create in the protected States an impression of exaggerated alarm. But the tone and substance of the replies which his Excellency's communication elicited showed that there was no reason for any such apprehensions. The Ruling Chiefs, on the contrary, appreciated and reciprocated the confidence reposed in them, and their replies, indeed, constitute an exceptionally interesting and instructive set of documents ; for the very diversity of origin and traditions and influence gives peculiar weight to the position assumed by the rulers of the Native States towards the forces of active unrest in India. Had those forces merely been engaged in a legitimate struggle for the enlargement of Indian rights and liberties, it is scarcely conceivable that the Ruling Princes and Chiefs should have passed judgment against them with such overwhelming unanimity.

It may be argued that in replying to a Viceregal *Kharita*, the Ruling Chiefs could hardly do less than recognize the existence of the "common danger" to which Lord Minto had drawn their attention. But the careful analysis of the influences behind the agitation and the practical suggestions for dealing with it which the majority of the replies contain, prove that their opinions are certainly not framed "to order." They represent the convictions and experience of a group of responsible Indians better situated in some respects to obtain accurate information about the doings and feelings of their fellow-countrymen than any Anglo-Indian administrators can be. The language of the Nizam is singularly apt and direct. "Once the forces of lawlessness and disorder are let loose there is no knowing where they will stop. It is true that, compared with the enormous population of India, the disaffected people are a very insignificant minority, but, given time and opportunity, there exists the danger of this small minority spreading its tentacles all over the country and inoculating with its poisonous doctrines the classes and masses hitherto untouched by this seditious movement." The Maharana of Udaipur, speaking with the authority of his unique position amongst Hindus as the premier Prince of Rajputana, not only condemns an agitation "which is detrimental to all good government and social administration," but declares it to be "a great disgrace to their name as also to their religious beliefs that, in spite of the great prosperity India has enjoyed under the British *régime*, people are acting in such an ungrateful way." No less emphatic is the Mahratta ruler of Gwalior:—"The question is undoubtedly a grave one, affecting as it does the future well-being of India," and "it particularly behoves those who preside over the destinies of the people and have large personal stakes to do all in their power to grapple with it vigorously." The Maharajah of Jaipur, one of the wisest of the older generation of Hindu rulers, agrees that "only a small fraction of the population has been contaminated by the seditious germ," but he adds significantly that "that fraction has, it seems, been carefully organized by able, rich, and unscrupulous men," and he does not hesitate to declare that "an organized and concerted campaign, offensive and defensive, against the common enemy is what is wanted."

According to the Rajah of Dewas, one of the most enlightened of the younger Hindu chiefs, "it is a well known fact that the endeavours of the seditious party are directed not only against the Paramount Power, but against all constituted forms of government in India, through an absolutely misunderstood sense of 'patriotism,' and through an attachment to the popular idea of 'government by the people,' when every level-headed Indian must admit that India generally has not in any way shown its fitness for a popular government." He goes so far even as to state his personal conviction that history and all "sound-minded" people agree that

India cannot really attain to the standard of popular government as understood by the West.

It is another Hindu ruler, the Rajah of Ratlam, who points out the close connexion, upon which I have had to lay repeated stress, between religious revivalism and sedition. He recognizes that "Hindus, and for the matter of that all Oriental peoples, are swayed more by religion than by anything else." Government have hitherto adopted, and rightly adopted, the policy of allowing perfect freedom in the matter of religious beliefs, but as the seditionists are seeking to connect their anarchical movement with religion, and the political *Sadhu* is abroad, it is high time to change the policy of non-interference in so-called religious affairs. The new religion which is now being preached, "with its worship of heroes like Shivaji and the doctrine of India for India alone," deserves, this Hindu Prince boldly declares, to be treated as Thuggism and Suttee were treated, which both claimed the sanction of religion. "It pains me," he adds, "to write as above, but already religion has played a prominent part in this matter, and religious books were found in almost every search made for weapons and bombs. The *rôle* of the priest or the *Sadhu* is most convenient, and rulers have bowed, and do bow, to religious preachers. These people generally distort the real import of religious precepts, and thereby vitiate the public mind. The founders are sly enough to flatter the Government by an occasional address breathing loyalty and friendship, but it is essential to check this religious propaganda."

The rulers of the Native States are not content merely to profess loyalty and reprobate disaffection. With the exception of the Gaekwar, whose reply, without striking any note of substantial dissent, is marked by a certain coolness that has won for him the applause of the Nationalist Press, they respond heartily to the Viceroy's request for suggestions as to the most effective measures to cope with the evil. Most of them put in the very forefront of their recommendations the necessity of checking the licence of the Indian Press, to which they attribute the main responsibility for the widening of the gulf between the rulers and the ruled. And it should be remembered that these opinions were expressed some months before the Imperial Government and the Government of India decided to introduce the new Press Act. The Nizam holds that newspapers publishing false allegations or exaggerated reports should be officially called upon "to print formal contradiction or correction as directed." For, in his Highness's opinion, "it is no longer safe or desirable to treat with silent contempt any perverse statement which is publicly made, because the spread of education on the one hand has created a general interest in the news of the country, and a section of the Press, on the other hand, deliberately disseminates news calculated to promote enmity between Europeans and Indians, or to excite hatred of Government and its officers in the ignorant and credulous minds." Several Chiefs recommend more summary proceedings and less publicity in the case of political offences, as, though such measures may appear arbitrary at first sight, "they are quite suited to the country." Several agree that a closer watch should be kept on "religious mendicants" who go about in the guise of *Sadhus* preaching sedition, and that a more intimate exchange of secret intelligence should take place with regard to the seditious propaganda between the different States and the Government of India. Others believe in the creation of counter-organizations to inform and encourage the loyal elements.

But it is perhaps on the question of education that some of the Ruling Chiefs speak with the greatest weight and authority, and there is nothing they more deeply deplore than the divorce of secular instruction from religious and moral training, which they hold responsible for much of the present mischief. "Strange as it may sound," says the Rajah of Dewas, "it is a well-known fact that the germs of the present unrest in India were laid by that benefactor of the human race, education." Another Chief is of opinion that, as the formation of character is the highest object of education, all public schools should be graded by the results they achieve in this direction rather than by high percentages in examinations; whilst others strongly recommend the extension of the residential college system and greater care in the selection of good teachers.

One may possibly not agree with all the opinions expressed or with all the recommendations made in this correspondence, but their general uniformity cannot fail to carry weight. It certainly carried weight with both the Government of India and the Imperial Government. Not only did it admittedly contribute to the enactment of the Indian Press Bill of February last, but it has probably also contributed to bring about a more general recognition of the urgency of the Indian educational problem. The effect produced in India itself by the publication of the views held by the rulers of Native States, many of whom enjoy great prestige and influence far beyond the limits of their immediate dominions, was naturally considerable. The "extremists" were lashed to fury, and none of the seditious leaflets directed against the "alien" rulers and "sun-dried bureaucrats" was more violent than one issued in reply to these utterances of the rulers of their own race. One of the ruling Chiefs to whom it had been sent gave me a copy of it as "a characteristic document." It is headed: "Choose, O Indian Princes." It begins, it is true, by assuring them that there is not as yet any cut-and-dried scheme for dealing with them.

No one but the voice of the Mother herself will and can determine when once She comes to herself and stands free what constitution shall be adopted by Her for the guidance of Her life after the revolution is over. . . . Without going into details we may mention this much, that whether the head of the Imperial Government of the Indian Nation be a President or a King depends upon how the revolution develops itself. . . . The Mother must be free, must be one and united, must make her will supreme. Then it may be that She gives out this Her will either wearing a kingly crown on Her head or a Republican mantle round Her sacred form.

But after being exhorted in impassioned accents either to sacrifice themselves in the great national struggle now at hand, or at the very least to stand back and keep the ring, they are warned as to the consequences of disregarding these admonitions :—

Forget not, O Princes ! that a strict account will be asked of your doings and non-doings, and a people newly-born will not fail to pay you in the coin you paid. Every one who shall have actively betrayed the trust of the people, disowned his fathers, and debased his blood by arraying himself against the Mother—he shall be crushed to dust and ashes. . . . Do you doubt our grim earnestness ? If so hear the name of Dhingra and be dumb. In the name of that martyr, O Indian Princes, we ask you to think solemnly and deeply upon these words. Choose as you will and you will reap what you sow. Choose whether you shall be the first of the nation's fathers or the last of the nation's tyrants.

In some less rabid quarters an attempt has been made to decry the views of the native rulers as emanating from petty Oriental despots, terrified by the onward march of the new Indian democracy. If so it is strange that whilst these " despots " make no secret of their attitude towards disaffection, they are equally outspoken on the necessity of a liberal and progressive policy. The Nizam himself states emphatically that he is " a great believer in conciliation and repression going hand in hand to cope with the present condition of India. While sedition should be localized and rooted out sternly, and even mercilessly, deep sympathy and unreserved reliance should manifest themselves in all dealings with loyal subjects without distinction of creed, caste, and colour." Unfortunately it requires at the present day more courage for an Indian to hold such language as that than to coquet, as many politicians do, with violence and crime. Indians in high position are peculiarly sensitive to printed attacks, perhaps because behind such attacks there often lurk forms of social pressure, rendered possible by their caste system, with which we, happily for ourselves, are totally unfamiliar. One of the most discouraging features of the present situation is that so few among the "moderate" politicians who are known to share and approve the views expressed by the Princes of India have had the moral courage to endorse them publicly.

The fearless response made by the ruling Chiefs to Lord Minto's appeal for advice and support in the repression of sedition conveys at the same time another lesson which we may well take to heart. The Government of India consulted them after the danger had arisen and become manifest. Is it not possible that, had we maintained closer touch with them in the past, had we appreciated more fully the value of their knowledge and experience, the danger might never have arisen or would never have attained such threatening proportions? At any rate, now that the consciousness of a common danger has drawn Princes and Government closer together, no time should be lost in establishing some machinery which would secure for the future a more sustained and intimate co-operation between them.

CHAPTER XVI.

Cross-Currents.

The political aspects of Indian unrest have compelled me to dwell chiefly upon the evil forces which it has generated. But contact with the West has acted as a powerful ferment for good as well as for evil upon every class of Indian society that has come more or less directly under its influence. Were it otherwise we should indeed have to admit the moral bankruptcy of our civilization. The forces of unrest are made up of many heterogeneous and often conflicting elements, and even in their most mischievous manifestations there are sometimes germs of good which it should be our business to preserve and to develop. Largely as the classes touched, however superficially, by Western education have of late years been invaded by a spirit of reaction and of revolt against all for which that education stands, they have not yet by any means been wholly conquered by it. It is the breath of the West that has stirred the spiritual and intellectual activity of which Hindu revivalism and political disaffection, glorified under the name of Nationalism, are unfortunately the most prominent and the most recent but not the only outcome. Another and much healthier outcome is the sense of social duty and social service which has grown up amongst many educated Indians of all races and creeds, and amongst none more markedly than amongst the Hindus. Traditions of mutual helpfulness are indeed deep-rooted in India as in all Oriental communities. Mutual helpfulness is the best feature of the caste system, of the Hindu family system, of the old Indian village system, and it explains the absence in a country where there is so much poverty of those abject forms of pauperism with which we are compelled at home to deal through the painful medium of our Poor Laws. But until the leaven of Western ideas had been imported into India mutual helpfulness was generally confined within the narrow limits of distinct and separate social units. It is now slowly expanding out of watertight compartments into a more spacious conception of the social interdependence of the different classes of the community. This expansion of the Indian's social horizon began with the social reform movement which had kindled the enthusiasm of an older generation in the '70's and '80's of the last century. Far from being, as some contend, a by-product of the more recent Nationalism, which had never been heard of at that period, its progress, as I have already shown, has been hampered not only by the reactionary tendencies of this Nationalism in religious and social matters, but by the diversion of some of the best energies of the country into the relatively barren field of political agitation.

Though social reform has been checked, it has not been altogether arrested, nor can it be arrested so long as British rule, by the mere fact of its existence, maintains the ascendency of Western ideals. Happily there are still plenty of educated Indians who realize that the liberation of Indian society from the trammels which are of its own making is much more urgent than its enfranchisement from an alien yoke. Even amongst politicians of almost every complexion the necessity of removing from the Indian social system the reproach of degrading anachronisms is finding at least theoretical recognition. Alongside of more conspicuous political organizations devoted mainly to political propaganda, other organizations have been quietly developing all over India whose chief purpose it is to grapple with social, religious, and economic problems which are not, or need not necessarily be, in any way connected with politics. Their voices are too often drowned by the louder clamour of the politicians pure and simple, and they attract little attention outside India. But no one who has spent any time in India can fail to be struck with the many-sided activities revealed in all the non-political conventions and conferences and congresses held annually all over the country. Within the last 12 months there have been philanthropic and religious conferences like the All India Temperance Conference, the Christian Endeavour Convention, the Theosophical Convention, social conferences like the Indian National Social Conference, the Moslem Educational Congress, and the Sikh Educational Conference, economic conferences like the Industrial Conference held at Lahore in connexion with the Punjab Industrial and Agricultural Exhibition, not to speak of many others, such as the Rajput Conference, the Hindu Punjab Conference, the Kshatrya Conference, the Parsee Conference, &c., which dealt with the narrower interests of particular castes or communities, but nevertheless gathered together representatives of those interests from all parts of India, or any rate from a whole province. Some of these meetings may be made to subserve political purposes. Others, like the Parsee Conference, betray reactionary tendencies in the most unexpected places, for the Parsee community, which has thriven more than any other on Western education and has prided itself upon being the most progressive and enlightened of all Indian communities, is the last one in which one would have looked for the triumph, however temporary, of a strangely benighted orthodoxy. But the majority of these gatherings represent an honest and earnest attempt to apply, as far as possible, the teachings of Western experience to the solution of Indian problems, and to subject Indian customs and beliefs to the test of modern criticism. They apply themselves, moreover, chiefly to questions in which no alien Government like that of India can take the initiative without serious risk of being altogether ahead of native opinion and arousing dangerous antagonism. As Mr. Lala Dev Raj, the chairman of the last Social Conference at Lahore, for instance, put it :—

> The reforms advocated here strike at those harmful and undesirable customs which are purely of our own creation and which must be bidden farewell to, as our eyes are being opened to them. If we cannot do that, we can hardly call ourselves a living community.

The results of all this activity may not so far have been very marked, but the mere fact that the supreme sanction of tradition, which was formerly almost undisputed, is now subjected to discussion is bound to make some impression, even upon those whose political concepts are based upon the immanent superiority of Hinduism. The new interpretation of the *Baghvat Gita*, though sometimes distorted to hideous ends, has itself been inspired by a broader appreciation of social duty than there was room for in the Hindu theory of life before it had been modified by Western influences. So long as the spirit of social endeavour kindled by men like Ram Mohun Roy and Keshab Chunder Sen and Mahadev Govind Ranade is kept alive, even though by much lesser men, we may well hope that the present wave of revolt will ultimately spend itself on the dead shore of a factious and artificial reaction, incompatible with the purpose to which their own best efforts were devoted, of bringing the social life of India into harmony with Western civilization.

A phenomenon which may prove to have a deep significance is that, side by side with these larger organizations for the promotion of social reform which only claim incidental service from their members, a number of smaller societies are growing up of which the members are bound together by much closer ties and more stringent obligations, and in some cases even by solemn vows to renounce the world and to devote themselves wholly to a life of social service. Many of them present features of special interest which deserve recognition, but I must be content to describe one of them to which the personality of its founder lends exceptional importance. This is the society of "The Servants of India," founded by Mr. Gokhale at Poona. Mr. Gokhale's career itself exemplifies the cross-currents that are often so perplexing a feature of Indian unrest. He is chiefly known in England as one of the leading and certainly most interesting figures in Indian politics. A Chitpavan Brahman by birth, with the blood of the old dominant caste of Maharashtra in his veins, he has often been, both in the Viceroy's Legislative Council and in that of his own Presidency, a severe and even bitter critic of an alien Government, of which he nevertheless admits the benefit, and even the necessity, for India. On the other hand, though he proclaims himself a Nationalist, and though, on one occasion at least, when he presided over the stormy session of the Indian National Congress at Calcutta in December, 1906, which endorsed the Bengalee boycott movement, he lent the weight of his authority to a policy that was difficult to reconcile with constitutional methods of opposition, his reason and his moral sense have always revolted against the reactionary appeals to religious prejudice and racial hatred by which men like Tilak have sought to stimulate a perverted form of Indian patriotism. Highly educated both as a Western and an Eastern scholar, he approaches perhaps more nearly than any of his fellow-countrymen to the Western type of doctrinaire, Radical in politics and agnostic in regard to religion, but with a dash of passion and enthusiasm which the Western doctrinaire is apt to lack. When Tilak opened his first campaign of unrest in the Deccan by attacking the Hindu reformers, he found few stouter opponents than Mr. Gokhale, who was one of Ranade's stanchest disciples and supporters. Nor did Tilak ever forgive him. His newspapers never ceased to pursue him with relentless ferocity, and only last year Mr. Gokhale had to appeal to the Law Courts for protection against the scurrilous libels of the "extremist" Press.

His own experiences in political life since he resigned his work as a professor at the Ferguson College in Poona in order to take a larger share in public affairs have probably helped to convince Mr. Gokhale that his fellow-countrymen for the most part still lack many essential qualifications for the successful discharge of those civic duties which are the corollary of the civic rights he claims for them. He does not, it is understood, desire to seek re-election to the Imperial Council at Calcutta after the expiry of its present powers, two years hence, as he wishes to devote himself chiefly to the educational work, which, in one form or another, has perhaps always been the most absorbing interest of his life. When he was a professor at the Ferguson College teaching was with him a vocation rather than a profession, and, if one may judge by his practice, he believes that only those who are prepared to set an example of selflessness and almost ascetic simplicity of life can hope to promote the moral and social as well as the political advancement of India. It is on these principles that he founded five years ago the "Servants of India" Society, recruited in the first instance amongst a few personal followers and supported hitherto by the voluntary contributions of his admirers. The objects of the Society as laid down by its promoters are "to train national missionaries for the service of India and to promote by all constitutional means the true interests of the Indian people." Its members "frankly accept the British connexion as ordained, in the inscrutable dispensation of Providence, for India's good," and they recognize that "self-government within the Empire and a higher life generally for their countrymen" constitute a goal which "cannot be attained without years of earnest and patient effort and sacrifices worthy of the cause." As to its immediate functions, "much of the work," it is stated, "must be directed towards building up in the country a higher type of character and capacity than is generally available at present," and to this end the Society "will train men prepared to devote their lives to the cause of the country in a religious spirit." The constitution of the Society recalls in fact that of some of the great religious societies of Christendom, and not least that of the Jesuits, though with this cardinal difference, that it is essentially non-sectarian and substitutes as its ideal the service of India for the service of God, much in the same way as the Japanese have to a large extent merged their religious creeds in an idealized cult of Japan.

Every "Servant of India" takes at the time of admission into the society the following seven vows :—

(*a*) That the country will always be first in his thoughts, and that he will give to her service the best that is in him.

(*b*) That in serving the country he will seek no personal advantage for himself.

(*c*) That he will regard all Indians as brothers and will work for the advancement of all, without distinction of caste or creed.

(*d*) That he will be content with such provision for himself and his family, if any, as the society may be able to make, and will devote no part of his energies to earning money for himself.

(*e*) That he will lead a pure personal life.

(*f*) That he will engage in no personal quarrel with any one.

(*g*) That he will always keep in view the aims of the society and watch over its interests with the utmost zeal, doing all he can to advance its work and never doing anything inconsistent with its objects.

The head of the society, called the First Member—who is Mr. Gokhale—is to hold office for life, and its affairs are to be conducted in accordance with by-laws framed for the purpose by the First Member, who will be assisted by a council of three, one of whom will be his own nominee, whilst two will be elected by the ordinary members. The powers assigned to the First Member are very extensive and include that of recommending the names of three ordinary members, one of whom, when the time comes, shall be chosen to succeed him. His authority is, in fact, the dominant one, whether over the probationers under training for a period of five years, three of which are to be spent at the society's home in Poona, or over the ordinary members admitted to the full privileges of the society, or over those who, as *attachés*, associates, and permanent assistants, are very closely affiliated to it without being actually received into membership. The scheme is, of course, at present in its infancy, as the society still numbers only about 25, the majority of whom have not yet completed their term of probation. Mr. Gokhale, however, hopes very soon to have 50 probationers constantly in residence, and he has already gathered together in the well-appointed buildings of the society's home just outside Poona, in close proximity to the Ferguson College, a group of young men, to some of whom he kindly introduced me, who have evidently caught the fervour of his enthusiasm. One of the latest recruits was by birth a Mahomedan, of whom Mr. Gokhale was specially proud, as he is very anxious that the society shall be, in fact as well as in theory, representative of all castes and creeds.

One of the first questions which this remarkable experiment suggests is whether the ideals which Mr. Gokhale sets before the "Servants of India" will suffice to supply the necessary driving power. Hitherto some form of religious faith and the hope of some heavenly reward have alone availed to induce men to renounce the world and all its material interests and surrender themselves to a life of rigorous and selfless discipline in the service of their fellow-creatures, or rather in the service of God through their fellow-creatures. Mr. Gokhale's society makes no claim to any religious sanction. Though Indian asceticism has from the most remote times found devotees willing to lead a life of far more complete self-annihilation than any that the most rigorous monastic orders of Christendom have ever imposed, or that, for the matter of that, Mr. Gokhale seeks to impose upon his followers, it has always been inspired by some religious conception. Will the "Servants of India" find the same permanent inspiration in the cult of an Indian Motherland, however highly spiritualized, that has no rewards to offer either in this world or in any other? On the political as well as other potentialities of such an organization as Mr. Gokhale contemplates there is no need to dwell. For the "Servants of India," moulded by one mind and trained to obey one will, are to go forth as missionaries throughout India, in the highways and byways, among the "untouchables" as well as among the higher classes, preaching to each and all the birth of an Indian nation.

CHAPTER XVII.

The Growth of Western Education.

The rising generation represent the India of the future, and though those who come within the orbit of the Western education we have introduced still constitute only a very small fraction of the whole youth of India, their numbers and their influence are growing steadily and are bound to go on growing. If we are losing our hold over them, it is a poor consolation to be told that we still retain our hold over their elders. I therefore regard the estrangement of the young Indian, and especially of the young Hindu who has passed or is passing through our schools and colleges, as the most alarming phenomenon of the present day, and I am convinced that of all the problems with which British statesmanship is confronted in India none is more difficult and more urgent than the educational problem. We are too deeply pledged now to the general principles upon which our educational policy in India is based for even its severest critics to contemplate the possibility of abandoning it But for this very reason it is all the more important that we should realize the grave defects of the existing system, or, as some would say, want of system, in order that we may, so far as possible, repair or mitigate them. There can be no turning back, and salvation lies not in doing less for Indian education, but in doing more and in doing it better.

Four very important features of the system deserve to be noted at the outset:—(1) Following the English practice, Government exercises no direct control over educational institutions other than those maintained by the State, though its influence is brought in several ways indirectly to bear upon all that are not prepared to reject the benefits which it can extend to them; (2) Government has concentrated its efforts mainly upon higher education, and has thus begun from the top in the over-sanguine belief that education would ultimately filter down from the higher to the lower strata of Indian society; (3) instruction in the various courses, mostly literary, which constitute higher education is conveyed through the medium of English, a tongue still absolutely foreign to the vast majority; and (4) education is generally confined to the training of the intellect and divorced not only, absolutely, from all religious teaching, but also, very largely, from all moral training and discipline, with the result that the vital side of education which consists in the formation of character has been almost entirely neglected.

To make the present situation intelligible, I must recapitulate, however briefly, the phases through which our Indian system of education has passed. The very scanty encouragement originally given to education by the East India Company was confined to promoting the study of the Oriental languages still used at that time in the Indian Courts of Law in order to qualify young Indians for Government employment and chiefly in the subordinate posts of the judicial service. After long and fierce controversies on the rival merits of the vernaculars and of English as the more suitable vehicle for the expansion of education, Macaulay's famous Minute of March 7, 1835, determined a revolution of which only very few at the time foresaw, however faintly, the ultimate consequences. Lord William Bentinck's Government decided that "the great object of the British Government ought to be the promotion of English literature and science, and that all the funds appropriated for the purpose of education would be best employed in English education alone."

Another influence—too often forgotten—had at least as large a share as Macaulay's in this tremendous departure. That was the influence of the great missionary, Dr. Alexander Duff, who inspired the prohibition of suttee and other measures which marked the withdrawal of the countenance originally given by the East India Company to religious practices incompatible, in the opinion of earnest Christians, with the sovereignty of a Christian Power. Duff had made up his mind, in direct opposition to Carey and other earlier missionaries, that the supremacy of the English language over the vernaculars must be established as a preliminary to the Christianization of India. He had himself opened in 1830 an English school in Calcutta with an immediate success which had confounded all his opponents. His authority was great both at home and in India, and was reflected equally in Lord Hardinge's Educational Order of 1844, which threw a large number of posts in the public service open to English-speaking Indians without distinction of race or creed, and in Sir Charles Wood's Educational Despatch of 1854, which resulted in the creation of a Department for Public Instruction, the foundation of the three senior Universities of Calcutta, Madras, and Bombay, the affiliation to them of schools and colleges for purposes of examination, and the inauguration of the "grant-in-aid" system for the encouragement of native educational enterprise by guaranteeing financial support according to a fixed scale to all schools that satisfied certain tests of efficiency in respect of secular instruction. Duff's influence had assured the supremacy of English in secular education, but he never succeeded in inducing Government to go a step beyond neutrality in regard to religious education, and though the remarkable successes which he had in the meantime achieved, not only as a teacher but as a missionary, amongst the highest classes of Calcutta society no doubt led him to hope that, even without any active co-operation from Government, the spread of English education would in itself involve the spread of both Christian ethics and Christian doctrine, he never ceased to preach the necessity of combining religious and moral with secular education or to prophesy the evils which would ensue from their divorce.

The system inaugurated by the Educational Minute of 1835 and developed in the Educational Orders of 1854 began well. The number of young Indians who took advantage of it was relatively small. They were drawn mostly from the better classes, and they were brought into direct contact with their English teachers, many of them very remarkable men whose influence naturally, and often unconsciously, helped to form the character of their pupils as well as to develop their intellect—and most of all, perhaps, in the mission schools; for the Christian missions were at that time the dominant factor in Indian educational work. In 1854 when there were only 12,000 scholars in all the Government schools, mission schools mustered four times that number and the rights they acquired, under the Orders of 1854, to participate in the new "grants-in-aid" helped them to retain the lead which in some respects, though not as to numbers, they still maintain. For more than 50 years after the Minute of 1835, and especially during the two or three decades that followed the Orders of 1854, the new system produced a stamp of men who seemed fully to justify the hopes of its original founders—not merely men with a sufficient knowledge of English to do subordinate work as clerks and minor *employés* of Government, but also men of great intellectual attainments and of high character, who filled with distinction the highest posts open to Indians in the public service, sat on the Bench, and practised at the Bar, and, in fact, made a mark for themselves in the various fields of intellectual activity developed by contact with the West. It is much to be regretted that no *data* have ever been collected to show what proportion men of this stamp bore to the aggregate number of students under the new system. The proportion was certainly small, but it was at any rate large enough to reflect credit upon the system as a whole and to disguise its inherent defects. It is characteristic of the narrowness of official interest in educational questions that, whereas abundant statistics are forthcoming on all subjects connected with material progress, no attempt seems to have been made to follow the results of Western education statistically into the after-life of high school pupils and college students. We know that a certain number have emerged into public distinction, but there is nothing to show, except in the most general way, how many have turned their education to humbler but still profitable account, or how many have turned it to no account at all.

Paradoxical as it may sound, it is the eagerness of young India to respond to our educational call that has led to the breakdown of the system in some of the most important functions of education. In its earlier stages those who claimed the benefit of the new system were chiefly drawn from the intellectual *élite*—*i.e.*, from the classes which had had the monopoly of knowledge, though it was not Western knowledge, before the introduction of Western education. With the success which the new system achieved the demand grew rapidly, and the quality of the output diminished as it increased in quantity. On the one hand education came to be regarded by the Indian public less and less as an end in itself, and more and more as merely an avenue either to lucrative careers or to the dignified security of appointments, however modest, under Government, and, in either case, to a higher social *status*, which ultimately acquired a definite money value in the matrimonial market. The grant-in-aid system led to the foundation of large numbers of schools and colleges under private native management, in which the native element became gradually supreme or at least vastly predominant, and it enabled them to adopt so low a scale of fees that many parents who had never dreamt of literacy for themselves were encouraged to try and secure for some at least of their children the benefit of this miraculous Open Sesame to every kind of worldly advancement. Much of the raw material pressed into secondary schools was quite unsuitable, and little or no attempt was made to sift it in the rough. Numbers therefore began to drop out somewhere on the way, disappointed of their more ambitious hopes and having acquired just enough new ideas to unfit them for the humbler work to which they might otherwise have been brought up [17]. On the other hand, whilst schools and colleges, chiefly under private native management, were multiplied in order to meet the growing demand, the instruction given in them tended to get petrified into mechanical standards, which were appraised solely or mainly by success in the examination lists. In fact, education in the higher sense of the term gave way to the mere cramming of undigested knowledge into more or less receptive brains with a view to an inordinate number of examinations, which marked the various stages of this artificial process. The personal factor also disappeared more and more in the relations between scholars and teachers as the teaching staff failed to keep pace with the enormous increase in numbers.

All these deteriorating influences, though they were perhaps not then so visible on the surface, were already at work in the 80's, when two important Government Commissions were held whose labours, with the most excellent intentions, were destined to have directly and indirectly, the most baneful effects upon Indian education. The one was the Education Commission of 1882-83, appointed by Lord Ripon, with Sir William Hunter as President, and the other the Public Service Commission of 1886-87, appointed by Lord Dufferin, with Sir Charles Aitchison as President. It is quite immaterial whether the steps taken by the Government of India during the subsequent decade were actually due to the recommendations of the Education Commission, or whether the Report of the Commission merely afforded a welcome opportunity to carry into practice the views that were then generally in the ascendant. The eloquence of the Commission, if I may borrow the language appropriately used to me by a very competent authority, was chiefly directed towards representing the important benefits that would be likely to accrue to Government and to education by the relaxation of Government's control over education, the withdrawal of Government from the management of schools, and the adoption of a general go-as-you-please policy. Amongst the definite results which we undoubtedly owe to the labours of that Commission was the acclimatization in India of Sir Robert Lowe's system of "payment by results," which was then already discredited in England. Just at the time when the transfer of the teacher's influence from European into native hands was being thus accelerated, the Public Service Commission, not a single member of which was an educational officer, produced a series of recommendations which had the effect of changing very much for the worse the position and prospects of Indians in the Educational Department. Before the Commission sat, Indians and Europeans used to work side by side in the superior graded service of the Department, and until quite recently they had drawn the same pay. The Commission abolished this equality and comradeship and put the Europeans and the Indians into separate pens. The European pen was named the Indian Educational Service, and the native pen was named the Provincial Educational Service. Into the Provincial Service were put Indians holding lower posts than any held by Europeans and with no prospect of ever rising to the *maximum* salaries hitherto within their reach. To pretend that equality was maintained under the new scheme is idle, and the grievance thus created has caused a bitterness which is not allayed by the fact that the Commission created analogous grievances in other branches of the public service. Nor was this all the mischief done. It quickened the impulse already given by the Education Commission by formally recommending that the recruitment of Englishmen for the Education Department should be reduced to a *minimum*, and, especially, that even fewer inspectors of schools than the totally inadequate number then existing should be recruited from England. It is interesting to note in view of subsequent developments that, whilst this recommendation was tacitly ignored by the Provincial Governments in some parts of India, as in Madras and in Bombay, it was accepted and applied in Bengal—*i.e.*, in the province where our educational system has displayed its gravest shortcomings.

From that time forward the dominant influence in secondary schools and colleges drifted steadily and rapidly out of the hands of Englishmen into those of Indians long before there was a sufficient supply of native teachers fitted either by tradition or by training to conduct an essentially Western system of education. Not only did the number of native teachers increase steadily and enormously, but that of the European teachers actually decreased. Dr. Ashutosh Mookerjee, the Vice-Chancellor of the Calcutta University, told me, for instance, that when he entered the Presidency College about 1880 all the professors, except a few specialists for purely Oriental subjects, were English, and the appointment, whilst he was there, of an Indian for the first time as an ordinary professor created quite a sensation. Last year there were only eight English professors as against 23 Indians, though, during the same 30 years, the number of pupils had increased from a little over 350 to close on 700—*i.e.*, it had nearly doubled. The Calcutta Presidency College is, even so, far better off in this respect than most colleges except the missionary institutions, in which the European staff of teachers has been maintained at a strength that explains their continued success. Out of 127 colleges there are 30 to-day with no Europeans at all on the staff, and these colleges contain about one-fifth of the students in all colleges. Of the other colleges 16 have only one European professor, 21 only two, and so forth. In the secondary schools the proportion of native to European teachers is even more overwhelming. From the point of view of mere instruction the results have been highly unsatisfactory. From the point of view of moral training and discipline and the formation of character they have been disastrous.

CHAPTER XVIII.

The Indian Student.

The fundamental weakness of our Indian educational system is that the average Indian student cannot bring his education into any direct relation with the world in which, outside the class or lecture room, he continues to live. For that world is still the old Indian world of his forefathers, and it is as far removed as the poles asunder from the Western world which claims his education. I am not speaking now of the relatively still very small class amongst whom Western ideas are already sufficiently acclimatized for the parents to be able to supplement in their own homes the education given to their children in our schools and colleges. Nor am I speaking of the students who live in hostels under the superintendence of high-minded Englishmen, and especially of missionaries such as those of the Oxford Mission in Calcutta, or the Madras Christian College, who have to reject scores of applicants for want of space. Those also form but a small minority. In Calcutta, for instance, out of 4,500 students barely 1,000 live in hostels, and not all hostels are by any means satisfactory. In the Indian Universities there is no collegiate life such as English Universities afford, and in India most of the secondary schools as well as colleges are non-residential. The majority of those who attend them, unless they live at home, have therefore to board out with friends or to live in promiscuous messes, or, as is too often the case, in lodgings of a very undesirable character, sometimes even in brothels, and almost always under conditions intellectually, morally, and physically deleterious.

Lest I may be accused of exaggeration or bias, I will appeal here to the testimony of Dr. Garfield Williams, a missionary of the highest repute and experience, and in profound sympathy with the natives of India. Speaking at the Missionary Conference at Calcutta last winter, he said :—

> The conditions and environment of the student in Calcutta are such as to make the formation of character almost impossible. . . . He is not a student in the best sense of the word, for he has not the scholarly instincts of a student —I speak, of course, of the average student, not of the exceptional one. His parents send him to the University to pass one or two examinations, and these have to be passed in order to enable him to attain a higher salary. . . . His work is sheer "grind." The acquisition of good notes for lectures is the first essential for him, and the professor who gives good clear-cut notes so that a man can dispense with any text-books is the popular professor—and for two reasons: first of all, it saves the expense of buying the text-book, and then, of course, it helps to get through the examination. That is a reason why two boys of the same village will go to different colleges because they can then "swap" notes. It is a very rare thing for a student to have money enough to buy more than one of the suggested books on a given subject for examination. He learns by heart one book and the notes of lectures of two or three of the favourite professors in Calcutta. There is many a man who has even got through his examinations without any text-book of any kind to help him, simply by committing to memory volumes of lecture notes. . . . I know of no student who labours more strenuously than the Bengalee student. The question is how to prevent this ridiculous wastage of students; how to prevent the production of this disappointed man who is a student only in name. He never had any desire to be a student in nature; he was brought up without that desire. . . and indeed, if he be a boy with real scholarly instincts, and he happens to fail in his examinations, it makes

it all the worse, for his parents will not recognize those scholarly instincts of his—all they want is a quick return for the money spent on his education, and he will have to make that return from a Rs.30 salary instead of a Rs.50 one.

Can there be anything more pathetic and more alarming than the picture that Dr. Williams draws of the student's actual life ?—

He gets up about 6, and having dressed (which is not a long process) he starts work. Until 10, if you go into his mess, you will see him "grinding" away at his text-book, under the most amazing conditions for work—usually stretched out upon his bed or sitting on the side of it. The room is almost always shared with some other occupant, usually with two or three or more other occupants, mostly engaged in the same task if they are students. At 10 the boy gets some food, and then goes off to his college for about four or five hours of lectures. A little after 3 in the afternoon he comes home to his mess, and between 3 and 5 is usually seen lounging about his room, dead tired but often engaged in discussion with his room-mates or devouring the newspaper, which is his only form of recreation and his only bit of excitement. At 5 he will go out for a short stroll down College-street or around College-square. This is his one piece of exercise, if such you can call it. At dusk he returns to his ill-lighted, stuffy room and continues his work, keeping it up, with a short interval for his evening meal, until he goes to bed, the hour of bed-time depending upon the proximity of his examination. A very large percentage when they actually sit for their examinations are nothing short of physical wrecks.

Dr. Williams proceeds to quote Dr. Mullick, an eminent Hindu physician who has devoted himself to helping young students :—

The places where the students live huddled up together are most hurtful to their constitutions. The houses are dirty, dingy, ill-ventilated, and crowded. Even in case of infectious sickness . . . they lie in the same place as others, some of whom they actually infect. Phthisis is getting alarmingly common among students owing to the sputum of infected persons being allowed to float about with the dust in crowded messes. . . . Most of them live in private messes where a hired cook and single servant have complete charge of his food and house-keeping, and things are stolen, foodstuffs are adulterated, badly cooked and badly served.

Dr. Williams, who states emphatically that "it is not exaggeration to say that the student is often half-starved," goes on to deal with the moral drawbacks of a life which is under no effective supervision and is not even under the restraints, implied in the term "good form," that play so important a part in Universities where there is a real collegiate life.

> When you segregate your young men by thousands in the heart of this "city of dreadful night," amid conditions of life which are most antagonistic to moral and physical well-being . . . the result is a foregone conclusion, and it does not only mean physical degeneration, it also means moral degeneration, and it becomes a most potent predisposing factor in political disease. Of that there can be no shadow of doubt.

The material conditions are not, it is true, nearly so bad in many other parts of India as they are in Bengal, and especially in Calcutta (though the Bengalees claim the intellectual primacy of India), and it is on the moral and physical evils produced by those conditions that Dr. Garfield Williams chiefly dwells. But the intellectual evils for all but a small minority are in their way quite as grave, and they are inherent to the system. Take the case of a boy brought up until he is old enough to go to school in some small town of the *mofussil*, anywhere in India, by parents who have never been drawn into any contact, however remote, with Western ideas or Western knowledge. From these purely Indian surroundings his parents, who are willing to stint themselves in order that their son may get a post under Government, send him to a secondary school, let us say in the chief town of the district, or in a University city. There again he boards w th friends of his family, if they have any, or in more or less reputab e lodgings amidst the same purely Indian surroundings, and his only contact with the Western world is through school-books in a foreign tongue, of which it is difficult enough for him to grasp even the literal meaning, let alone the spirit, which his native teachers have themselves too often only very partially imbibed and are therefore quite unable to communicate [18]. From the secondary school he passes for his University course, if he gets so far, in precisely the same circumstances into a college which is merely a higher form of school. Whilst attending college our student still continues to live amidst the same purely Indian surroundings, and his contact with the Western world is still limited to his text-books. Even the best native teacher can hardly interpret that Western world to him as a trained European can, and unless our student intends to become a doctor or an engineer, and has to pass through the schools of medicine or engineering, where he is bound to be a good deal under English teachers, he may perfectly well, and very often does, go through his whole course of studies in school and in college without ever coming into personal contact with an Englishman. How can he be expected under such conditions to assimilate Western knowledge or to form even a remote conception of the customs and traditions, let alone the ideals, embodied in Western knowledge?

Try and imagine for a moment, however absurd it may seem, what would have been the effect upon the brains of the youth of our own country if it had been subject to Chinese rule for the last 100 years, and the Chinese, without interfering with our own social customs or with our religious beliefs, had taken charge of higher education and insisted upon conveying to our youth a course of purely Chinese instruction imparted through Chinese text-books, and taught mainly by Englishmen, for the most part only one degree more familiar than their pupils with the inwardness of Chinese thought and Chinese ethics. The effect could hardly have been more bewildering than the effect produced in many cases similar to that which I have instanced on the brain of the Indian youth when he emerges from our schools and colleges.

It may be said that such cases are extreme cases, but extreme as they are, they are not exceptional. The exceptions must be sought rather amongst the small minority, who, in spite of all these drawbacks, display such a wonderful gift of assimilation, or, it might perhaps be more correctly termed, of intuition, that they are able to transport themselves into a new world of thought, or at any rate to see into it, as it were, through a glass darkly. But the number of those who possess this gift has probably always been small, and smaller still, with the reduction of the European element in the teaching staff, is the number growing of those who have a fair chance of developing that gift, even if nature has endowed them with it. A comparison of the Census Report of 1901 with the figures given in the Educational Statistics for 1901-2 shows that the total number of Europeans then engaged in Indian educational work was barely 500, of whom less than half were employed by Government, whilst that of the Indians engaged in similar work in colleges and secondary schools alone was about 27,500. As the number of Indian students and scholars receiving higher education amounts to three-quarters of a million, it is obvious that so slight a European leaven, whatever its quality—and its quality is not always what it should be—can produce but little impression upon so huge a mass.

Our present system of Indian education in fact presents in an exaggerated form, from the point of view of the cultivation of the intellect, most of the defects alleged against a classical education by its bitterest opponents in Western countries, where, after all, the classics form only a part, however important, of the curriculum, and neither Latin nor Greek is the only medium for the teaching of every subject. From the point of view of the formation of character according to Western standards, and even from that of physical improvement, the case is even worse. In Western countries the education given in our schools, from the Board school to the University, is always more or less on the same plane as that of the class from which the boys who attend them are drawn. It is merely the continuation and the complement of the education our children receive in their own homes from the moment of their birth, and it moves on the same lines as the world in which they live and move and have their being. In India, with rare exceptions, it is not so, but exactly the reverse.

On the deficiencies of the system, from the moral point of view, a new and terribly lurid light has been shed within the last few years. There has been no more deplorable feature in the present political agitation than the active part taken in it by Indian schoolboys and students. It has been a prominent feature everywhere, but nowhere more so than in the Bengal provinces, where from the very outset of the boycott movement in 1905 picketing of the most aggressive character was conducted by bands of young Hindus who ought to have been doing their lessons. That was only the beginning, and the state of utter demoralization that was ultimately reached may be gathered from the following statements in the last Provincial Report on Education (1908-9), issued by the Government of Eastern Bengal :—

> On the 7th of August [1908] most of the Hindu students abstained from attending the college and high schools at Comilla as a demonstration in connexion with the boycott anniversary. Immediately afterwards, on the date of the execution of the Muzafferpur murderer, the boys of several schools in the province attended barefooted and without shirts and in some cases fasting. . . . At Jamalpur the demonstration lasted a week. . . . Later in the year, on the occasion of the execution of one of the Alipur murderers, the pupils of the Sandip Cargill school made a similar demonstration.

The report adds, in a sanguine vein, that, as a result of various disciplinary measures, a marked improvement had subsequently taken place, but quite recent events, during the great conspiracy trial at Dacca, show that something more than disciplinary measures is required to eradicate the spirit which inspired such occurrences.

The heaviest responsibility rests on those who, claiming to be the intellectual leaders of the country, not only instigated its youth to take part in political campaigns, but actually placed them in the forefront of the fray. However reprehensible from our British point of view other features of a seditious agitation may be, to none does so high a degree of moral culpability attach as to the deliberate efforts made by Hindu politicians to undermine the fundamental principles of authority by stirring up the passions or appealing to the religious sentiment of inexperienced youth at the most emotional period of life [19]. Even the fact that political murders have been invariably perpetrated by misguided youths of the student class is hardly as ominous as the homage paid to the murderers' memories by whole schools and colleges. Most ominous of all is the tolerance, and sometimes the encouragement, extended to such demonstrations by schoolmasters and professors. These are symptoms that point to a grave moral disease amongst the teachers as well as the taught, which we can only ignore at our peril and at the sacrifice of our duty towards the people of India. In his last two Convocation speeches, Dr. Ashutosh Mookerjee has himself felt constrained to lay special stress on the question of teachers and politics. Alluding in 1909 to " the lamentable events of the last 12 months," he maintained, " without hesitation," that " the most strenuous efforts must be unfalteringly made by all persons truly interested in the future of the rising generation to protect our youths from the hands of irresponsible people who recklessly seek to seduce our students from the path of academic life and to plant in their immature minds the poisonous seeds of hatred against constituted Government." This year he was even more outspoken, and laid it down that even the teacher " who scrupulously abstains from political matters within his class-room, but at the same time devotes much or all of his leisure hours to political activities and agitation, and whose name and speeches are prominently before the world in connexion with political organizations and functions," fails in his duty towards his pupils; for "their minds will inevitably be attracted towards political affairs and political agitation if they evidently constitute the main life-interest and life-work of one who stands towards them in a position of authority." Teachers should therefore avoid everything that tends "to impart to the minds of our boys a premature bias towards politics."

A most admirable exhortation; but I had an opportunity of estimating the weight that it carried with some of the political leaders of Bengal when I accepted an invitation from Mr. Surendranath Banerjee to meet a few Bengalee students in an informal way and have a talk with them. They were bright, pleasant lads, and, if they had been left to themselves, I might have had an interesting talk with them about their studies and their prospects in life, but Mr. Banerjee and several other politicians who were present insisted upon giving to the conversation a political turn of a disagreeably controversial character which seemed to me entirely out of place.

The mischievous incitements of politicians would not, however, have fallen on to such receptive soil if economic conditions, for which we are ourselves at least partly responsible, had not helped to create an atmosphere in which political disaffection is easily bred amongst both teachers and taught. The rapid rise in the cost of living has affected no class more injuriously than the old clerkly castes from which the teaching staff and the scholars of our schools and colleges are mainly recruited. Their material position now often compares unfavourably with that of the skilled workman and even of the daily labourer, whose higher wages have generally kept pace with the appreciation of the necessaries of life. This is a cause of great bitterness even amongst those who at the end of their protracted course of studies get some small billet for their pains. The bitterness is, of course, far greater amongst those who fail altogether. The rapid expansion of an educational system that has developed far in excess of the immediate purpose for which it was originally introduced was bound to result in a great deal of disappointment for the vast number of Indians who regarded it merely as an avenue to Government employment. For the demand outran the supply, and the deterioration in the quality of education consequent upon this too rapid expansion helped at the same time to restrict the possible demand. F.A.'s (First Arts) and even B.A.'s are now too often drugs in the market. Nothing is more pathetic than the hardships to which both the young Indian and his parents will subject themselves in order that he may reach the coveted goal of University distinctions, but unfortunately, as such distinctions are often achieved merely by a process of sterile cramming which leaves the recipients quite unable to turn mere feats of memory to any practical account, the sacrifices prove to have been made in vain. Whilst the skilled artisan, and even the unskilled labourer, can often command from 12 annas to 1 rupee (1s. to 1s. 4d.) a day, the youth who has sweated himself and his family through the whole course of higher education frequently looks in vain for employment at Rs.30 (£2) and even at Rs.20 a month. In Calcutta not a few have been taken on by philanthropic Hindus to do mechanical labour in jute mills at Rs.15 a month simply to keep them from starvation. Things have in fact reached this pitch, that our educational system is now turning out year by year a semi-educated proletariat which is not only unemployed, but in many cases almost unemployable. A Hindu gentleman who is one of the highest authorities on education told me that in Bengal, where this evil has reached the most serious dimensions, he estimates the number of these unemployed at over 40,000. This is an evil which no change in the relative number of Europeans and natives employed in Government and other services could materially affect. Even if every Englishman left India, it would present just as grave a problem to the rulers of the country, except that the bitterness engendered would not be able to vent itself, as it too often does now, on the alien rulers who have imported the alien system of education by which many of those who fail believe themselves to have been cruelly duped.

Similar causes have operated to produce discontent amongst the teachers, who in turn inoculate their pupils with the virus of disaffection. It was much easier to multiply schools and colleges than to train a competent teaching staff. Official reports seldom care to look unpleasant facts in the face, and the periodical reports both of the Imperial Department of Public Education and of the Provincial Departments have always been inclined to lay more stress upon the multiplication of educational institutions and the growth in the numbers of pupils and students than upon the weak points of the system. Nevertheless, there is one unsatisfactory feature that the most confirmed optimists cannot ignore. Hardly a single one of these reports but makes some reference to the deficiencies and incapacity of the native teaching staff. The last quinquennial report issued by Mr. Orange, the able Director-General of Public Education, who is now leaving India, contains a terse but very significant passage. "Speaking generally," he writes, "it may be said that the qualifications and the pay of the teachers in secondary schools are below any standard that could be thought reasonable; and the inquiries which are now being made into the subject have revealed a state of things that is scandalous in Bengal and Eastern Bengal, and is unsatisfactory in every province." Very little information is forthcoming as to the actual qualifications or pay of the teachers. It appears, however, from the inspection of high schools by the Calcutta University that out of one group of 3,054 teachers over 2,100 receive salaries of less than 30 rupees (£2) a month. One cannot, therefore, be surprised to hear that in Bengal "only men of poor attainments adopt the profession, and the few who are well qualified only take up work in schools as a stepping-stone to some more remunerative career." That career is frequently found in the Press, where the disgruntled ex-schoolmaster adds his quota of gall to the literature of disaffection. But he is still more dangerous when he remains a schoolmaster and uses his position to teach disaffection to his pupils either by precept or by example.

I have already alluded to the unfortunate effect of the recommendations of the Public Service Commission of 1886-7 on the native side of the Education Service. But if it has become more difficult to attract to it the right type of Indians, it has either become almost as difficult to attract the right type of Europeans, or the influence they are able to exercise has materially diminished. In the first place, their numbers are quite inadequate. Out of about 500 Europeans actually engaged in educational work in India less than half are in the service of the State. Many of them are admittedly very capable men, and not a few possess high University credentials. But so long as the Indian Educational Service is regarded and treated as an inferior branch of the public service, we cannot expect its general tone to be what it should be in view of the supreme importance of the functions it has to discharge. One is often told that the conditions are at least as attractive as those offered by an educational career at home. Even if that be so, it would not affect my contention that, considering how immeasurably more difficult is the task of training the youth of an entirely alien race according to Western standards, and how vital that task is for the future of British rule in India, the conditions should be such as to attract, not average men, but the very best men that we can produce. As it is, the Education Department cannot be said to attract the best men, for these go into the Civil Service, and only those, as a rule, enter the Educational Service who either, having made up their minds early to seek a career in India, have failed to pass the Civil Service examinations, or, having originally intended to take up the teaching profession in England, are subsequently induced to come out to India by disappointments at home or by the often illusory hope of bettering their material prospects. When they arrive they begin work without any knowledge of the character and customs of the people. Some are employed in inspection and others as professors, and the latter especially are apt to lose heart when they realize the thanklessness of their task and their social isolation. In some cases indifference is the worst result, but in others—happily rare—they themselves, I am assured, catch the surrounding contagion of discontent, and their influence tends rather to promote than to counteract the estrangement of the rising generation committed to their charge. Some men, no doubt, rise superior to all these adverse conditions and, in comparing the men of the present day with those of the past, one is apt to remember only the few whose names still live in the educational annals of India and to forget the many who have passed away without making any mark. The fact, however, remains that nowadays the Europeans who have the greatest influence over their Indian pupils are chiefly to be found amongst the missionaries with whom teaching is not so much a profession as a vocation.

CHAPTER XIX.

SOME MEASURES OF EDUCATIONAL REFORM.

Though already in 1889, when Lord Lansdowne was Viceroy, an important resolution, drafted by Sir Anthony (now Lord) MacDonnell as Secretary to Government, was issued, drawing attention to some of the most glaring defects of our educational system from the point of view of intellectual training and of discipline, and containing valuable recommendations for remedying them, it seems to have had very little practical effect. A more fruitful attempt to deal with the question was made during Lord Curzon's Viceroyalty. He summoned and presided over an Educational Conference, of which the results were embodied in a Government Resolution issued on March 11, 1904, and in the Universities Act of the same year. They were received at the time with a violent outburst of indignation by Indian politicians, who claim to represent the educated intellect of the country. The least that Lord Curzon was charged with was a deliberate attempt to throttle higher education in India. This factious outcry has now died away, except amongst the irreconcilables, and Dr. Ashutosh Mookerjee, an authority whom even Hindu partisanship can hardly repudiate, declared in his last Convocation speech that the new regulations which are now being brought into operation, far from bearing out the apprehensions of "alarmist prophets," have been distinctly beneficial to the better and stronger class of students.

To summarize very briefly the work of the Conference, it recognized in the first place the importance of the vernaculars as the proper medium for instruction in the lower stages of education, whilst maintaining the supremacy of English in the higher stages. It sought to give a more practical character to high-school training by promoting the "modern side," hitherto overshadowed by a mainly literary curriculum, and it endeavoured to make the school courses self-sufficing and self-contained instead of merely a stepping-stone to the University courses. To this end secondary schools were encouraged to give more importance to School Final Examinations as a general test of proficiency and not to regard their courses as almost exclusively preparatory to the University Entrance Examination. Great stress was also laid upon the improvement of training colleges for teachers as well as upon the development of special schools for industrial, commercial, and agricultural instruction. Nor were the ethics of education altogether forgotten in their bearings upon the maintenance of healthy discipline. Government emphasized the great importance of a large extension of the system of hostels or boarding-houses, under proper supervision, in connexion with colleges and secondary schools, as a protection against the moral dangers of life in large towns; and whilst provision was made for the more rigorous inspection of schools to test their qualifications both for Government grants-in-aid and for affiliation to Universities, certain reforms were also introduced into the constitution and management of the Universities themselves.

The results already achieved are not inconsiderable. The provision of hostels, in which Lord Curzon was deeply interested, has made great progress, and one may hope that the conditions of student life described by Dr. Garfield Williams in Calcutta are typical of a state of things already doomed to disappear, though at the present rate of progress it can only disappear very slowly. In Madras there is a fine building for the Presidency College students and also for those of the Madras Christian College. In Bombay Government are giving money for the extension of the boarding accommodation of the three chief colleges. In Allahabad, Agra, Lucknow, Meerut, Bareilly, Lahore, and many other centres old residential buildings are being extended or new ones erected. The new Dacca College, in the capital of Eastern Bengal, is one of the most conspicuous and noteworthy results of the Partition. In Calcutta itself little has been done except in the missionary institutions; and it is certainly very discouraging to note that an excellent and very urgent scheme for removing the Presidency College, the premier college of Bengal, from the slums in which it is at present in every way most injuriously confined, to a healthy suburban site has been shelved by the Bengal Government partly under financial pressure and partly because of the lukewarmness of native opinion. What is no doubt really wanted is the wholesale removal of all the Colleges connected with the Calcutta University altogether from their present surroundings, but to refuse to make a beginning with the Presidency College is merely to prove once more that *le mieux est l'ennemi du bien*.

In regard to the University Entrance Examinations, the latest Madras returns, which were alone sufficiently complete to illustrate the effect of the new regulations, showed that the increased stringency of the tests had resulted in a healthy decrease in the number of matriculations, whilst the standard had been materially raised. In Calcutta the University inspection of schools and colleges and the exercise by the Universities of their discretionary powers in matters of affiliation have grown much more effective. That the powers of the University Senates have not been unduly curtailed is only too clearly shown on the other hand by the effective resistance hitherto offered at Bombay to the scheme of reforms proposed by Sir George Clarke. To the most important features of the scheme, which were the provision of a course of practical science for all first-year students, a systematic bifurcation of courses, the lightening of the number of subjects in order to secure somewhat more thoroughness, and compulsory teaching of Indian history and polity, no serious objection could be raised, but the politicians on the Senate effectively blocked discussion.

A great deal still remains to be done, and can be done, on the lines of the resolution of 1904. The speed at which it can be done must, no doubt, be governed in some directions by financial considerations. The extension of the hostel system, for instance, which is indispensable to the removal of some of the worst moral and physical influences upon education, is largely a matter of money. So is too to some extent the strengthening of the educational staff, European and native, which is also urgently needed. The best Indians cannot be attracted unless they are offered a living wage in some measure consonant with the dignity of so important a profession, and our schools and colleges will continue to be too often nursery grounds of sedition so long as we do not redress the legitimate grievances of teachers on starvation wages. But though improved prospects may attract better men in the future, the actual inefficiency of a huge army of native teachers, far too hastily recruited and imperfectly trained, can at best be but slowly mended. We want more and better training colleges for native teachers, but that is not all. The great Mahomedan College at

Aligarh, one of the best educational institutions in India, partly because it is wholly residential, has obtained excellent results by sending some of its students who intend to return as teachers to study Western educational methods in Europe, after they have completed their course in India. The same practice might be extended elsewhere.

To raise the standard of the Europeans in the Educational Service something more than a mere improvement of material conditions is required. Additions are being made to both the teaching and the inspecting staff. But what is above all needed is to get men to join who regard teaching not merely as a livelihood, but as a vocation, and to inform them with a better understanding both of the people whose children they have to train and of the character and methods of the Government they have to serve. This can hardly be done except by associating the Educational Service much more closely with what are now regarded as the higher branches of the public service in India. No Englishmen are in closer touch with the realities of Indian life than Indian civilians, and means must be found to break down the wall which now rigidly separates the Educational Service from the Civil Service. Opportunities might usefully be given to young Englishmen when they first join the Educational Service in India to acquire a more intimate knowledge of Indian administrative work, as well as of the character and customs and language of the people amongst whom their lot is to be cast, by serving an apprenticeship with civilians in the *mofussil*. The appointment of such a very able civilian as Mr. Harcourt Butler to be the first Minister of Education in India may be taken as an indication that Lord Morley realizes the importance of rescuing the Educational Service from the watertight compartment in which it has hitherto been much too closely confined. We can hardly hope to restore English influence over education to the position which it originally occupied.

There are 1,200 high schools for boys in India to-day, of which only 220 are under public management, and, even for the latter, it would be difficult to provide an English headmaster apiece. What we can do is to follow up the policy which has been lately resumed of increasing the number of high schools under Government control, until we have at least one in every district, and in every large centre one with an English headmaster which should be the model school for the division.

A much vexed question is whether it is impossible to raise the fees charged for higher education with a view to checking the wastage which results from the introduction into our schools and colleges of so much unsuitable raw material. The fees now charged for the University course are admittedly very low, even for Indian standards. The total cost of maintaining an Indian student throughout his four years' college course ranges from a *minimum* of £40 to a *maximum* of £110—*i.e.*, from £10 to £27 10s. per annum. The actual fees for tuition vary from three to twelve rupees (4s. to 16s.) a month in different colleges. Very large contributions, amounting roughly to double the total aggregate of fees, have therefore to be made from public funds towards the cost of collegiate education. Is it fair to throw so heavy a burden on the Indian taxpayer for the benefit of a very small section of the population amongst whom, moreover, many must be able to afford the whole, or at least a larger proportion, of the cost of their children's education? Is it wise by making higher instruction so cheap to tempt parents to educate children often of poor or mediocre abilities out of their own plane of life? Would it not be better at any rate to raise the fees generally and to devote the sums yielded by such increase to exhibitions and scholarships for the benefit of the few amongst the humbler classes who show exceptional promise?

Against this it is urged that it would be entirely at variance with Indian traditions to associate standards of knowledge with standards of wealth, and, in practice, education has, I understand, been found to be worst where the fees bear the greatest proportion to the total expenditure. The same arguments equally apply for and against raising the fees in secondary schools. In regard to the latter, however, the opponents of any general increase of fees make, nevertheless, a suggestion which deserves consideration. In many schools the fees begin at a very low figure—eight annas (8d.) a month in the lowest forms and rise to three, four, and even five rupees (4s., 5s. 4d., and 6s. 8d.) a month in the highest forms. It is this initial cheapness which induces so many thoughtless parents to send their boys to secondary schools without having considered whether they can afford to keep them through the whole course, whilst it fosters the notion that badly paid and badly qualified teachers are good enough for the early, which are often the most important, stages of a boy's education. To obviate these evils it is suggested that the fees for all forms should be equalized.

I shall have occasion later on to point out the immense importance of giving greater encouragement to scientific and technical education. Government service and the liberal professions are already overstocked, and it is absolutely necessary to check the tendency of young Indians to go in for a merely literary education for which, even if it were more thorough than it can be under existing conditions, there is no longer any sufficient outlet. The demand which is arising all over India for commercial and industrial development should afford an unrivalled opportunity of deflecting education into more useful and practical channels.

Some better machinery than exists at present seems also to be required to bring the Educational Service into touch with parents. Education can nowhere be a question of mere pedagogics, and least of all in India. Yet there is evidently a strong tendency to treat it as such. To take only one instance, the tasks imposed upon schoolboys and students by the exigencies of an elaborate curriculum are often excessive, and there have been cases when the intervention of other authorities has been necessary to bring the education officers to listen to the reasonable grievances of parents. If in these and other matters parents were more freely consulted, they would probably be more disposed to give education officers the support of their parental authority. There are many points upon which native opinion would not be so easily misled by irreconcilable politicians if greater trouble were taken to explain the questions at issue.

What is evidently much wanted is greater elasticity. In a country like India, which is an aggregation of many widely different countries, the needs and the wishes of the people must differ very widely and cannot be met by cast-iron regulations, however admirable in theory. It is earnestly to be hoped that the creation of a separate portfolio in the Government of India will not involve the strengthening of the centralizing tendencies which have been the bane of Indian education since the days of Macaulay, himself one of the greatest theorists that ever lived. We cannot afford to relax the very little control we exercise over education, but education is just one of the matters in which Provincial Governments should be trusted to ascertain, and to give effect to, the local requirements of the people. In another direction, however, the creation of a Ministry for Education should be all to the good. If any real and comprehensive improvements are to be carried out they will cost a great deal of money, and in the ordinary sense of the term it will not be reproductive expenditure, though no expenditure, if wisely applied, can yield more valuable results. As a member of Council—*i.e.*, as a member of the Government of India—Mr. Butler must carry much greater weight in recommending the necessary expenditure than a Director-General of Public Education or than a Provincial Governor, especially as the expenditure will probably have to be defrayed largely out of

Imperial and not merely out of Provincial funds. If the educational problem is the most vital and the most urgent one of all at the present hour in India, it stands to reason that no more disastrous blunder could be made than to stint the new department created for its solution.

CHAPTER XX.

The Question of Religious Education.

There remains one vital aspect of the educational problem which was left untouched by the Educational Resolution of 1904, and has been left untouched ever since we entered three-quarters of a century ago on an educational experiment unparalleled in the world's history—a more arduous experiment even than that of governing the 300 millions of India with a handful of Englishmen. Many nations have conquered remote dependencies inhabited by alien races, imposed their laws upon them, and held them in peaceful subjection, though even this has never been done on the same scale of magnitude as by the British rulers of India. We alone have attempted to educate them in our own literature and science and to make them by education the intellectual partners of the civilization that subdued them. Of the two tasks, that of government and that of education, the latter is not by any means the easier. For good government involves as little interference as possible with the beliefs and customs and traditions of the people, whereas good education means the substitution for them of the intellectual and moral conceptions of what we regard as our higher civilization. Good government represents to that extent a process of conservation; good education must be partially a destructive, almost a revolutionary, process. Yet upon the more difficult and delicate problems of education we have hitherto, it is to be feared, bestowed less thought and less vigilance than upon administrative problems in India. The purpose we have had in view is presumably that which Dr. Ashutosh Mookerjee admirably defined in his last address to the University of Calcutta as "the raising up of loyal and honourable citizens for the welfare of the State." But is it a purpose which those responsible for our Indian system of education have kept steadily before them? Is it a purpose that could possibly be achieved by the *laisser faire* policy of the State in regard to the moral and religious side of education? If so, how is it that we have had of late such alarming evidence of our frequent failure to achieve it?

The divorce of education from religion is still on its trial in Western countries, which rely upon a highly-developed code of ethics and an inherited sense of social and civic duty to supply the place of religious sanctions. In India, as almost everywhere in the East, religion in some form or another, from the fetish worship of the primitive hill tribes to the Pantheistic philosophy of the most cultured Brahman or the stern Monotheism of the orthodox Moslem, is the dominant force in the life both of every individual and of every separate community to which the individual belongs. Religion is, in fact, the basic element of Indian life, and morality apart from religion is an almost impossible conception for all but an infinitesimal fraction of Western-educated Indians. Hence, even if the attempt had been or were in the future made to instil ethical notions into the minds of the Indian youth independently of all religious teaching, it could only result in failure. For the Hindu, perhaps more than for any other, religion governs life from the hour of his birth to that of his death. His birth and his death are in fact only links in a long chain of existences inexorably governed by religion. His religion may seem to us to consist chiefly of ritual and ceremonial observances which sterilize any higher spiritual life. But even if such an impression is not due mainly to our own want of understanding, the very fact that every common act of his daily life is a religious observance, just as the caste into which he is born has been determined by the degree in which he has fulfilled similar religious observances in a former cycle of lives, shows how completely his religion permeates his existence. The whole world in which he lives and moves and has his being, in so far as it is not a mere illusion of the senses, is for him an emanation of the omnipresent deity that he worships in a thousand different shapes, from the grotesque to the sublime.

Yet in a country where religion is the sovereign influence we have, from the beginning, absolutely ignored it in education. It is no doubt quite impossible for the State in a country like India with so many creeds and sects, whose tenets are often repugnant to all our own conceptions not only of religion but of morality, to take any direct part in providing the religious instruction which would be acceptable to Indian parents. But was it necessary altogether to exclude such instruction from our schools and colleges? Has not its exclusion tended to create in the minds of many Indians the belief that our professions of religious neutrality are a pretence, and that, however rigorously the State may abstain from all attempts to use education as a medium for Christian propaganda, it nevertheless uses it to undermine the faith of the rising generations in their own ancestral creeds? Even if they acquit us of any deliberate purpose, are they not at any rate entitled to say that such have been too often the results? Did not the incipient revolt against all the traditions of Hinduism that followed the introduction of Western education help to engender the wholesale reaction against Western influcnces which underlies the present unrest?

Few problems illustrate more strikingly the tremendous difficulties that beset a Government such as ours in India. On the one hand, Indian religious conceptions are in many ways so diametrically opposed to all that British rule stands for that the State cannot actively lend itself to maintain or promote them. On the other hand, they provide the ties which hold the whole fabric of Indian society together, and which cannot be hastily loosened without serious injury and even danger to the State. This has been made patent to the most careless observer by the events of the last few years that have revealed, as with a lurid flash of lightning, the extent to which the demoralization of our schools and colleges had proceeded. If any Englishman has doubts as to the connexion in this matter of cause and effect, let him ask respectable Indian parents who hold aloof from politics. They have long complained that the spirit of reverence and the respect for parental authority are being killed by an educational system which may train the intellect and impart useful worldly knowledge, but withdraws their youths from the actual supervision and control of the parents or of the *guru*, who for spiritual guidance stood *in loco parentis* under the old Hindu system of education, and estranges them from all the ideas of their own Hindu world [20]. That parents often genuinely resent the banishment of all religious influence from our schools and colleges appears from the fact that many of them prefer to Government institutions those conducted by missionaries in which, though no attempt is made to proselytize, a religious, albeit a Christian, atmosphere is to some extent maintained. It is on similar grounds also that the promoters of the new movement in favour of "National Schools" advocate the maintenance of schools which purchase complete immunity from Government control by renouncing all the advantages of grants-in-aid and of University affiliation. They have been started mainly under the patronage of "advanced" politicians, and have too often turned out to be mere hot-beds of sedition, but their *raison d'être* is alleged to be the right of Hindu parents to bring up Hindu children in a Hindu atmosphere.

From the opposite pole in politics, most of the ruling chiefs in their replies to Lord Minto's request for their opinions on the growth of disaffection call attention to this aspect of education, and the Hindu princes especially lay great stress on the neglect of religious and moral instruction. I will quote only the Maharajah of Jaipur, a Hindu ruler universally revered for his high character and great experience :—

> My next point has reference to the neglect there seems to be of religious education, a point to which I drew your Excellency's attention at the State banquet at Jaipur on the 29th October, 1909. I must say I have great faith in a system of education in which secular and religious instruction are harmoniously combined, as the formation of character entirely depends upon a basework of religion, and the noble ideals which our sacred books put before the younger generation will, I fervently hope, make them loyal and dutiful citizens of the Empire. Such ideals must inevitably have their effect on impressionable young men, and it is perhaps due to such ideals that sedition and anarchy have obtained so small a footing in the Native States as a whole. In the Chiefs' College Conference, held at the Mayo College in 1904, I impressed upon my colleagues the necessity of religious education for the sons of the chiefs and nobles of Rajputana, and it should be one of the principal objects in all schools for the Pandits and the Moulvies to instil in the minds of their pupils correct notions as to the duty they owe to the community they belong to and to their Sovereign.

In this respect the ruling chiefs unquestionably reflect the views which prevail amongst the better-class Indians in British India as well as in the Native States. The Government of India cannot afford to disregard them. The Resolution of 1904, it is true, laid it down again definitely that "in Government institutions, the instruction is and must continue to be exclusively secular." But much has happened since 1904 to reveal the evils which our educational system has engendered and to lend weight to the representations made by responsible exponents of sober Indian opinion in favour of one of the remedies which it is clearly within our power to apply. Nor need we really depart from our time-honoured principle of neutrality in religious matters. All we have to do is to set apart, in the curriculum of our schools and colleges, certain hours during which they will be open, on specified conditions, for religious instruction in the creed in which the parents desire their children to be brought up. There is no call for compulsion. This is just one of the questions in which the greatest latitude should be left to local Governments, who are more closely in touch than the Central Government with the sentiment and wishes of the different communities. I am assured that there would be little difficulty in forming local committees to settle whether there was a sufficiently strong feeling amongst parents in favour of a course of religious instruction and to determine the lines upon which it should be given. Some supervision would have to be exercised by the State, but in the Educational Service there are, it is to be hoped, enough capable and enlightened representatives of the different creeds to exercise the necessary amount of supervision in a spirit both of sympathy for the spiritual needs of their people and of loyalty to the Government they serve. It may be objected that there are so many jarring sects, so many divisions of caste, that it would be impossible ever to secure an agreement as to the form to be imparted to religious instruction. Let us recognize but not overrate the difficulty. In each of the principal religions of India a substantial basis can be found to serve as a common denominator between different groups, as, for instance, in the Koran for all Mahomedans and in the Shastras for the great majority of high-caste Hindus. At any rate, if the effort is made and fails through no fault of ours, but through the inability of

Indian parents to reconcile their religious differences, the responsibility to them will no longer lie with us.

Another objection will probably be raised by earnest Christians who would hold themselves bound in conscience to protest against any facilities being given by a Christian State for instruction in religious beliefs which they reprobate. Some of these austere religionists may even go so far as to contend that, rather than tolerate the teaching of "false doctrines," it is better to deprive Indian children of all religious teaching. To censure of this sort, however, the State already lays itself open in India. There are educational institutions—and some of the best, like the Mahomedan College at Aligurh—maintained by denominational communities on purpose to secure religious education. Yet the State withdraws from them neither recognition nor assistance because pupils are taught to be good Mahomedans or good Hindus. Why should it be wrong to make religious instruction permissive in other Indian schools which are not wholly or mainly supported by private endeavour? Is not the "harmonious combination of secular and religious instruction" for which the Maharajah of Jaipur pleads better calculated than our present policy of *laisser faire* to refine and purify Indian religious conceptions, and to bring about that approximation of Eastern to Western ideals, towards which the best Indian minds were tending before the present revolt against Western ascendency?

Here is surely a question bound up with all the mainsprings of Indian life in which we may be rightly asked "to govern according to Indian ideas." Can we expect that the youth of India will grow up to be law-abiding citizens if we deprive them of what their parents hold to be "the keystone to the formation of character"? Can we close our eyes to what so many responsible Indians regard as one of the chief causes of the demoralization which has crept into our schools and colleges? The State can, doubtless, exact in many ways more loyal co-operation from Indian teachers in safeguarding their pupils from the virus of disaffection. It can, for instance, intimate that it will cease to recruit public servants from schools in which sedition is shown to be rife. It can hold them collectively responsible, as some Indians themselves recommend for crimes perpetrated by youths whom they have helped to pervert. But these are rigorous measures that we can hardly take with a good conscience so long as our educational system can be charged with neglecting or undermining, however unintentionally, the fabric upon which Indian conceptions of morality are based. So long as we take no steps to refute a charge which, in view of recent evidence, can no longer be dismissed as wholly unfounded, can we expect education to fulfil the purpose rightly assigned to it by Dr. Mookerjee—" the raising up of loyal and honourable citizens for the welfare of the State?"

CHAPTER XXI.

Primary Education.

It is too late in the day now to discuss whether it was wise to begin our educational policy as we did from the top and to devote so much of our energies and resources to secondary at the expense of primary education. The result has certainly been to widen the gulf which divides the different classes of Indian society and to give to those who have acquired some veneer, however superficial, of Western education the only articulate voice, often quite out of proportion to their importance, as the interpreters of Indian interests and desires. One million is a liberal estimate of the number of Indians who have acquired and retained some knowledge of English ; whilst at the last census, out of a total population of 294 millions, less than sixteen millions could read and write in any language—not fifteen millions out of the whole male population and not one million out of the whole female population—and this modest amount of literacy is mainly confined to a few privileged castes.

With the growth of a school of Indian politicians bent upon undermining British rule, the almost inconceivable ignorance in which the masses are still plunged has become a real danger to the State, for it has proved an all too receptive soil for the calumnies and lies of the political agitator, who, too well educated himself to believe what he retails to others, knows exactly the form of calumny and lie most likely to appeal to the credulity of his uninformed fellow-countrymen. I refer especially to such very widespread and widely believed stories as that Government disseminates plague by poisoning the wells and that it introduces into the plague inoculation serum drugs which destroy virility in order to keep down the birth-rate. No one has put this point more strongly than Lord Curzon :—

> What is the greatest danger in India ? What is the source of suspicion, superstition, outbreaks, crime—yes, and also of much of the agrarian discontent and suffering amongst the masses ? It is ignorance. And what is the only antidote to ignorance ? Knowledge.

Curiously enough, it was one of Lord Curzon's bitterest opponents who corroborated him on this point by relating in the course of a recent debate how, when the Chinsurah Bridge was built some years ago over the Hughli, "the people believed that hundreds and thousands of men were being sacrificed and their heads cut off and carried to the river to be put under the piers to give the bridge stability, so that the goddess might appreciate the gift and let the piers remain." And he added :—"I know that ignorant people were afraid to go out at nights, lest they might be seized and their heads cut off and thrown under the piers of the Hughli Bridge."

It was, however, on more general considerations, as is his wont, that Mr. Gokhale moved his resolution in the first Session of the Imperial Council at Calcutta last winter for making elementary education free and compulsory, and for the early appointment of a committee to frame definite proposals.

> Three movements [he claimed] have combined to give to mass education the place which it occupies at present amongst the duties of the State—the humanitarian movement which reformed prisons and liberated the slave, the democratic movement which admitted large masses of men to a participation in Government, and the industrial movement which brought home to nations the recognition that

the general spread of education in a country, even when it did not proceed beyond the elementary stage, meant the increased efficiency of the worker.

The last of these three considerations is, perhaps, that which just now carries the most weight with moderate men in India, where the general demand for industrial and commercial development is growing loud and insistent, and Mr. Gokhale's resolution met with very general support from his Mahomedan, as well as from his Hindu, colleagues. But, in the minds of disaffeeted politicians, another consideration is, it must be feared, also present, to which utterance is not openly given. It is the hope that the extension of primary schools may serve, as has that of secondary schools, to promote the dissemination of seditious doctrines, especially amongst the "depressed eastes" to which the political agitator has so far but rarely secured access.

Whatever danger may lie in that direction, it cannot be allowed to affect the policy of Government, who gave to Mr. Gokhale's resolution a sufficiently sympathetic reception to induce him to withdraw it for the present. To the principle of extending primary education the Government of India have indeed long been committed, and increased efforts were recommended, both in the Educational Despatch of 1854 and by the Education Commission of 1883. Stress was equally laid upon it by the Resolution of 1904 under Lord Curzon, who already, in 1902, had caused additional grants, amounting to more than a quarter of a million sterling, to be given to provincial Governments for the purpose. Under Lord Minto's administration Government seemed at one moment to have gone very much further and to have accepted at any rate the principle of free education, for in 1907 the Finance Member conveyed in Council an assurance from the Secretary of State that "notwithstanding the absence of Budget provision, if a suitable scheme should be prepared and sanctioned by him, he will be ready to allow it to bc carried into effect in the course of the year, provided that the finaneial position permits." It was rather unfortunate that hopes should be so prematurely raised, and it would surely have been wiser to consult the local Governments before than after such a pronouncement. For when they were consulted their replies, especially as to the abolition of fees, were mostly unfavourable, and this year also Government, whilst expressing its good will, felt bound to defer any decision until the question had been more fully studied and the financial situation had improved.

The present situation is certainly unsatisfactory. In 1882 there were 85,000 primary schools in India recognized by the Educational Department which gave elementary education to about 2,000,000 pupils. In 1907, according to the last quinquennial report, the total attendance had increased to 3,631,000 ; but though the increase appears very considerable, the Director-General of Education had to admit that, assuming progress to be maintained at the present rate, " several generations would still elapse before all the boys of school age were in school." And Mr. Gokhale's resolution applies, at least ultimately, to girls as well as to boys ! Now in British India—*i.e.*, without counting the Native States—the total number of boys of school-going age on the basis of the four years' eourse proposed for India would be nearly 12 millions, and there must be about an equal number of girls. The total cost to the State according to the estimates of local Governments would be no less than £15,000,000 per annum, whilst non-recurring expenditure would amount to £18,000,000. The fees at present paid by parents for primary education, which is already free in some parts of India and in certain circumstances, make up only about £210,000 per annum. The whole of the enormous difference would, therefore, be thrown upon the Indian taxpayers, who now have to find for primary education less than £650,000 per annum. Even Mr. Gokhale does not, of course, propose that this educational and financial revolution should be effected by a stroke of the pen, and one of his

Hindu colleagues held that it would be contrary to all Hindu traditions for parents to avail themselves of free education if they could afford to pay a reasonable sum for it.

But even if the state of Indian finances were likely within any appreciable time to warrant an approximate approach to such vast expenditure, or if Government could entertain the suggestions made by Mr. Gokhale for meeting it, partly by raising the import duties from 5 to 7½ per cent. and imposing other taxes, and partly by wholesale retrenchment in other departments, the financial difficulty is not the only one to be overcome. Model schoolhouses could no doubt be built all over India, if the money were forthcoming, instead of the wretched accommodation which exists now, and is so inadequate that in the Bombay Presideney alone there are said to be 100,000 boys for whom parents want, but cannot obtain, primary education. But what of the teachers ? These cannot be improvised, however many millions Government may be prepared to spend. There is an even greater deficiency of good teachers than of good schoolhouses, and, in some respects, the value of primary education still more than that of secondary education depends upon good teachers—teachers who are capable of explaining what they teach and not merely of reeling off by rote, and imperfectly, to their pupils lessons which they themselves imperfectly understand. The total number of teachers engaged in primary education exceeds 100,000, but their salaries barely average Rs.8 (10s. 8d.) a month. So miserable a pittance abundantly explains their inefficiency. But there it is, and a new army of teachers—nearly half a million altogether—would have to be trained before primary education, whether free and compulsory, as Mr. Gokhale would have it, or optional and for payment, as others propose, could be usefully placed within the reach of the millions of Indian children of a school-going age.

In this as in all other matters, the Government of

India cannot afford to stand still, and will have to take Indian opinion more and more into account. But whilst there is a very general consensus that more should be done by the State for primary education, there is no unanimity as to its being made free and compulsory. Various Indian members of Council have expressed themselves against it on different grounds. Some contend that many parents cannot afford, as bread-winners, to be deprived of the help of their children. According to others, there is already much complaint amongst parents that school-going boys do not make good agriculturists and affect to consider work in the fields as beneath their dignity. Others, again, ask, and with some reason, who is going to care for boys of that age who may have to leave their homes and be removed from parental control in order to attend school. There is, doubtless, something in all these objections. Assuming that Government can do more than it has hitherto done to further primary education, the wisest course would be to improve the quality rather than the quantity, and, most of all, the quality of the teachers. Here, again, uniformity should be avoided rather than ensued. No primary curriculum can be evolved which will meet the needs alike of the rural population and of the townsfolk, or of the different parts of India with their varying conditions of climate and temperament. Even more than with regard to secondary schools, the needs of parents must be consulted, and the greatest latitude given to provincial Governments to vary the system in a practical spirit and in accordance with local requirements. Nor can the opinion, strongly held by many parents, be overlooked that religious instruction cannot be safely excluded from the training of such young children. Some of the objects to be kept specially in view have been well stated by Mr. Orange, the Director-General of Public Education :—

We desire to see, if not in every village, within reach of every village, a school, not an exotic, but a village school, in which the village itself can take pride, and of which the first purpose will be to train up good men and women and good citizens; and the second, to impart useful knowledge, not forgetting while doing so to train the eye and the hand so that the children when they leave school, whether for the field or the workshop, will have begun to learn the value of accurate observation and to feel the joy of intelligent and exact manual work.

This is undoubtedly the goal towards which primary education should be directed, but it can only be reached by steady and continuous effort spread over a long term of years. Otherwise we shall discover, again too late, that, as in the case of secondary education, most haste is worst speed.

I shall not attempt to deal with the question of female education, either primary or secondary, for it is so intimately bound up with the peculiarities of Indian, and especially Hindu, society, that it would be difficult for the State to take any vigorous initiative without running a great risk of alarming and alienating native opinion [21]. Owing to Indian social customs and to the practice of early marriage, or at least of early seclusion, for girls, their education presents immense practical difficulties which do not exist in the case of boys. Hence the slow progress it has made. At the last census only eight per thousand women could read and write; and in the whole of India only about half a million girls, or four out of every 100 of a school-going age, even on the basis of a four years' course, are receiving any kind of education. Of such as do go to school nine out of ten only go to primary schools. Mr. Gokhale himself has abandoned the idea of making primary education compulsory for girls as well as for boys. Female education is just one of the questions upon which Indian opinion must be left to ripen, Government giving, in proportion as it ripens, such assistance as can be legitimately expected. It has long engaged the attention of enlightened Indians, and in some communities, especially amongst the Aryas of the Punjab, some headway is being made. The Parsees, of course, as in all educational and philanthropic developments, have always been in the van. With the growth of Western education the Indian woman of the higher classes cannot indefinitely lag behind, and, if only to make their daughters more eligible for marriage, the most conservative Indian parents will be compelled to educate them, as some have already done, so that they shall not be separated from their male partners by an unfathomable gulf of intellectual inferiority. In Calcutta, in Bombay, in Madras, and indeed in all the principal cities of India, one may already meet native ladies, both Hindu and Mahomedan, of education and refinement, who, however few their numbers, are shining examples of what Indian womanhood can rise to when once it is emancipated from the trammels of antiquated custom.

CHAPTER XXII.

SWADESHI AND ECONOMIC PROGRESS.

Was it not Talleyrand who said that speech had been given to man in order to enable him to disguise his thoughts? Indian politicians are no Talleyrands, but they sometimes seem to have framed their vocabulary on purpose to disguise political conceptions which most of them for various reasons shrink from defining at present with decision. We have already seen how elastic is the word *Swaraj*, self-government, or rather self-rule. In the mouth of the "moderates" of the Indian National Congress it means, we are assured, only a pious aspiration towards the same position which our self-governing Colonies enjoy within the Empire. For the "advanced" politician *Swaraj* means a transition stage which he hopes and believes must infallibly lead to a complete severance of the ties that unite India to the Empire. For the "extremists" it means the immediate and violent emancipation of India from British rule, and absolute independence. So it is with the term *Swadeshi*, which means anything from the perfectly legitimate and commendable encouragement of Indian trade and industry to the complete exclusion of foreign, and especially of British, goods by a "national" and often forcible "boycott" as part of a political campaign against British rule.

Political *Swadeshi* bases itself upon a Nationalist legend that a "golden age" prevailed in India before we appeared on the scene, and that British rule has deliberately drained India of her wealth. Even if we have to admit that Indian home industries have suffered heavily from the old commercial policy of the East India Company and from the formidable competition of the organized and scientific processes of British industry, this legend hardly deserves to be treated seriously. The *reductio ad absurdum* of the argument has certainly been reached when Mr. Keir Hardie alleges that Indian loans raised in England constitute "a regular soaking drain upon India because the interest is paid to bondholders in this country [England], and is not therefore benefiting the people from whom it is taken." I can only commend this sapient contention to our self-governing Colonies, who have all had recourse in turn to British capital for the development of their resources, and paid interest on their loans to British bondholders without being apparently conscious of any "soaking drain." The supposed "drain" is estimated in various ways, but a common method adopted is to lay stress upon the excess of exports over imports [22]. Lord Curzon has rightly pointed out that economically this test is quite fallacious; and that in the richest country in the world, America, the value of the exports exceeds the imports by over £100,000,000 per annum. Home charges represent three-fourths of the "drain," and these may be calculated at about £18,000,000 annually. Of this sum, £6,750,000 is paid in interest on railway capital; but the railways are a source of profit, and the payment comes from the railway passenger. Moreover, in course of time, the Indian railways will become, and are becoming, a property of enormous value to the State. The interest on India's public debt is £3,000,000, but it has to be remembered how much India has benefited by expenditure which has proved reproductive. Sir Bampfylde Fuller has stated that the lowest estimate of the increase in produce obtained through irrigation works alone is estimated at £30,000,000 annually. In the last 50 years the total volume of Indian trade, imports and exports, has increased from £40,000,000 to £200,000,000. The remaining items are roughly, home military charges, £2,000,000 ; India Office, &c., £250,000 ; leave allowances, £750,000 ; pensions, £4,000,000. A considerable part of these pensions represent merely deferred pay. Moreover, unlike some other countries, *e.g.*, the United States, where £32,000,000 are spent on pensions, mostly unearned, India has had good value, brimming over, for her pensions. The private remittances to England, which must be added to these sums, are not treated in any other country as an economic loss. No American economist would so regard the enormous annual sums remitted by immigrants to Ireland, Italy, and other European countries, or the vast annual expenditure of American tourists in Europe. Indian immigrants remit £400,000 annually to India from the Straits Settlements and Malay States alone, and considerable sums must be sent from East and South Africa and Ceylon, as well as smaller sums from Mauritius and the West Indies. Yet these colonies do not apparently complain about a "drain" to India.

What India is entitled to ask is whether Indian loans have been expended for the benefit of the Indian people, and the answer is conclusive. India possesses to-day assets in the shape of railways, irrigation canals, and other public works which, as marketable properties, represent more than her total indebtedness, without even taking into account the enormous value of the "unearned increment" they have produced for the benefit of the people of India. If, therefore, we look at the Government of India for a moment as merely a board of directors conducting a great development business on behalf of the Indian people, they can certainly show an excellent balance-sheet. Let us admit that some of the "home charges" may be open to discussion, and I shall have a word or two or say about them later on. But taken altogether they may fairly be regarded as the not unreasonable cost of administering a concern which, if we wished to liquidate it and to retire from business to-morrow, would leave a handsome surplus to India after paying off the whole debt contracted in her name. The case was stated very fairly by the late Mr. Ranade, whose teachings all but the most "advanced" politicians still profess to reverence, when he delivered the inaugural address at the first Industrial Conference held just 20 years ago at Poona :—

> There are some people who think that as long as we have a heavy tribute to pay to England which takes away nearly 20 crores of our surplus exports, we are doomed, and can do nothing to help ourselves. This is, however, hardly a fair or manly position to take up. A portion of the burden represents interest on moneys advanced to, or invested in, our country, and so far from complaining, we have reason to be thankful that we have a creditor who supplies our needs at such a low rate of interest. Another portion represents the value of stores supplied to us, the like of which we cannot produce here. The remainder is alleged to be more or less necessary for the purpose of administration, defence, and payment of pensions, and, though there is good cause for complaint that it is not all necessary, we should not forget the fact that we are enabled by reason of this British connexion to levy an equivalent tribute from China by our opium monopoly.

If India must now forgo this tribute from China, it is not at any rate the fault of the Government of India that the whole cost of the awakening of the national conscience in England to the iniquity of the opium traffic is being thrown upon India.

The question is not whether we have done well, but whether we might not have done better, and whether the economic development of India, industrial, commercial, and agricultural, has kept pace with that of the rest of the world. If the answer in this case is more doubtful, we have to bear in mind the idiosyncrasies of the Indian people and especially of the educated classes. Indians have been as a rule disinclined to invest their money

17

in commerce or industry or in scientific forms of agriculture. It is estimated that the hoarded wealth of India amounts, at a conservative calculation, to £300,000,000, and this probably represents gold alone. The annual absorption of gold by India is very great. Lord Rothschild remarked to the Currency Commission that none of the smooth gold bars sent to India ever came back. There is, in addition, an enormous sum hoarded in silver rupees and silver ornaments. It is no uncommon sight, in the cities of Upper India, to see a child wearing only one ragged, dirty garment, but loaded with massive silver ornaments. Indians who have money and do not merely hoard it prefer to lend it out, often at usurious rates of interest, to their needy or thriftless fellow-countrymen. Until quite recently the educated classes have held almost entirely aloof from any but the liberal professions. Science in any form has been rarely taken up by University students, and for every B.Sc. the honours lists have shown probably a hundred B.A.'s. The Indian National Congress itself, as it represented mainly those classes, naturally displayed the same tendencies, and for a long time it devoted its energies to so-called political problems rather than to practical economic questions. Hence the almost complete failure of the Western-educated Indian to achieve any marked success in commercial and industrial undertakings, and nowhere has that failure been more complete than in Bengal, where it would be difficult to quote more than one really brilliant exception. Hence also no doubt some of the political bitterness which those classes display. Within the last few years, however, the politician has realized that, whilst commercial and industrial development was steadily expanding and the demand for it was increasing on all sides, he was left standing on a barren shore. He has done his best, or rather his worst, to convert *Swadeshi* into a political weapon. His efforts have only been temporarily and partially successful. But we may rest assured that long after this spurious political *Swadeshi* has disappeared, the legitimate form of *Swadeshi* will endure—the *Swadeshi* that does not boycott imported goods merely because they come from England, but is bent on stimulating the production in India of articles of the same or of better quality which can be sold cheaper, and can, therefore, beat the imported goods in the Indian markets.

To this form of *Swadeshi* it is undoubtedly the duty and the interest of the Government of India to respond. We are bound as trustees for the people of India to promote Indian trade and industry by all the means in our power, and we are equally bound to help to open up new fields of activity for the young Indians whom our educational system has diverted from the old paths, and who no longer find for their rapidly increasing numbers any sufficient outlet in the public services and liberal professions which originally absorbed them. No reforms in our educational system can be permanently effective unless we check the growth of the intellectual proletariat, which plays so large a part in Indian unrest, by diverting the energies of young India into new and healthier channels. At the same time there can be no better material antidote to the spread of disaffection than the prosperity which would attend the expansion of trade and industry and give to increasing numbers amongst the Western-educated classes a direct interest in the maintenance of law and order. There are amongst those classes too many who, having little or nothing to lose, are naturally prone to fish in the troubled waters of sedition.

In regard to agriculture, which is, and is bound to remain, the greatest of all Indian industries, for it supports 70, and perhaps 80, per cent. of the whole population, the Government of India have no reason to be ashamed of their record. Famines can never be banished from a country where vast tracts are entirely dependent upon an extremely uncertain rainfall, and the population is equally dependent upon the fruits of the soil. But besides the scientific organization of famine relief, the public works policy of Government has been steadily and chiefly directed to the reduction of famine areas. Not only has the construction of a great system of railways facilitated the introduction of foodstuffs into remote famine-stricken districts, but irrigation works, devised on a scale and with a skill which have made India the premier school of irrigation for the rest of the world, have added enormously both to the area of cultivation and to that where cultivation is secured against failure of the rainfall. The arid valley of the Indus has been converted into a perennial granary, and in the Punjab alone irrigation canals have already added 8,000,000 acres of unusual fertility to the land under tillage, and have given to 5,000,000 acres more the protection against drought in years of deficient rainfall which they formerly lacked. Plantations of tea, coffee, cinchona, &c., and the cultivation of jute have added within the last 25 years some £30,000,000 a year to the value of Indian exports. Jute alone covers the whole of the so-called "drain."

The fact, nevertheless, cannot be denied, though it is an unpleasant admission, that a large proportion of the immense agricultural population of India have remained miserably poor. Indian politicians ascribe this poverty to the crushing burden of the land revenue collected by Government—a burden which has been shown to work out only to about 1s. 8d. per acre of crop and is being steadily reduced in relation to the gross revenue of the country—but they say nothing about the exactions of the native landlord, who has, for instance in Bengal, monopolized at the expense of the peasantry almost the whole benefit of the Permanent Settlement. Some very significant facts with regard to *rayatwari* landlords were brought out in a debate this year in the Legislative Council of Madras, when Mr. Atkinson, in rep'y to one of his Hindu colleagues who had been denouncing the Government assessments in certain villages, produced an overwhelming array of figures to show that in those very villages the rents exacted by native landlords varied between eight and eleven times the amount which they paid to Government. Nor do Indian politicians say much about the native money-lender, who is far more responsible than the tax-gatherer for the poverty of the peasant. Still less do they say about the extravagance of native customs, partly religious and partly social, which makes the peasant an easy prey to the money-lender, to whom he is too often driven when he has a child to marry or a parent to bury or a Brahman to entertain. Indebtedness is the great curse of Indian agriculture, and the peasant's chief necessity is cheap credit obtained on a system that will not cause him to sink deeper into the mire. Here again it is not Indian politicians, but the British rulers of India who have found a solution, and it is of such importance and promise that it deserves more than mere passing mention.

It has been found in the adaptation to Indian requirements of the well-known Raffeisen system. Sir William Wedderburn was, I believe, actually the earliest advocate of this movement, but the first practical experiments were made in Madras as a result of exhaustive investigation by Sir Frederick Nicholson and in the United Provinces when Sir Antony (now Lord) MacDonnell was Lieutenant-Governor, and one of the many measures passed by Lord Curzon for the benefit of the humbler classes in India, with little or no support from the politicians and often in despite of their vehement opposition, whilst Nationalist newspapers jeered at "a scheme for extracting money from wealthy natives in order that Government might make a show of benevolence at other people's expense," was an Act giving legal sanction to the operations of a system of co-operaive banks and credit societies. It found a healthy basis ready made in the Indian village system, and though it would never have succeeded without the informing energy and integrity of "sun-dried bureaucrats" and the countenance given to it by Government, it has had the cordial support of many capable native gentlemen. It is now only eight years old, but it has begun to spread with amazing rapidity. The report of the Calcutta Conference of Registrars last winter showed that the number of societies of all kinds had risen from 1,357 in the preceding year to 2,008, and their aggregate working capital from 44 lakhs to nearly 81 (one lakh or Rs.100,000=£6,666). The new movement is, of course, still only in its infancy, but it is full of promise. The money-lender, who was at first bitterly hostile, is beginning to realize that by providing capital for the co-operative banks he can get, on the whole, an adequate return with much better security for his money than in the old days of great gains and, also, great losses. One of the healthiest features is that, notwithstanding the great expansion of the system during the last twelvemonth, the additional working capital required was mainly provided by private individuals and only a very small amount by Government. Another hopeful feature is that the money saved to the peasant by the lower interest he has to pay on his debts pending repayment is now going into modern machinery and improved methods of agriculture. The new system appeals most strongly to poor and heavily indebted villages, and in the Punjab, where the results are really remarkable, especially in some of the backward Mahomedan districts, it is hoped that within a few years nearly half the peasant indebtedness, estimated at 25 to 30 millions sterling, will have been wiped off.

Practical education is, however, as urgently needed for Indian agriculture as for any other form of Indian industry. The selection of land and of seeds, the use of suitable manures, an intelligent rotation of crops, the adoption of better methods and less antiquated implements can only be brought about by practical education, and the demand for it is one that Government will hear put forward with growing insistency by the new Councils on which Indian landowners have been wisely granted the special representation that the agricultural interests of India so abundantly deserve.

It was the "sun-dried bureaucrat" again who in regard to Indian industries as well as to Indian agriculture preached and practised sound *Swadeshi* before the word had ever been brought into vogue by the Indian politician. The veteran Sir George Birdwood, Sir George Watt, Sir Edward Buck, and many others have stood forth for years as the champions of Indian art and Indian home industries. As far back as 1883, a Resolution was passed by Government expressing its desire "to give the utmost encouragement to every effort to substitute for articles now obtained from Europe articles of *bona fide* local manufacture or indigenous origin." In 1886, a special Economic Department was created to keep up the elaborate survey of the economic products of India which Sir George Watt had just completed under State direction. But the most important administrative measure was the creation under Lord Curzon of a separate portfolio of Commerce and Industry in the Government of India, to which a civilian, Sir John Hewett, was appointed with very conspicuous success. It was also under Lord Curzon that the most vigorous impulse was given to technical education of which the claims had already been advocated by many distinguished Anglo-Indian officials, such as Sir Antony MacDonnell and Sir Auckland Colvin. The results of an exhaustive inquiry conducted throughout India by a Committee of carefully selected officers were embodied in the Educational Resolution of 1904. Particular stress was laid upon the importance of industrial, commercial, and art and craft schools as the preparatory stages of technical education, for which, in its higher forms, provision had already been made in such institutions as the engineering colleges at Sibpur, Rurki, Jubbulpore, and Madras, the College of Science at Poona, and the Technical Institute of Bombay. Until then the record of technical schools had too often resembled the description which Mr. Butler, the new Minister of Education, tersely gave of that of the Lucknow Industrial School—" a record of inconstant purpose with breaks of unconcern." Not only did the question of technical education receive more systematic treatment, but a special assignment of Rs.244,000 a year was made in 1905 by the Government of India in aid of the provincial revenues for its improvement and extension. It was not, however, until the liberality of the late Mr. J. N. Tata and his sons, one of the best-known Parsee families of Bombay, recently placed a considerable income for the purpose at the disposal of Government that steps have been taken to establish an " Indian Institute of Science " worthy of the name, to which the Mysore Government, who have given a site for it in Bangalore, as well as the Government of India, have promised handsome financial assistance.

Whilst the encouragement given to Indian technical education has until quite lately proceeded far more from the British rulers of India than from any native quarter, it has been also until quite lately British capital and British enterprise that have contributed mostly to the development of Indian industry and commerce. The amount of British capital invested in India for its commercial and industrial development has been estimated at £350,000,000, and this capital incidentally furnishes employment for large numbers of Indians. Half a million are employed on the railways alone. Another half million work on the tea estates. The Bombay and Ahmedabad cotton mills represent at the present day the only important and successful application of Indian capital and Indian enterprise to industrial development. The woollen, cotton, and leather industries of Cawnpore, which has become one of the chief manufacturing centres of India, and the great jute industry of Bengal were promoted almost exclusively by B.itish, and not by indigenous effort. Real *Swadeshi*, stimulated by British teaching and by British enterpri e, was thus already in full swing when the Indian politician took up the cry and too often perverted it to criminal purposes, and, though he may have helped to rouse his sluggish fellow-countrymen to healthy as well as to mischievous activity, it may be doubted whether any good he has done has not been more than counterbalanced by the injurious effect upon capital of a violent and often openly seditious agitation. Mr. Gokhale himself seems to have awakened to this danger, when in an eloquent speech delivered by him at Lucknow, in support of *Swadeshi* in 1907, he protested, rather late in the day, against the " narrow, exclusive, and intolerant spirit " in which some advocates of the cause were seeking to promote it, and laid stress upon the importance of capital as well as of enterprise and skill as an indispensable factor of success. British investments are large, but not so large as they might and should be, and the reluctance to invest in India grows with the uneasiness caused by political unrest.

That an immense field lies open in India for industrial development need scarcely be argued. It has been explored with great knowledge and ability in a very instructive article contributed last January to the *Asiatic Quarterly Review* by Mr. A. C. Chatterjec, an Indian member of the Civil Service. Amongst the many instances he gives of industries clamouring for the benefits of applied science, I will quote only the treatment of oil seeds, the manufacture of paper from wood pulp and wood meal, the development of leather factories and tanneries, as well as of both vegetable and chemical dyes, the sugar industry, and metal work—all of which, if properly instructed and directed, would enable India to convert her own raw materials with profit into finished products either for home consumption or for exportation abroad. It is at least equally important for India to save her home industries, and especially her hand-weaving industry, the wholesale destruction of which under the pressure of the Lancashire power loom has thrown so many poor people on to the already overcrowded land. Here, as Mr. Chatterjee wisely remarks, combination and organization are badly needed, for "the hand industry has the greatest chances of survival when it adopts the methods of the power industry without actual resort to power machinery." The articles on the Indian industrial problem in *Science Progress* for April and July, by Mr. Alfred Chatterton, Director of Industries, Madras, are also worth careful attention. He remarks quite truly that her inexhaustible supplies of cheap labour are "India's greatest asset"; but he too wisely holds that the factory system of the West should only be guardedly extended and under careful precautions. The Government of India have at present under consideration important legislative measures for preventing the undue exploitation of both child and adult labour—measures which are already being denounced by the native Press as "restrictive" legislation devised by the "English cotton kings" in order to "stifle the indigenous industries of India in their infancy"!

What Government can do for the pioneering of new industries is shown by the success of the State dairies in Northern India and of Mr. Chatterton's experiments in the manufacturing of aluminium in Madras. There is an urgent demand at present for industrial research laboratories and experimental work all over India, and above all for better and more practical education. But it would seem that, in this direction, the impetus given by Lord Curzon has somewhat slackened under Lord Minto's administration, owing, doubtless, to the absorbing claims of the political situation and of political reforms.

In speaking in the Calcutta Council on a resolution for the establishment of a great Polytechnic College, the Home Member was able to point to a fairly long list of measures taken at no small cost by the State to promote technical education in all parts of India, and he rightly urged that there would be little use in creating a sort of technical University until a larger proportion of students had qualified for it by taking advantage of the more elementary courses already provided for them. His answer would, however, have been more convincing could he have shown that existing institutions are always adequately equipped and that considered schemes which have the support of the best Indian as well as of the best official opinion are not subjected to merely dilatory objections at headquarters. Three years ago, after the Naini Tal Industrial Conference, the most representative ever perhaps held in India, Sir John Hewett, who had been made Lieutenant-Governor of the United Provinces after having been the first to hold the new portfolio of Commerce and Industry, developed a scheme for the creation of a Technological College at Cawnpore, which met with unanimous approval. Nothing has yet been done to give effect to it, and it was not only the Indian but many of the European members, official as well as unofficial, of the Viceroy's Legislative Council who sympathized with Mr. Mudholkar's protest when he asked with some bitterness what must be the impression produced in India by the shelving of a scheme that was supported by men of local experience, by the head of the Provincial Government, and by the Government of India, because people living 6,000 miles away did not consider it to be absolutely flawless.

In one direction at any rate, India can rightly demand that Government should be left an entirely free hand—namely, in regard to the very large orders which have to be placed every year by the great spending departments. It has now been laid down by the Secretary of State that Indian industry should supply the needs of Government in respect of all articles that are, in whole or in part, locally manufactured. But Indian industry would be able to supply much more if the Government of India were in a position to give it more assured support.

The case of the Bengal Iron and Steel Company has been quoted to me, which was compelled to close down its steel works and to reduce the number of its iron furnaces in blast from four to two because the promises of support received from Government when the company took over the works proved to be largely and quite inexcusably illusory. For works of this kind cannot be run at present in India unless they can depend upon the hearty support of Government, which, through the Railways and Public Works Department, is the main, and, indeed, the only, consumer on a large scale.

At the present moment, Messrs. Tata are making a truly gigantic endeavour to acclimatize the iron and steel industry in India by the erection of immense works at Sakti in Bengal, where they have within easy reach a practically unlimited supply of the four necessary raw materials—iron ore, coking coal, flux, and manganese ore. To utilize these, plant is being set up of a yearly capacity of 120,000 tons of foundry iron, rails, shapes, and merchant bars, and plans have been drawn out for an industrial city of 20,000 inhabitants. The enterprise is entirely in Indian hands with an initial share capital of £1,545,000 administered by an Indian board of directors, who have engaged American experts to organize the works. Government has granted various railway facilities to the company and has placed with them an order for 200,000 tons of rails for periodical delivery. Upon the future of these works will probably depend for many years to come the success of the metallurgical and other kindred industries of India, and it is to be hoped that Government will be allowed to give them all reasonable assistance without interference from home. Another purely Indian enterprise—also under the auspices of Messrs. Tata—is a great scheme for catching the rainfall of the Western Ghats and creating a hydro-electric supply of power which will, amongst other uses, drive most of the Bombay mills.

In regard to minor Indian industries, hints have,

I am assured, too frequently been sent out from England that the claims of British industry to Government support must not be forgotten. Even now no change has been made in the regulations which compel the Government of India to purchase all articles not wholly or partly manufactured in India through the Stores Department of the India Office. The delay thus caused in itself represents a serious loss, for it appears to take an average of nine months for any order through that Department to be carried out, and further delays arise whenever some modification in the original indent is required. Nowadays merchants in India keep for ordinary purposes of trade such large collections of samples that in nine cases out of ten Government Departments could settle at once upon what they want and their orders would be carried out both more quickly and more cheaply. The maintenance of these antiquated regulations, which are very injurious to Indian trade, is attributed by Indians mainly to the influence of powerful vested interests in England.

The time would also seem to have arrived when, with the development of Indian trade and industry, private contracts might with advantage be substituted for the more expensive and slower activities of the Public Works Department. Work done by that Department is bound to be more expensive, for its enormous establishment has to be maintained on the same footing whether financial conditions allow or do not allow Government to embark on large public works expenditure, and when they do not, the proportion of establishment charges to the actual cost of works is ruinous. When the Calcutta Port Trust and other institutions of the same character put out to contract immense works running every year into millions, why, it is asked, should not Government do the same ? Some works like irrigation works may properly be reserved for the Public Works Department, but to mobilize the Department whenever a bungalow has to be built or a road made by Government, is surely ridiculous.

Indian opinion is at present just in the mood when reasonable concessions of this kind would make an excellent impression; and, if they are not made spontaneously, the enlarged Indian Councils will soon exert pressure to obtain them.

CHAPTER XXIII.

THE FINANCIAL AND FISCAL RELATIONS BETWEEN INDIA AND GREAT BRITAIN.

When Lord Morley introduced his Indian reforms scheme, a section at least of the party to which he belongs supported it not only on general grounds, but more especially in the belief that it would strengthen the hands of the Imperial Government in dealing with the hide-bound officialism of which the Government of India is in the eyes of some British Radicals the visible embodiment. None of them, probably, anticipated that the boot would be on the other leg. If the Government of India have sometimes sacrificed Indian interests to British interests, it has been almost exclusively in connexion with the financial and fiscal relations between the two countries, and often against the better judgment and sense of justice of Anglo-Indian officials. In this respect the enlarged Indian Councils will lend far greater weight than in the past to any representations which the Government of India may make at Whitehall.

Even in the course of its first session at Calcutta the Imperial Council has given abundant indications of its attitude. In the Budget debate, Sir Vithaldas Thackersey, one of the Indian elected members from

Bombay, remarked very pointedly that "there is an impression abroad that, in deciding most important questions of economic and financial policy, the Government are obliged to be guided by political exigencies." Official secrets have a way of leaking out in India, and Sir Vithaldas knew what he was talking about when he added with regard to the Budget under discussion—"It is generally believed that, if the Government of India had had a freer hand, they would have preferred the raising of the general tariff or a duty on sugar, which would have been less objectionable than the levying of the proposed enhanced duties in the teeth of the practically unanimous opposition of the non-official members of this Council and of the public generally."

It is certainly unfortunate that on the first occasion on which the Government of India had to lay a financial statement before the enlarged Council, Indian members should have come to the conclusion that the unpopular Budget submitted to them was not the one originally proposed by the Indian Finance Department, but that it had been imposed upon that Department by the Secretary of State in deference to the exigencies of British party politics. Equally unfortunate is it that the financial difficulties which this Budget had to meet were mainly due to the loss of revenue on opium in consequence of the arrangements made by Great Britain with China, in which Indian interests had received very scant consideration. Not only had Sir Edward Baker, when he was Finance Minister three years ago, given an assurance that the new opium policy would be carried out without any resort to extra taxation, but there is a strong feeling in India that the praiseworthy motives which have induced the Imperial Government to come to terms with China on the subject of the opium trade would be still more creditable to the British people had not the Indian taxpayer been left, with his fellow-sufferers in Hong-kong and Singapore, to bear the whole cost of British mo al rectitude. The Imperial Council did not confine itself, either, to criticism of what had happened. Sir Vithaldas Thackersey had probably every Indian and many official members with him when he made the following very clear intimation as to the future :—" We are prepared to bear our burdens, and all that we ask is that the country should be allowed greater freedom in choosing the methods of raising revenue. I am unable to see how it will be injurious to the interests of Government if this Council is allowed a more real share as regards what articles shall be taxed and what duties shall be paid."

It is upon such questions as these that the voice of the enlarged Councils will in future cause much more frequent embarrassment to the Imperial Government than to the Government of India, and I shall be much surprised if they have not to listen to it in regard to various "home charges" with which the Government of India have from time to time very reluctantly agreed to burden Indian finance at the bidding of Whitehall. The Indian Nationalist Press has not been alone in describing the recent imposition on the Indian taxpayer of a capitation allowance amounting to £300,000 a year to meet the increased cost of the British soldier as "the renewed attempt of a rapacious War Office to raid the helpless Indian Treasury," and even the increase in the pay of the native soldier, which Lord Kitchener obtained for him, does not prevent him and his friends from drawing their own comparison between the squalor of the quarters in which he is still housed and the relatively luxurious barracks built for Tommy Atkins under Lord Kitchener's administration at the expense of the Indian taxpayer. It is no secret that the Government of India have also frequently remonstrated in vain when India has been charged full measure and overflowing in respect of military operations in which the part borne by her has been governed less by her own direct interests than by the necessity of making up with the help of Indian contingents the deficiencies of our military organization at home. It was no Indian politician but the Government of India who expressed the opinion that :—

> The Imperial Government keeps in India and quarters upon the revenues of that country as large a portion of its army as it thinks can possibly be required to maintain its dominion there ; that it habitually treats that army as a reserve force available for Imperial purposes ; that it has uniformly detached European regiments from the garrison of India to take part in Imperial wars whenever it has been found necessary or convenient to do so ; and, more than this, that it has drawn not less freely upon the native army of India, towards the maintenance of which it contributes nothing, to aid in contests outside of India with which the Indian Government has had little or no concern.

All these are, however, but secondary issues to the much larger one which the creation of the new Councils must tend to bring to the front with all the force of the increased weight given to them by the recent reforms. For that issue will raise the whole principle of our fiscal relations with India, if it results in a demand for the protection of Indian industries against the competition of imported manufactures by an autonomous tariff. It must be remembered that the desire for Protection is no new thing in India. Whether we like it or not, whether we be Free Traders or Tariff Reformers, we have to reckon with the fact that almost every Indian is a Protectionist at heart, whatever he may be in theory. The Indian National Congress has hitherto fought shy of making Protection a prominent plank of its platform, lest it should offend its political friends in England. Yet as far back as 1902 a politician as careful as Mr. Surendranath Banerjee to avoid in his public utterances anything that might alienate British Radicalism, declared in his inaugural address at the 18th session of the Congress that " if we had a potential voice in the government of our own country there would be no question as to what policy we should follow. We would unhesitatingly adopt a policy of Protection." This note has been accentuated since the political campaign in favour of militant Swadeshism, and when English Radicals sympathize with the *Swadeshi* boycott as a protest against the Partition of Bengal, they would do well to recollect that, before Indian audiences, the most violent forms of *Swadeshi* are constantly defended on the ground that British industrial greed, of which Free Trade is alleged to be the highest expression, has left no other weapons to India for the defence of her material interests. Mr. Lala Lajpat Rai, who has the merit of often speaking with great frankness, addressed himself once in the following terms to "those estimable gentlemen in India who believe in the righteousness of the British nation as represented by the electors of Great Britain and Ireland, and who are afraid of offending them by the boycott of English-made goods":

> If there are any two classes into which the British nation can roughly be divided they are either manufacturers or the working men. Both are interested in keeping the Indian market open for the sale and consumption of their manufactures. They are said to be the only friends to whom we can appeal against the injustice of the Anglo-Indian bureaucracy. Offend them, we are told, and you are undone. You lose the good will of the only classes who can help you and who are prepared to listen to your grievances. But, boycott or no boycott, any movement calculated to increase the manufacturing power of India is likely to incur the displeasure of the British elector. He is a very well-educated animal, a keen man of business, who can at once see through things likely to affect his pocket, however cleverly they may be put or arranged by those who hold an interest which is really adverse to his. He is not likely to be hoodwinked by the cry of *Swadeshi* minus the boycott, because, really speaking, if effectively worked and organized, both are one and the same thing.

That *Swadeshi* as understood by educated Indians of all classes and of all political complexions means in some form or other Protection was made clear even in the Imperial Council. The Finance Member, Sir Fleetwood Wilson, was himself fain to pay homage to it, but his sympathy did not disarm Mr. Chitnavis, an Indian member whose speech deserves to be recorded, as it embodied the opinions entertained by 99 out of every 100 Indians who are interested in economic questions and by a very large number of Anglo-Indians, both official and non-official :—

The country must be grateful to him [the Finance Member] for his sympathetic attitude towards Indian industries. "I think *Swadeshi* is good, and if the outcome of the changes I have laid before the Council result in some encouragement of Indian industries, I for one shall not regret it." For a Finance Minister to say even so much is not a small thing in the present state of India's dependence upon the most pronounced and determined Free Trade country in the world. . . . At the same time we regret the absence of fiscal autonomy for India and the limitations under which this Government has to frame its industrial policy. We regret that Government cannot give the country a protective tariff forthwith. However excellent Free Trade may be for a country in an advanced stage of industrial development, it must be conceded that Protection is necessary for the success and development of infant industries. Even pronounced protagonists of Free Trade do not view this idea with disfavour. That Indian manufacturing industry is in its infancy does not admit of controversy. Why should not India, then, claim special protection for her undeveloped industry? Even countries remarkable for their industrial enterprise and excellence protect their industries. The United States and Germany are decidedly Protectionist. The British Colonies have protective tariffs. . . protective in purpose, scope, and effect. They are not, like the Indian import duties, levied for revenue purposes. The Indian appeal for Protection cannot in the circumstances be unreasonable. The development of the industries is a matter of great moment to the Empire, and the popular leanings towards Protectionism ought to engage the sympathy of Government. The imposition of import duties for revenue purposes is sanctioned by precedent and principle alike. . . . And yet for a small import duty of 3½ per cent. upon cotton goods a countervailing Excise duty upon home manufactures is imposed in disregard of Indian public opinion, and the latest pronouncement of the Secretary of State has dispelled all expectations of the righting of this wrong.

No measure has done greater injury to the cause of

Free Trade in India or more permanent discredit to British rule than this Excise duty on Indian manufactured cotton, for none has done more to undermine Indian faith in the principles of justice upon which British rule claims, and, on the whole, most legitimately claims, to be based. In obedience to British Free Trade principles, all import duties were finally abolished in India at the beginning of the eighties, except on liquors and on salt, which were subject to an internal Excise duty. In 1894, however, the Government of India were compelled by financial stress to revive the greater part of the old 5 per cent. tariff on imports, excluding cottons, until the end of the year when cottons were included and under pressure from England Lord Elgin's Government had to agree to levy a countervailing Excise duty of 5 per cent. on cotton fabrics manufactured in Indian power mills. After a good deal of heated correspondence the Government of India were induced in February, 1896, to reduce the duty on cotton manufactured goods imported from abroad to 3½ per cent., with the same reduction of the Indian Excise duty, whilst cotton yarns were altogether freed from duty. This arrangement is still in force.

Rightly or wrongly, every Indian believes that the Excise duty was imposed upon India for the selfish benefit of the British cotton manufacturer and under the pressure of British party politics. He believes, as was once sarcastically remarked by an Indian member of the Viceroy's Legislative Council, that, so long as Lancashire sends 60 members to Westminster, the British Government will always have 60 reasons for maintaining the Excise duty. To the English argument that the duty is "only a small one" the Indian reply is that, according to the results of an elaborate statistical inquiry conducted at the instance of the late Mr. Jamsetjee N. Tata, a 3½ per cent. Excise duty on cotton cloth is equivalent to a 7 per cent. duty on capital invested in weaving under Indian conditions. The profits are very fluctuating and the depreciation of plant is considerable. Equally fallacious is another argument that the duty is in reality paid by Englishmen. The capital engaged in the Indian cotton industry is, it is contended, not British, but almost exclusively Indian, and a large proportion is held by not over-affluent Indian shareholders.

There is nothing to choose between the records of the two great political parties at home in their treatment of England's financial and fiscal relations with India, and English Tariff Reformers have as a rule shown little more disposition than English Free Traders to study Indian interests. In fact, until Mr. M. de P. Webb, a member of the Bombay Legislative Council, published under the title of "India and the Empire" an able exposition of the Tariff problem in relation to India, very few Tariff Reformers seemed even to take India into account in their schemes of Imperial preference. I hope, therefore, to be absolved from all suspicion of party bias in drawing attention to a question which is, I believe, destined to play in the near future a most important—perhaps even a determining—part in the relations of India to the British Empire.

One of the first things that struck me on my return to India this year—and struck me most forcibly—was the universality and vehemence of the demand for a new economic policy directed with energy and system to the expansion of Indian trade and industry. It is a demand with which the great majority of Anglo-Indian officials are in full sympathy, and it is in fact largely the outcome of their own efforts to stimulate Indian interest in the question. There is very little doubt that the Government of India would be disposed to respond to it speedily and heartily on the lines I have already briefly indicated. Will the Imperial Government and the British democracy lend them a helping hand or even leave a free hand to them? If not, we shall assuredly find ourselves confronted with an equally universal and vehement demand for Protection pure and simple by the erection of an Indian Tariff wall against the competition of imported manufactures. I need hardly point out how the rejection of such a demand would be exploited by the political agitator or how it would rally to the side of active disaffection some of the most conservative and influential classes in India. For if, as those Englishmen who claim a monopoly of sympathy with the people of India are continually preaching, we must be prepared to sacrifice administrative efficiency to sympathy, how could we shelter ourselves on an economic issue behind theories of the greater economic efficiency of Free Trade ? If we are to try "to govern India in accordance with Indian ideas"—a principle with which I humbly but fully agree—how could we justify the refusal to India of the fiscal autonomy for which there is a far more widespread and genuine demand than for political autonomy ?

CHAPTER XXIV.

THE POSITION OF INDIANS IN THE EMPIRE.

The problems of Indian administration are in themselves difficult enough to solve, but even more difficult are some of the problems connected with the relations of India and her peoples to the rest of the Empire. One of these has assumed during the last few years a character of extreme gravity, which neither the Imperial Government nor the British public seems to have at all adequately grasped.

"I think," said Mr. Gokhale in moving his resolution for the prohibition of Indian indentured labour for Natal, "I am stating the plain truth when I say that no single question of our time has evoked more bitter feelings throughout India—feelings in the presence of which the best friends of British rule have had to remain helpless—than the continued ill-treatment of Indians in South Africa."

Every Indian member of the Viceroy's Legislative Council who spoke during that debate, whatever race or creed or caste he represented, endorsed the truth of Mr. Gokhale's statement, and had a vote been taken on the resolution it would have had what no other resolution moved during the whole session would have secured—the unanimous support of the whole body of Indian members and the sympathy of every English member, official as well as unofficial. The Government of India wisely averted a division by accepting the resolution. Not a single attempt was made either by the Viceroy in the chair or by other representatives of Government to controvert either Mr. Gokhale's statement or the overwhelming array of facts showing the nature and extent of the ill-treatment of Indians in South Africa, which was presented by the mover of the resolution and by every Indian speaker who followed him. The whole tone of the debate was extremely dignified and self-restrained, but no Englishman can have listened to it without a deep sense of humiliation. For the first time in history the Government of India had to sit dumb whilst judgment was pronounced in default against the Imperial Government upon a question which has stirred the resentment of every single community of our Indian Empire. It was the one question which called forth very deep feeling in the Indian National Congress at Lahore last December, where subscriptions and donations flowed in freely to defray the expenses of a campaign throughout India, and it figured just as prominently in the proceedings of the All-India Moslem League, which held its annual meeting there in the following month. In fact, Mahomedans have the additional grievance that the laws of the Transvaal discriminate by name against those of their faith. There is scarcely a city of any importance in India in which public meetings have not testified to the interest and indignation which the subject arouses in every class of Indian audience.

This is a very grave fact. I need not enter into the details of the question. They are well known. There may be some exaggerations, Indian immigrants may not always be drawn from desirable classes, there may be differences of opinion as to the wisdom of the attitude taken up by some of the Indians in South Africa, and Englishmen may sympathize with the desire of British and Dutch colonists to check the growth of another alien population in their midst. But that the Indian has not received there the just treatment to which he is entitled as a subject of the British Crown, and that disabilities and indignities are heaped upon him because he is an Indian, are broad facts that are not and cannot be disputed. The resolution adopted by the Imperial Council, with the sanction of the Government of India, was formally directed against Natal because it is only in regard to Natal that India possesses an effective weapon of retaliation in withholding the supply of indentured labour which is indispensable to the prosperity of that colony. But the Indian grievance is not confined to Natal ; it is even greater in the Transvaal. Still less is it confined to the particular class of Indians who emigrate as indentured labourers to South Africa. What Indians feel most bitterly is that however well educated, however respectable and even distinguished may be an Indian who goes to or resides in South Africa, and especially in the Transvaal, he is treated as an outcast and is at the mercy of harsh laws and regulations framed for his oppression and often interpreted with extra harshness by the officials who are left to apply them. This bitterness is intensified by the recollection that, before the South African War, the wrongs of British Indians in the Transvaal figured prominently in the catalogue of charges brought by the Imperial Government against the Kruger *régime* and contributed not a little to precipitate its downfall. In prosecuting the South African War Great Britain drew freely upon India for assistance of every kind except actual Indian combatants. Not only was it the loyalty of India that enabled the British troops who saved Natal to be embarked hurriedly at Bombay, but it was the constant supply from India of stores of all kinds, of transport columns, of hospital bearers, &c., which, to a great extent, made up throughout the war for the deficiencies of the British War Office. There are monuments erected in South Africa which testify to the devotion of

British Indians who, though non-combatants, laid down their lives in the cause of the Empire. Yet, as far as the British Indians are concerned, the end of it all has been that their lot in the Transvaal since it became a British Colony is harder than it was in the old Kruger days, and the British colonists in the Transvaal, who were ready enough to use Indian grievances as a stick with which to beat Krugerism, have now joined hands with the Dutch in refusing to redress them. The Government of India have repeatedly urged upon the Imperial Government the gravity of this question, and Lord Curzon especially pressed upon his friends, when they were in office, the vital importance of effecting some acceptable settlement whilst the Transvaal was still a Crown Colony, and, therefore, more amenable to the influence of the Mother Country than it would be likely to prove when once endowed with self-government. Yet the Imperial Government after a succession of half-hearted and ineffective protests have now finally acquiesced in the perpetuation and even the aggravation of wrongs which some ten years ago they solemnly declared to be intolerable.

Apart from the sense of justice upon which Englishmen pride themselves, it is impossible to overlook the disastrous consequences of this *gran rifiuto* for the prestige of British rule in India. One of the Indian Members of Council, Mr. Dadabhoy, indicated them in terms as moderate as they were significant :—

> In 1899 Lord Lansdowne feared the moral consequences in India of a conviction of the powerlessness of the British *Raj* to save the Indian settlers in the Transvaal from oppression and harsh treatment. That was when there was peace all over this country, when sedition, much more anarchism, was an unheard-of evil. If the situation was disquieting then, what is it now when the urgent problem of the moment is how to put down and prevent the growth of unrest in the land ? The masses do not understand the niceties of the relations between the Mother Country and the Colonies ; they do not comprehend the legal technicalities. The British *Raj* has so far revealed itself to them as a power whose influence is irresistible, and when they find that, with all its traditional

omnipotence, it has not succeeded in securing to their countrymen—admittedly a peaceable and decent body of settlers who rendered valuable services during the war—equal treatment at the hands of a small Dependency, they become disheartened and attribute the failure to the European colonist's influence over the Home Government. That is an impression which is fraught with incalculable potentialities of mischief and which British statesmanship should do everything in its power to dispel. The present political situation in India adds special urgency to the case.

No comments of mine could add to the significance of this warning.

The measure contemplated by Mr. Gokhale's resolution may have some direct effect upon Natal, whose leading statesmen have repeatedly acknowledged the immense value of Indian indentured labour to the Colony, and may indirectly affect public opinion in the Transvaal. But behind the immediate question of the worse or better treatment of Indians in South Africa stand much larger questions, which Mr. Gokhale did not hesitate to state with equal frankness :—

Behind all the grievances of which I have spoken to-day three questions of vital importance emerge to view. First, what is the *status* of us Indians in this Empire? Secondly, what is the extent of the responsibility which lies on the Imperial Government to ensure to us just and humane and, gradually, even equal treatment in this Empire? And, thirdly, how far are the self-governing members of this Empire bound by its cardinal principles, or are they to share in its privileges only and not to bear their share of the disadvantages?

These issues have been raised in their most acute form in South Africa, but they exist also in Australia, and even in Canada, where many Indians suffered heavily from the outburst of anti-Asiatic feeling which swept along the Pacific Coast a couple of years ago. They involve the position of Asiatic subjects of the Crown in all the self-governing Dominions and indirectly in many of the Crown Colonies, for they affect the relations of the white and coloured races throughout the Empire.

Here, however, I must confine myself to the Indian aspects. I have discussed them with a good many Indians, and they are quite alive to the difficulties of the situation. Though they resent the colour bar, they realize the strength of the feeling there is in the Colonies in favour of preserving the white race from intermixture with non-white races. It is, in fact, a feeling they themselves in some ways share, for, in India, the unfortunate Eurasian meets with even less sympathy from Indians than from Europeans. Indian susceptibilities may even find some consolation in the fact that Colonial dislike of the Indian immigrant is to a great extent due to his best qualities. " Indians," said Mr. Mudholkar, appealing to Lord Minto, " are hated, as your Lordship's predecessor pointed out, on account of their very virtues. It is because they are sober, thrifty, industrious, more attentive to their business than the white men that their presence in the Colonies is considered intolerable." Educated Indians know how little hold the Mother Country has over her Colonies in these matters. They know that both British and Anglo-Indian statesmen have recognized their grievances without being able to secure their redress, and it is interesting to note how warm were the tributes paid in the Imperial Council to the energy with which Lord Curzon had upheld their cause, by some of those who were most bitterly opposed to him when he was in India. They know, on the other hand, that though the British Labour Party can afford to profess great sympathy for Indian political aspirations in India, it has never tried—or, if it has tried, it has signally failed—to exercise the slightest influence in favour of Indian claims to fair treatment with its allies in the Colonies, where the Labour Party is always the most uncompromising advocate of a policy of exclusion and oppression, and they know the power which the Labour Party wields in all our Colonies.

They are, therefore, I believe, ready to reckon with the realities of the situation, and to agree with Lord Curzon that "the common rights of British citizenship cannot be held to override the rights of self-protection conceded to self-governing Colonies"—rights which, moreover, are often exercised to the detriment of immigrants from the Mother Country itself. They will, on the other hand, urge the withholding of Indian labour if the Colonies are unwilling to treat it with fairness and humanity, and they argue, rightly enough, that India, to whom the emigration of tens of thousands of her people is not an unmixed advantage, will lose far less than Colonies whose development will be starved by the loss of labour they cannot themselves supply. An influential Indian Member stated in Council that they have accepted the view that complete freedom of immigration is beyond the pale of practical politics, and is not to be pressed as things stand. All that they ask, he added, in the Transvaal is for the old Indian residents to be allowed to live peaceably, as in Cape Colony for instance, without being treated like habitual criminals, and for men of education and position to be allowed to come in, so that they may have teachers, ministers of religion, and doctors for themselves and their people. In Natal they ask for the maintenance of the rights and privileges they have had for years and years. On such lines a practical working arrangement with the Colonies should not be beyond the bounds of possibility. But what Indians also demand is that laws and regulations of an exceptional character which may be accepted in regard to immigration shall not be applicable to Indians who merely wish to travel in the Colonies. An Indian of very high position whom every one from the King downwards welcomes when he comes to England, wished a few years ago to visit Australia, but before doing so he wrote to a friend there to inquire whether he would be subjected to any unpleasant formalities. The answer he received discouraged him. These are the sort of difficulties which Indians claim should be removed, and one practical suggestion I have heard put forward is that, on certain principles to be laid down by mutual agreement between the Imperial Government, the Governments of the Dominions, and the Government of India, the latter should have power to issue passports to Indian subjects which would be recognized and would exempt them from all vexatious formalities throughout the Empire.

The whole question is one that cannot be allowed to drag on indefinitely without grave danger to the Empire. It evidently cannot be solved without the co-operation of the Colonies. Next year the Imperial Conference meets again in the capital of the Empire. If, in the meantime, the Imperial Government were to enter into communication with the Government of India and with the Crown Colonies, so many of whom are closely interested in Indian labour, they should be in a position to lay before the representatives of the Dominions assembled in London next March considered proposals which would afford a basis for discussion and, one may hope, for a definite agreement. A recognition of the right of Colonial Governments to regulate the conditions on which British Indians may be allowed admission as indentured labourers or for permanent residence ought to secure guarantees for the equitable and humane treatment of those who have been already admitted, or shall hereafter be admitted, and also an undertaking that Indians of good position armed with specified credentials from the Government of India, travelling either for pleasure or for purposes of scientific study or on business or with other legitimate motives, would be allowed to enter and travel about for a reasonable period without let or hindrance of any sort. That is the *minimum* which would, I believe, satisfy the best Indian opinion, and it is inconceivable that if the situation were freely and frankly explained to our Colonial kinsmen they would reject a settlement so essential to the interests and to the credit of the whole Empire in relation to India.

CHAPTER XXV.

Social and Official Relations.

On few subjects are more ignorant or malevolent statements made than on the attitude of Englishmen in India towards the natives of the country. That social relations between Englishmen and Indians seldom grow intimate is true enough, but not that the fault lies mainly with Englishmen. At the risk of being trite, I must recall a few elementary considerations.

The bedrock difficulty is that Indian customs prevent any kind of intimacy between English and Indian families. Even in England the relations between men who are excluded from acquaintance with each other's families can rarely be called intimate, and except in the very few cases of Indian families that are altogether Westernized, Indian habits rigidly exclude Englishmen from admission into the homes of Indian gentlemen, whether Hindu or Mahomedan. Intercourse between Indian and English ladies is in the same way almost entirely confined to formal visits paid by the latter to the zenana and the harem, and to so-called *Purdah* parties, given in English houses, in which Indian ladies are entertained as far as possible under the same conditions that prevail in their own homes—*i.e.*, to the total exclusion of all males. So long as Indian ladies are condemned to a life of complete seclusion the interests they have in common with their English visitors must necessarily be very few. On the other hand, it is not surprising that Englishmen, knowing the views that many Indian men entertain with regard to the position of women, do not care to encourage them to visit their own houses on a footing of intimacy that would necessarily bring them into more or less familiar contact with their English wives and sisters and daughters. There is very much to admire in the family relations, and especially in the filial relations, that exist in an Indian home, whether Hindu or Mahomedan, but it is idle to pretend that Indian ideas with regard to the relations between the sexes are the same as ours. In these circumstances any social fusion between even the better classes of the two races seems to be for the present out of the question.

Very sincere and creditable efforts are now, it is true, being made on both sides to diminish the gulf that divides English and Indian society, and I have been at various gatherings which were attended by Englishmen and Englishwomen and by Indians, among whom there was sometimes even a sprinkling of Indian ladies. But the English host and hostess invariably found it difficult to prevent their Indian guests forming groups of their own, and each group seemed to be as reluctant to mingle with other Indian groups of a different class or caste as with their English fellow-guests. Indian society has been for centuries split up by race and caste and creed distinctions into so many watertight compartments that it does not care for the Western forms of social intercourse, which tend to ignore those distinctions. It is Indians themselves who regard us, much more than we regard ourselves, as a separate caste. Moreover, for the ordinary and somewhat desultory conversation which plays so large a part in Western sociability the Indian has very little understanding. He always imagines that conversation must have some definite purpose, and though he has, far more than most Englishmen, the gift of ready and courteous speech, and often will talk for a long time both discursively and pleasantly, it is almost always as a preliminary to the introduction of some particular topic in which his personal interests are more or less directly involved. A question which causes a good deal of soreness is the rigid exclusion of Indians from many Anglo-Indian clubs. But though a little more elasticity as to the entertainment of Indian "guests" might reasonably be conceded to Indian susceptibilities, a club is after all just as much as his house an Englishman's castle, and it is only in India that any one would venture to suggest that a club should not settle its rules of membership as it thinks fit. In the large cities at least there should, however, be room for clubs which, like the Calcutta Club at Calcutta, serve the very useful purpose of bringing together by mutual consent the higher classes of Indians and Englishmen, official and non-official. Yet even there the exigencies of caste observances, especially in the case of Hindus, militate against the more convivial forms of intercourse which the Englishman particularly affects. There are not a few Hindu members who will talk or play bridge with their English fellow-members into the small hours of the morning, but who consider themselves bound in conscience not to sit down to dinner with them; whilst some will doubtless feel obliged to perform ceremonial ablutions when they go home. Others again, for similar reasons, would decline to join any European club. They are no more to be blamed than Englishmen who prefer to reserve membership of their clubs to Europeans, but the fact remains and has to be reckoned with.

The best and most satisfactory relations are those maintained between Englishmen and Indians who understand and respect each other's peculiarities. No class of Englishman in India fulfils those conditions more fully than the Indian Civil Service. It is, I know, the *bête noire* of the Indian politician, and even Englishmen who ought to know better seem to think that, once they have labelled it a "bureaucracy," that barbarous name is enough to hang it—or enough, at least, to lend plausibility to the charge that Anglo-Indian administrators are arrogant and harsh in their personal dealings with Indians and ignorant and unsympathetic in their methods of government.

That the English civilian goes out to India with a tolerably high intellectual and moral equipment can hardly be disputed, for he represents the pick of the young men who qualify for our Civil Service at home as well as abroad, and in respect of character, integrity, and intelligence the British Civil Service can challenge comparison with that of any other country in the world. Why should he suddenly change into a narrow-minded, petty tyrant as soon as he sets foot in India? A great part at least of his career is spent in the very closest contact with the people, for he often lives for years together in remote districts where he has practically no other society than that of natives. He generally knows and speaks fluently more than one vernacular, though, owing to the multiplicity of Indian languages—there are five, for instance, in the Bombay Presidency alone—he may find himself suddenly transferred to a district in which the vernaculars he has learnt are of no use to him. Part of his time is always spent "in camp"—*i.e.*, moving about from village to village, receiving petitions, investigating cases, listening to complaints. Perhaps none of the ordinary duties of administration bring him so closely into touch with the people as the collection of land revenue, for it is there that his sense of fairness comes most conspicuously into play and wins recognition. Hence, for instance, in Bengal one of the bad results of the "Permanent Settlement" of the land revenue, which leaves no room for the Collector's ordinary work, has been that the people and the civilian know generally less about each other than in other parts of India. Few Indians venture to impugn the Englishman's integrity and impartiality in adjudging cases in which material interests are concerned, or in settling differences between natives; and nowhere are those qualities more valuable and more highly appreciated than in a country accustomed for centuries to every form of oppression and of social pressure for which the multitudinous claims of caste and family open up endless opportunities. As he has no permanent ties of his own in India, it does not matter to him personally whether the individual case he has to settle goes in favour of A or of B, or whether the native official, whom he appoints or promotes, belongs to this or to that caste. The people know this, and because they have learned to trust the Englishman's sense of fair play, they appeal, whenever they get the chance, to the European official rather than to one of their own race. But it is especially in times of stress, in the evil days of famine or of plague, that they turn to him for help. Nowhere is the "sun-dried bureaucrat" seen to better advantage than in the famine or plague camp, where the "bureaucrat" would come hopelessly to grief, but where the English civilian, not being a "bureaucrat," triumphs over difficulties by sheer force of character and power of initiative. It is just in such emergencies, for which the most elaborate "regulations" cannot wholly provide, that the superiority of the European over the native official is most conspicuous. If "Padgett, M.P.", would go out to India in the hot rather than in the cold weather, and instead of either merely enjoying the splendid hospitality of the chief centres of Anglo-Indian society, or borrowing his views of British administration from the Indian politicians of the large cities, would spend some of his time with a civilian in an up-country station and follow his daily round of work amidst the real people of India, he would probably come home with very different and much more accurate ideas of what India is and of what the relations are between the Anglo-Indian official and the natives of the country.

Far from having flooded India, as is often alleged,

with a horde of overpaid officials, we may justly claim that no Western nation has ever attempted to govern an alien dependency with a smaller staff of its own race, or has admitted the subject races to so large a participation in its public services. The whole vast machinery of executive and judicial administration in British India employs over 1,250,000 Indians, and only a little more than 5,000 Englishmen altogether, of whom about one-sixth constitute what is called *par excellence* the Civil Service of India. Not the least remarkable achievement of British rule has been the building up of a great body of Indian public servants capable of rising to offices of great trust. Not only, for instance, do Indian Judges sit on the Bench in the High Courts on terms of complete equality with their European colleagues, but magisterial work all over India is done chiefly by Indians. The same holds good of the Revenue Department and of the much, and often very unjustly, abused Department of Police; and, in fact, as Anglo-Indian officials are the first to acknowledge, there is not a department which could be carried on to-day without the loyal and intelligent co-operation of the Indian public servant. There is room for improving the position of Indians, not only, as I have already pointed out, in the Educational Department, but probably in every branch of the "Provincial" service, which corresponds roughly with what was formerly called the "Uncovenanted" service. As far back as 1879 Lord Lytton laid down rules which gave to natives of India one-sixth of the appointments until then reserved for the "Covenanted" service, and we have certainly not yet reached the limit of the number of Indians who may ultimately with advantage be employed in the different branches of the public service; but few who know the defects as well as the good qualities of the native will deny that to reduce hastily the European leaven in any department would be to jeopardize its moral as well as its administrative efficiency. The condition of the police, for instance, is a case in point, for any survival of the bad old native traditions is due very largely to the insufficiency of European control. Mr. Gokhale has himself admitted as one of the reasons for founding his society of "Servants of India" the necessity of "building up a higher type of character and capacity than is generally available in the country." For the same reason we must move slowly and cautiously in substituting Indians for Europeans in the very small number of posts which the latter still occupy. That the highest offices of executive control must be very largely held by Englishmen so long as we continue to be responsible for the government of India is admitted by all but the most "advanced" Indian politicians, and it is to qualify for and to hold such positions that the Indian Civil Service—formerly the "Covenanted" service—is maintained. It consists of a small *élite* of barely 1,200 men, mostly, but not exclusively, Englishmen, for it includes nearly 100 Indians. It is recruited by competitive examinations held in England, and this is one of the chief grievances of Indians. But in order to preserve the very high standard it has hitherto maintained, it seems essential that Indians who wish to enter it should have had not only the Western education which Indian Universities might be expected to provide, but the thoroughly English training which India certainly does not as yet supply.

In the eyes of the disaffected Indian politician the really unpardonable sin of the Civil Service is that it constitutes the bulwark of British rule, the one permanent link between the Government of India and the manifold millions entrusted to their care. I have already had occasion to show, incidentally, how unfounded is the charge that, through ignorance and want of sympathy, the British civilian is callous to the real interests and sentiments of the people in dealing with the larger problems of Indian statesmanship. The contrary is the case, for to him belongs the credit of almost every measure passed during the last 50 years for the benefit of the Indian masses, and passed frequently in the teeth of vehement opposition from the Indian politician. Nor is it surprising that it should be so. For the Indian politician—generally a townsman—is, as a rule, drawn from and represents classes that have very little in common with the great bulk of the people, who are agriculturists. The British civilian, on the other hand, often spends the best years of his life in rural districts, seldom even visited by the politician, and therefore knows much more about the needs and the feelings of the people among whom he lives and moves. In the best sense of the word he is in fact the one real democrat in India. The very fact that he is a bird of passage in the country makes him absolutely independent of the class interests and personal bias to which the politician is almost always liable. Moreover, the chief, and perfectly legitimate, object to which the Anglo-Indian administrator is bound to address himself is, as Mr. Bepin Chandra Pal once candidly admitted, to capture "the heart, the mind of the people . . . to secure, if not the allegiance, at least the passive, the generous acquiescence of the general mass of the population." To make his meaning perfectly clear, Mr. Pal instanced the rural reforms, the agricultural banks and other things which had been done in Lord Curzon's time, "to captivate the mind of the teeming masses," and he added that "he is a foolish politician in India who allows the Government to capture the mind of the masses to the exclusion of his own influence and his own countrymen." Mr. Pal is from his point of view perfectly logical, and so were the writers in the *Yugantar*, who, when they elaborated their scheme of revolutionary propaganda, declared that the first step must be to undermine the confidence of the people in their rulers and to destroy the spirit of contentedness under an alien yoke. But could there be a more striking tribute to the intelligent and sympathetic treatment of the interests of the Indian masses by their British rulers than such admissions on the part of the enemies of British rule?

From this point of view nothing but good should result from the larger opportunities given by the recent reforms for the discussion of Indian questions in the enlarged Councils, so long as the Indian representatives in these Councils are drawn, as far as possible, from the different classes which, to some extent, reflect the different interests of the multitudinous communities that make up the people of India. The British civilian will have a much better chance than he has hitherto had of meeting his detractors in the open, and, if one may judge by the proceedings last winter, when the Councils met for the first time under the new conditions, there is little reason to fear, as many did at first, that he will be taken at a disadvantage in debate owing to the greater fluency and rhetorical resourcefulness of the Indian politician. It was not only in the Imperial Council in Calcutta that the official members, having the better case and stating it quite simply, proved more than a match for the more exuberant eloquence of their opponents. On the contrary, the personal contact established in the enlarged Councils between the Anglo-Indian official and the better class of Indian politician may well serve to diminish the prejudices which exist on both sides. It is, I believe, quite a mistake to suppose that the British civilian generally resents the recent reforms, though he may very well resent the spirit of hostility and suspicion in which they were advocated and welcomed in some quarters, as if they were specially directed against the European element in the Civil Service. A practical difficulty is the heavy call which attendance in Council will make upon Civil servants who have to represent Government in these assemblies. Already for many years past the amount of work, and especially of office work, has steadily increased and without any corresponding increase of the establishment. Hence the civilian has less time to receive Indian visitors, and he is often obliged to curtail the period he spends during the year in camp. Hence also the growing frequency of transfers and of officiating or temporary appointments. There are, in fact, to-day barely enough men to go round, and, obviously, the more frequently a man is moved, the less chance he has of getting thoroughly acquainted with the people among whom he has to work in a country such as India, where within the limits of the same province you may find half a dozen widely different communities speaking different languages and having different creeds and customs. Perhaps, too, for the same reasons, there is a tendency towards over-centralization in the "Secretariats" or permanent departments at the seat of government, whether in Simla or in the provincial capitals, and the less favoured civilian who bears the heat and burden of the day in the *mofussil* is both more dependent upon them and more jealous of the many advantages they naturally enjoy. Posts and telegraphs and the multiplying of "regulations" everywhere tend to weaken personal initiative. Nor can it be denied that with the increased facilities of travel to and from Europe civilians no longer look upon India quite so much as their home. The local *liaisons*, not uncommon in pre-Mutiny days, are now things of the past, and the married man of to-day who has to send his children home for their education, and often his wife too, either on account of the climate or to look after the children, is naturally more disposed to count up his years of service and to retire on his pension at the earliest opportunity. The increased cost of living in India and the depreciation of the rupee have also made the service less attractive from the purely pecuniary point of view, whilst in other ways it must suffer indirectly from such changes as the reduction of the European staff in the Indian Medical Department. The substitution of Indian for European doctors in outlying stations where there are no European practitioners is a distinct hardship for married officials, as there is a good deal more than mere prejudice to explain the reluctance of Englishwomen to be treated by native medical advisers. Nor is it possible to disguise the soreness caused throughout the

Indian Civil Service by the recent appointment of a young member of the English Civil Service to one of the very highest posts in India. No one questions Mr. Clark's ability, but is he really more able than every one of the many men who passed with him, and for many years before him, through the same door into the public service and elected to work in India rather than at home ? No Minister would have thought of promoting him now to an Under-Secretaryship of State in England, and apart from the grave reflection upon the Indian Civil Service—and the belief generally entertained amongst Indians that it was meant to be a reflection upon the Indian Civil Service—his appointment to a far higher Indian office implies a grave misconception of the proper functions of a Council which constitutes the Government of India.

None of these minor considerations, however, will substantially affect the future of the Indian Civil Service if only it continues to receive from public opinion at home, and from the Imperial Government as well as from the Government of India, the loyal support and encouragement which the admirable work it performs, often under very trying conditions, deserves. An unfortunate impression has undoubtedly been created during the last few years in the Indian Civil Service that there is no longer the same assurance of such support and encouragement either from Whitehall or from Simla, whilst the attacks of irresponsible partisans have redoubled in intensity and virulence, and have found a louder and louder echo both on the platform and in the Press at home. The loss of contact between the Government of India and Anglo-Indian administrators has been as painfully felt as the frigid tone of many official utterances in Parliament, which have seemed inspired by a desire more often to avoid party embarrassments at Westminster than to protect public servants, who have no means of defending themselves, against even the grossest forms of misrepresentation and calumny, leading straight to the revolver and the bomb of the political assassin. The British civilian is not going to be frightened by one more risk added to the vicissitudes of an Indian career, but can you expect him to be proof against discouragement when many of his fellow-countrymen exhaust their ingenuity in extenuating or in casting upon him the primary responsibility for the new Indian gospel of murder which is being preached against him? Mr. Montagu was well inspired in protesting against such "hostile, unsympathetic, and cowardly criticism" as was conveyed in Mr. Mackarness's pamphlet; but this pamphlet was mere sour milk compared with the vitriol which the native Press had been allowed to pour forth day after day on the British official in India before any action was taken by Government to defend him.

The new Viceroy, who himself belongs to one of the most important branches of the British Civil Service, may be trusted to display in his handling of the British civilian the tact and sympathy required to sustain him in the performance of arduous duties which are bound to become more complex and exacting as our system of government departs further from the old patriarchal type. Our task in India must grow more and more difficult, and will demand more than ever the best men that we can give to its accomplishment. The material prizes which an Indian career has to offer may be fewer and less valuable, whilst the pressure of work, the penalties of exile, the hardship of frequent separation from kith and kin, the drawbacks of an always trying and often treacherous climate, will for the most part not diminish. But the many-sided interests and the real magnitude and loftiness of the work to be done in India will continue to attract the best Englishmen so long as they can rely upon fair treatment at the hands of the Mother Country. If that failed them there would speedily be an end not only to the Indian Civil Service, but to British rule itself. For the sword cannot govern. It can only maintain government, and can maintain it only as long as government itself retains the respect and acquiescence of the great masses of the Indian peoples which have been won, not by generals or by Secretaries of State, or even by Viceroys, but by the patient and often obscure spadework of the Indian Civil Service—by its integrity, its courage, its knowledge, its efficiency, and its unfailing sense of justice.

Complaints of the aloofness of the British civilian very seldom proceed either from Indians of the upper classes or from the humbler folk. They generally proceed from the new, more or less Western-educated middle class whose attitude towards British officials is seldom calculated to promote cordial relations ; and they are also sometimes inspired by another class of Indian who, one may hope, will before long have vanished, but whom of all others the civilian is bound to keep at arm's length. There are men who would get a hold upon him, if he is a young man, by luring him into intrigues with native women, or by inveigling him into the meshes of the native moneylender, or who, by less reprehensible means, strive to establish themselves on a footing of intimacy with him merely in order to sell to other Indians the influence which they acquire or pretend to have acquired over him. Cases of this kind are no doubt rare, and growing more and more rare, as social conditions are passing away which in earlier days favoured them. Less objectionable, but nevertheless to be kept also at arm's length, is the far more numerous class of natives known in India as *umedwars*, who are always anxious to seize on to the coat-tails of the Anglo-Indian official in order to heighten their own social *status*, and, if possible, to wheedle out of Government some of those minor titles or honorific distinctions to which Indian society attaches so much importance.

In other branches of the public service selection has not always operated as successfully as the competitive system for the Civil Service. Men are too often sent out as lawyers or as doctors, or even, as I have already pointed out, to join the Education Department, with inadequate qualifications, and they are allowed to enter upon their work without any knowledge of the language and customs of the people. Such cases are generally the result of carelessness or ignorance at home, but some of them, I fear, can only be described as "jobs"—and there is no room in India for jobs. The untravelled Indian is also brought into contact to-day with an entirely different class of Englishman. The globe-trotter, who is often an American, though the native cannot be expected to distinguish between him and the Englishman, constantly sins from sheer ignorance against the customs of the country. Then, again, with railways and telegraphs and the growth of commerce and industry a type of Englishman has been imported to fill subordinate positions in which some technical knowledge is required, who, whatever his good qualities, is much rougher and generally much more strongly imbued with, or more prone to display, a sense of racial superiority. Nor is he kept under the same discipline as Tommy Atkins, who is generally an easy-going fellow, and looks upon the native with good-natured, if somewhat contemptuous, amusement, though he, too, is sometimes a rough customer when he gets "above himself," or when his temper is ruffled by prickly heat, that most common but irritating of hot-weather ailments. In this connexion the remarkable growth of temperance among British soldiers in India is doubly satisfactory.

On the whole, the relations between the lower classes of Europeans and natives in the large cities, where they practically alone come into contact, seldom give rise to serious trouble; and it is between Europeans and natives of the higher classes that, unfortunately, personal disputes from time to time occur, which unquestionably produce a great deal of bad blood—disputes in which Englishmen have forgotten not only the most elementary rules of decent behaviour, but the self-respect which our position in India makes it doubly obligatory on every

Englishman to observe in his dealings with Indians. Some of these incidents have been wilfully exaggerated, others have been wantonly invented. Most of them have taken place in the course of railway journeys, and without wishing to palliate them, one may reasonably point out that, even in Europe, people, when travelling, will often behave with a rudeness which they would be ashamed to display in other circumstances, and that long railway journeys in the stifling heat of India sometimes subject the temper to a strain unknown in more temperate climates. In some cases, too, it is our ignorance of native customs which causes the trouble, and the habits of even high-class Indians are now and then unpleasant. A few months ago, I shared a railway compartment one night with an Indian gentleman of good position and pleasant address, belonging to a sect which carries to the most extreme lengths the respect for all forms of life, however repulsive. Had I been a stranger to India and ignorant of these conscientious eccentricities, I might well have objected very strongly to some of the proceedings of my companion, who spent a good deal of his time in searching his person and his garments for certain forms of animal life, which he carefully deposited in a little silver box carried for this special purpose. Nevertheless it must be admitted that there have been from time to time cases of brutality towards natives sufficiently gross and inexcusable to create a very deplorable impression. I have met educated Indians who, though they have had no unpleasant experiences of the kind themselves, prefer to avoid entering a railway carriage occupied by Europeans lest they should expose themselves even to the chance of insulting treatment. On the other hand, speaking from personal experience as well as from what I have heard on unimpeachable authority, I have no hesitation in saying that there are evil-disposed Indians, especially of late years, who deliberately seek to provoke disagreeable incidents by their own misbehaviour, either in the hope of levying blackmail or in order to make political capital by posing as the victims of English brutality. But even when Englishmen put themselves entirely in the wrong, there is perhaps a tendency amongst Anglo-Indians—chiefly amongst the non-official community—to treat such cases with undue leniency, and it is one of the curious ironies of fate that Lord Curzon, whom the Nationalist Press has singled out for constant abuse and denunciation as the prototype of official tyranny, was the one Viceroy who more than any other jeopardized his popularity with his fellow-countrymen in India by insisting upon rigorous justice being done where Indians had, in his opinion, suffered wrongs of this kind at the hands of Europeans.

It is a lamentable fact that, amongst Indians, the greatest bitterness with regard to the social relations between the two races often proceeds from those who have been educated in England. There is, first of all, the young Indian who, having mixed freely with the best type of Englishmen and Englishwomen, finds himself on his return to India quite out of touch with his own people, and yet has to live their life. Cases of this kind are especially pathetic, when, having imbibed European ideals of womanhood, he is obliged to marry some girl chosen by his parents, with whom, however estimable she may be, he has nothing in common. Such is the contrariety of human nature that he usually visits his unhappiness, not on the social system which has resumed its hold upon him, but on the civilization which has killed his belief in it. Then there is the very mischievous type of young Indian who, having been left to his own devices in England, and without any good introductions, brings back to India and retails there impressions of English society, male and female, gathered from the very undesirable surroundings into which he has drifted in London and other large cities. It is he who is often responsible for one of the most deplorable features in the propaganda of the seditious Press—namely, the scandalous libels upon the character of

English domestic life, and especially upon the morality of English womanhood—by which it is sought to undermine popular respect for and confidence in the Englishman. But our own responsibility must also be very great, so long as we allow the young Indian who comes to England to drift hopelessly, without help or guidance, among the rocks and shoals of English life. Men of our own race, and carefully picked men, come from our oversea Dominions to study in our colleges, and we have a special organization to look after their moral and material welfare. For years past we have allowed young Indians to come and go, and no responsible hand has been stretched out to save them from the manifold temptations of an entirely alien society in which isolation is almost bound to spell degradation and bitterness.

Considering, however, the many inevitable causes of friction and the inherent imperfections of human nature, whether white or coloured, one may safely say that between Englishmen of all conditions and Indians of all conditions there often and, indeed, generally exist pleasanter relations than are to be found elsewhere between people of any two races so widely removed. They are never closer than when special circumstances help to break down the barriers. The common instincts and the common dangers of their profession create often singularly strong ties of regard and affection between the sepoy of all ranks and his British officers—especially on campaign. In domestic tribulations, as well as in public calamities, Indians, at least of the lower classes, will often turn more readily and confidently for help to the Englishman who lives amongst them than to their own people. I need not quote instances of the extraordinary influence which many European missionaries have acquired by their devoted labours amongst the poor, the sick, and the suffering, and in former times, perhaps more than in recent times, even with Indians of the higher classes. In ordinary circumstances we have to recognize the existence on both sides of obstacles to anything like intimacy. Many Indian ideas and habits are repugnant to us, but so also are many of ours to them. Indians have their own conceptions of dignity and propriety which our social customs frequently offend. If Englishmen and Englishwomen in high places in India would exert their influence to invest the social life of Europeans in the chief resorts of Anglo-Indian society with a little more decorum and seriousness, they would probably be doing better service to a good understanding between the two races in social matters than by trying to break down by sheer insistence, however well meant, the barriers which diametrically opposite forms of civilization have placed between them.

CHAPTER XXVI.

The Government of India.

In the very able speech in which, on July 27, Mr. Montagu, the new Under-Secretary of State for India, introduced the Indian Budget in the House of Commons, one passage referred to the relations between the Secretary of State and the Viceroy in terms which have deservedly attracted very great attention[23]. Differences of opinion, sometimes of an acute character, have at intervals occurred between Secretaries of State and Viceroys as to their relative attributions. Mr. Montagu's language, however, would seem to constitute an assertion of the powers of the Secretary of State far in excess not only of past practice but of any reasonable interpretation of legislative enactments on the subject. After congratulating Lord Minto on the completion of a "difficult reign," Mr. Montagu said :—

> The relations of a Viceroy to the Secretary of State are intimate and responsible. The Act of Parliament says "That the Secretary of State in Council shall superintend, direct, and control all acts, operations, and concerns which in any way relate to or concern the government or revenues of India, and all grants of salaries, gratuities, and allowances, and all other payments and charges whatever out of or on the revenues of India." It will be seen how wide, how far-reaching, and how complete these powers are. Lord Morley and his Council, working through the agency of Lord Minto,

have accomplished much. . . . I believe that men of all parties will be grateful that Lord Morley remains to carry out the policy he has initiated.

It is to be regretted in the first place that Mr. Montagu should not have been more careful to make his quotation accurate. For, as quoted by him, the Act would make it obligatory upon the Secretary of State to supervise practically every act of the Government of India, whereas the powers of the Secretary of State, who has succeeded to the powers of the old Board of Control of the East India Company, are discretionary powers. The statute from which the Secretary of State actually derives his powers is the Government of India Act, 1858, wh ch under section 3 declares that the Secretary of State "shall have and perform all such or the like powers and duties in any wise relating to the government or revenues of India and all such or the like powers over all officers appointed or continued under this Act as might or should have been exercised or performed" by the Company and Board of Control, and those powers and duties are defined in the following terms in the Act of 1833 (3 and 4 William IV., c. 85, sec. 25), which Mr. Montagu would seem to have had in his mind, though he quoted it imperfectly: "The said Board [of Control] shall have and be invested with full power and authority to superintend, direct, and control all acts, operations, and concerns, &c." The difference, as has been very properly pointed out in the *Manchester Guardian*, no unfriendly critic of the present Administration, is "between exercising control and the power to exercise control, between 'shall' and 'may.' If these words of the Act were to be abbreviated, the right abbreviation would have been 'may.' This is the word used by Sir Courtenay Ilbert in his summary of the Secretary of State's powers (The Government of India, p. 145):— '. . . the Secretary of State may, subject to the provisions embodied in this digest, superintend, direct, and control all acts, operations, and concerns, &c.'

This difference between 'shall' and 'may' is, of course, vital. 'Shall' implies that the Secretary of State is standing over the Viceroy in everything he does; 'may' simply reserves to him the right of control where he disapproves. 'Shall' imparts an agency of an inferior order; 'may' safeguards the rights of the Crown and Parliament without impairing the dignity of the Viceregal office."

Of greater importance, however, is the construction which Mr. Montagu places on these statutes. There are three fundamental objections to the doctrine of "agency" which he propounds in regard to the functions of the Viceroy. In the first place, it ignores one of the most important features of his office—one, indeed, to which supreme importance attaches in a country such as India, where the sentiment of reverence for the Sovereign is rooted in the most ancient traditions of all races and creeds. The Viceroy is the direct and personal representative of the King-Emperor, and in that capacity, at any rate, it would certainly be improper to describe him as the "agent" of the Secretary of State. From this point of view, any attempt to lower his office would tend dangerously to weaken the prestige of the Crown, which, to put it on the lowest grounds, is one of the greatest assets of the British *Raj*. In the second place, Mr. Montagu ignores equally another distinctive feature of the Viceroy's office, especially important in regard to his relations with the Secretary of State—namely, that, in his executive as well as in his legislative capacity, the Viceroy is not a mere individual, but the Governor-General in Council. Mr. Montagu omitted to quote the important section of the Act of 1833, confirmed in subsequent enactments, which declared that :—

> The superintendence, direction, and control of the whole civil and military government of all the said territories and revenues in India shall be and is hereby vested in a Governor-General and Councillors to be styled "the Governor-General of India in Council."

The only title recognized by statute to the Viceroy is that of Governor-General in Council, and how material is this conjunction of the Governor-General with his Council is shown by the exceptional character of the circumstances in which power is given to the Governor-General to act on his own responsibility alone, and by the extreme rareness of the cases in which a Governor-General has exercised that power.

Thus, on the one hand, Mr. Montagu forgets the Crown when he talks of the Secretary of State acting through the agency of the Viceroy; and, on the other hand, he forgets the Governor-General in Council when he talks of the relations between the Viceroy and the Secretary of State—whose proper designation, moreover, is Secretary of State in Council, for, like the Governor-General, the Secretary of State has a Council intimately associated with him by statute in the discharge of his constitutional functions. Though the cases in which the Secretary of State cannot act without the concurrence of the Council of India, who sit with him at the India Office, are limited to matters involving the grant or appropriation of revenues, and in other matters he is not absolutely bound to consult them and still less to accept their recommendations, the Act of Parliament quoted by Mr. Montagu clearly implies that, in the exercise of all the functions which it assigns to him, he is expected to act generally in consultation and in concert with his Council, since those functions are assigned to him specifically as Secretary of State in Council.

Now, as to the nature of the relations between the Governor-General in Council and the Secretary of State in Council as above defined by statute. The ultimate responsibility for Indian government, as Mr. Montagu intimated, rests unquestionably with the Imperial Government represented by the Secretary of State for India, and therefore, in the last resort, with the people of the United Kingdom represented by Parliament. The question is, What is in theory and practice the proper mode of discharging this "ultimate responsibility" for Indian government? It is not a question which can be authoritatively answered, but, if we may infer an answer from the spirit of legislative enactments and from the usage that has hitherto prevailed, it may still be summed up in the same language in which John Stuart Mill described the function of the Home Government in the days of the old East India Company—"The principal function of the Home Government is not to direct the details of administration, but to scrutinize and revise the past acts of the Indian Governments; to lay down principles and to issue general instructions for their future guidance, and to give or refuse sanction to great political measures which are referred home for approval." This seems undoubtedly to be the view of the relations, inherited from the East India Company, between the Secretary of State and the Government of India which has been accepted and acted upon on both sides until recently. Nor is any other view compatible with the Charter Act of 1833, or with the Government of India Act of 1858, which, in all matters pertinent to this issue, was based upon, and confirmed the principles of the earlier statute. The Secretary of State exercises general guidance and control, but, as Mill laid it down no less forcibly, "the Executive Government of India is and must be seated in India itself." Such relations are clearly very different from those of principal and agent which Mr. Montagu would apparently wish to substitute for them.

Besides the special emphasis he laid on his definition of the relations between the Viceroy and the Secretary of State, other reasons have led to the belief that the Under-Secretary, who spoke with a full sense of his responsibility as the representative of the Secretary of State, was giving calculated expression to the views of his chief. I am not going to anticipate the duties of the historian, whose business it will be to establish the share of initiative and responsibility that belong to Lord

Morley and Lord Minto respectively in regard to the Indian policy of the last five years. Whilst something more than an impression generally prevails both at home and in India that Mr. Montagu's definition does in fact very largely apply to the relations between the present Viceroy and the Secretary of State, and that every measure carried out in India has originated in Whitehall, it is only fair to bear in mind that Lord Morley has never himself put forward any such claim, nor has Lord Minto ever admitted it. The Viceroy, on the contrary, has been at pains to emphasize on several occasions his share, and indeed to claim for himself the initiative, of all the principal measures carried out during his tenure of office, and especially of the new scheme of Indian reforms, of which the paternity is ascribed by most people to Lord Morley.

The Secretary of State's great personality may partly account for the belief that he has entirely overshadowed the Viceroy, all the more in that he has certainly overshadowed the Council of India as never before. But if Lord Minto has reason to complain of the prevalence of this belief, he cannot be unaware that he too has helped to build it up by neglecting to associate his own Council with himself as closely as even his most masterful predecessors had hitherto been careful to do.

Lord Minto's position has no doubt been one of very peculiar difficulty, and no one will grudge him the warm tribute paid to him by Mr. Montagu. Whatever the merits of the great controversy between Lord Curzon and Lord Kitchener, the overruling of the Government of India by the Home Government on a question of such magnitude and the circumstances in which Lord Curzon was compelled to resign had dealt a very heavy blow to the authority and prestige of the Viceregal office in India. Within a few weeks of Lord Minto's arrival in India the Unionist Government who had appointed him fell, and a Liberal Government came into power who could not be expected to display any special consideration for their predecessors' nominee unless he showed himself to be in sympathy with their policy. Lord Minto's friends can therefore very reasonably argue that his chief anxiety was, quite legitimately, to avoid any kind of friction with the new Secretary of State which might have led to the supersession of another Viceroy so soon after the unfortunate crisis that had ended in Lord Curzon's resignation. If this was the object that Lord Minto had in view, his attitude has certainly been most successful, for Lord Morley has repeatedly testified to the loyalty and cordiality with which the Viceroy has constantly co-operated with him. That the Secretary of State and the Viceroy have, nevertheless, not always seen eye to eye with regard to the interference of the India Office in the details of Indian administration appears clearly from a telegram read out by Lord Morley himself in the House of Lords on February 23, 1909. In the course of this telegram, which acknowledged in the most generous terms the strong support of the Secretary of State in all dealings with sedition, the Viceroy made the following curious admission :—"The question of the control of Indian administration by the Secretary of State, mixed up as it is with the old difficulties of centralization, we may very possibly look at from different points of view." The curtain fell upon this restrained attempt to assert what Lord Minto evidently regarded eighteen months ago as his legitimate position, and to the public eye it has not been raised again since then. But in India certainly the fear is often expressed in responsible quarters that, notwithstanding the courageous support which Lord Morley has given to legislative measures for dealing with the worst forms of seditious agitation, their effect has been occasionally weakened by that interference from home in the details of Indian administration of which Lord Minto's telegram contains the only admission known to the public.

It is difficult to believe that Lord Minto's position would not have been stronger had he not allowed the

Governor-General in Council to suffer such frequent eclipses. The Governor-General's Council during Lord Minto's tenure of office may have been exceptionally weak, and there will always be a serious element of weakness in it so long as membership of Council is not recognized to be the crowning stage of an Indian career. So long as it is, as at present too frequently happens, merely a stepping-stone to a Lieutenant-Governorship, it is idle to expect that the hope of advancement will not sometimes act as a restraint upon the independence and sense of individual responsibility which a seat in Council demands. In any case, the effacement of Council during the last few years behind the Viceroy has not been calculated to dispel the widespread impression that, both in Calcutta and in Whitehall, there has been a tendency to substitute for the constitutional relations between the Governor-General in Council and the Secretary of State in Council more informal and personal relations between Lord Minto and Lord Morley, which, however excellent, are difficult to reconcile with the principles essential to the maintenance of a strong Government of India. Private letters and private telegrams are very useful helps to a mutual understanding, but they cannot safely supplant, or encroach upon, the more formal and regular methods of communication, officially recorded for future reference, in consultation and concert with the Councils on either side, as by statute established.

There is a twofold danger in any eclipse, even partial, of the Governor-General in Council. One of the remarks I have heard most frequently all over India, and from Indians as well as from Englishmen, is that "there is no longer any Government of India"; and it is a remark which, however exaggerated in form, contains a certain element of truth. To whatever extent the Viceroy, in his relations with Whitehall, detaches himself from his Council, to that extent the centre of executive stability is displaced and the door is opened to that constant interference from home in the details of Indian administration which is all the more to be deprecated if there appear to be any suspicion of party pressure. Lord Morley has so often and so courageously stood up for sound principles of Indian government against the fierce attacks of the extreme wing of his party, and he has shown, on the whole, so much moderation and insight in his larger schemes of constructive statesmanship, whilst Lord Minto has won for himself so much personal regard during a very difficult period, that criticism may appear invidious. But the tone adopted, especially during the first years of Lord Morley's administration, in official replies to insidious Parliamentary questions aimed at Indian administrators, the alacrity with which they were transmitted from the India Office to Calcutta, the acquiescence with which they were received there, and the capital made out of them by political agitators when they were spread broadcast over India contributed largely to undermine the principle of authority upon which, as Lord Morley has himself admitted, Indian government must rest. For the impression was thus created in India that there was no detail of Indian administration upon which an appeal might not be successfully made through Parliament to the Secretary of State over the head of the Government of India. Now if, as Lord Morley has also admitted, Parliamentary government is inconceivable in India, it is equally inconceivable that Indian government can be carried on under a running fire of malevolent or ignorant criticism from a Parliament 6,000 miles away. That is certainly not the sort of Parliamentary control contemplated in the legislative enactments which guarantee the "ultimate responsibility" of the Secretary of State.

At the same time the effacement of the Viceroy's Executive Council has weakened that collective authority of the Government of India without which its voice must fail to carry full weight in Whitehall. Every experienced Anglo-Indian administrator, for instance, had been quick to realize what were bound to be the consequences of the unbridled licence of the extremist Press and of an openly seditious propaganda. Yet the Government of India under Lord Minto lacked the cohesion necessary to secure the sanction of the Secretary of State to adequate legislative action, repugnant to party traditions at home, until we had already begun to reap the bloody harvest of an exaggerated tolerance, and with the Viceroy himself the views of the ruling chiefs seem to have carried greater weight in urging action on the Secretary of State than the opinions recorded at a much earlier date by men entitled to his confidence and entrusted under his orders with the administration of British India.

Even i' one could always be certain of having men of transcendent ability at the India Office and at Government House in Calcutta, it is impossible that they should safely dispense w:th the permanent corrective to their personal judgment and temperament—not to speak of outside pressure—which their respective Councils have been created by law to supply. Let us take first of all the case of the Viceroy. His position as the head of the Government of India may be likened to that of the Prime Minister at home, and the position of the Viceroy's Executive Council to that of the Ministers who, as heads of the principal executive Departments, form the Cabinet over wh ch the Prime Minister presides. But no head of the Executive at home stands so much in need of capable and experienced advisers as the Viceroy, who generally goes out to India without any personal knowledge of the vast sub-continent and the 300 million people whom he is sent out to govern for five years with very far-reaching powers, and often without any administrative experience, though he has to take charge of the most complicated administrative machine in the world. Even when he has gone out to India, his opportunities of getting to know the country and its peoples are actually very scant. He spends more than six months of the year at Simla, an essentially European and ultra-official hill-station perched up in the clouds and entirely out of touch with Indian life, and another four months he spends in Calcutta, which, again, is only partially Indian, or, at any rate, presents but one aspect of the many-sided life of India. It takes a month for the great public departments to transport themselves and their archives from Calcutta to Simla at the beginning of the hot weather, and another month in the autumn for the pilgrimage back from the hills to Calcutta. It is only during these two months that the Viceroy can travel about freely and make himself acquainted with other parts of the vast Dependency committed to his care, and, though railways have shortened distances, rapid journeys in special trains with great ceremonial programmes at every halting point scarcely afford the same opportunities as the more leisurely progress of olden days, when the Governor-General's camp, as it moved from place to place, was open to visitors from the whole surrounding country. Moreover, the machinery of administration grows every year more ponderous and complicated, and the Viceroy, unless he is endowed with an almost superhuman power and quickness of work, is apt to find himself entangled in the meshes of never-ending routine. It is in order to supply the knowledge and experience which a Viceroy in most cases lacks when he first goes out, and in some cases is never able to acquire during his whole tenure of office, that his Executive Council is so constituted, in theory and as far as possible in practice, that it combines with administrative experience in the several Departments over which members respectively preside such a knowledge collectively of the whole of India that the Viceroy can rely upon expert advice and assistance in the transaction of public business and, not least, in applying with due regard for Indian conditions the principles of policy laid down for his guidance by the Home Government. These were the grounds upon which Lord Morley justified the appointment to the

Viceroy's Executive Council of an Indian member who, besides being thoroughly qualified to take charge of the special portfolio entrusted to him, would bring into Council a special and intimate knowledge of native opinion and sentiment. These are the grounds upon which, by the way, Lord Morley cannot possibly justify the appointment of Mr. Clark as Member for Commerce and Industry, for a young subordinate official, however brilliant, of an English public Department cannot bring into the Viceroy's Executive Council either special or general knowledge of Indian affairs. Such an appointment must to that extent weaken rather than strengthen the Government of India.

The same arguments which apply in India to the conjunction of the Governor-General with his Council apply, *mutatis mutandis,* with scarcely less force to the importance of the part assigned to the Council of India as advisers of the Secretary of State at the India Office.

If we look at the Morley-Minto *régime* from another point of view, it is passing strange that the tendency to concentrate the direction of affairs in India in the hands of the Viceroy and to subject the Viceroy in turn to the closer and more immediate control of the Secretary of State, whilst simultaneously diminishing *pro tanto* the influence of their respective Councils, should have manifested itself just at this time, when it is Lord Morley who presides over the India Office. For no statesman has ever proclaimed a more ardent belief in the virtues of decentralization than Lord Morley, and Lord Morley himself is largely responsible for legislative reforms which will not only strengthen the hands of the provincial Governments in their dealings with the Government of India, but will enable and, indeed, force the Government of India to assume on many vital questions an attitude of increased independence towards the Imperial Government. The more we are determined to govern India in accordance with Indian ideas and with Indian interests, the more we must rely upon a strong, intelligent, and self-reliant Government of India. The peculiar conditions of India exclude the possibility of Indian self-government on colonial lines, but what we may, and probably must, look forward to at no distant date is that, with the larger share in legislation and administration secured to Indians by such measures as the Indian Councils Act, the Government of India will speak with growing authority as the exponent of the best Indian opinion within the limits compatible with the maintenance of British rule, and that its voice will therefore ultimately carry scarcely less weight at home in the determination of Indian policy than the voice of our self-governing Dominions already carries in all questions concerning their internal development.

The future of India lies in the greatest possible decentralization in India subject to the general, but unmeddlesome, control of the Governor-General in Council, and in the greatest possible freedom of the Government of India from all interference from home, except in regard to those broad principles of policy which it must always rest with the Imperial Government, represented by the Secretary of State in Council, to determine. It is only in that way that, to use one of Mr. Montagu's phrases, we can hope successfully to " yoke " to our own " democratic " system " a Government so complex and irresponsible to the peoples which it governs as the Government of India."

CHAPTER XXVII.

CONCLUSIONS.

No Viceroy has for fifty years gone out to India at so critical a moment as that at which Lord Hardinge of Penshurst is about to take up the reins of government. In one respect only is he more favoured than most of his predecessors. The Anglo-Russian agreement, of which he himself helped to lay the foundations when he was Ambassador at St. Petersburg, has removed the greatest of all the dangers that threatened the external security of India and the peace of Central Asia during the greater part of the nineteenth century. It does not, however, follow that the Government of India can look forward with absolute confidence to continued immunity from all external troubles. Save for the Tibetan expedition and one or two small punitive expeditions against Pathan tribes, there have been no military operations on the Indian frontier since the Terai campaign was brought to a close in 1898. But signs are, unfortunately, not wanting of a serious recrudescence of restlessness on the North-West Frontier, where the very necessary measures taken to cut off supplies of arms from the Persian Gulf have contributed to stimulate the chronic turbulence of the unruly tribesmen. There is no definite evidence at present that they are receiving direct encouragement from Cabul, but it is at least doubtful whether the somewhat exaggerated deference shown to the Ameer on the occasion of his visit three years ago to India has permanently improved our relations with him, and though he is no longer able to play off Russia and England against each other, he has not yet brought himself to signify his adhesion to the Convention which defined our understanding with Russia in regard to Afghan affairs. The condition of Persia, and especially of the southern provinces, has created a situation which cannot be indefinitely tolerated, whilst the provocative temper displayed by the Turkish authorities under the new *régime* at various points on the Persian Gulf is only too well calculated to produce unpleasant complications, however anxious we must be to avoid them, if only in view of the feeling which any estrangement between Mahomedan Powers and Great Britain inevitably produces amongst Indian Moslems. The high-handed action of China in Tibet, and, indeed, all along the north-eastern borderland of our Indian Empire, has introduced a fresh element of potential trouble which the Government of India cannot safely disregard, for we are bound not only to protect our own frontiers, but also to safeguard the interests of Nepal and Bhutan, where, as well as in Sikkim, the fate of Tibet and the flight of the Dalai Lama have caused no slight perturbation. In Nepal especially, which is one of the most valuable recruiting grounds of the Indian Army, Chinese ascendency cannot be allowed to overshadow British influence. Lord Hardinge is by profession a peacemaker, and how efficient a peacemaker he proved himself to be at St. Petersburg during the Russo-Japanese war will only be fully known when the historian has access to the secret records of that critical period of Anglo-Russian relations. But it must not be forgotten that the maintenance of peace along such a vast and still largely unsettled borderland as that of India may at any moment be frustrated by disturbing forces over which the most peacefully disposed Viceroy has little or no control.

Peace and sound finance, which is inseparable from peace, have certainly never been more essential to India than at the present juncture. For without them the difficulty of solving the most absorbing and urgent of the internal problems of India will be immeasurably enhanced. There is a lull in the storm of unrest, but after the repeated disappointments to which official optimism has been subjected within the last few years, he would be a sanguine prophet who would venture to assert that this lull presages a permanent return to more normal conditions. Has the creation of a new political machinery which gives a vastly enlarged scope to the activities of Indian constitutional reformers, definitely rallied the waverers and restored courage and confidence to the representatives of sober and law-abiding opinion, or will they continue to follow the lead of impatient visionaries clamouring, as Lord Morley once put it, for the moon which we cannot give them? Have the forces of aggressive disaffection been actually disarmed by the so-called measures of "repression," or have they merely been compelled for the time being to cover their tracks and modify their tactics, until the relaxation of official vigilance or the play of party politics in England or some great international crisis opens up a fresh opportunity for militant sedition? To these momentous questions the next five years will doubtless go far to furnish a conclusive answer, and it will be determined in no small measure by the statesmanship, patience, and firmness which Lord Hardinge will bring to the discharge of the constitutional functions assigned to him as Viceroy—*i.e.*, as the personal representative of the King Emperor, and as Governor-General in Council—*i.e.*, as the head of the Government of India.

I have attempted, however imperfectly, to trace to their sources some of the chief currents and cross-currents of the great confused movement which is stirring the stagnant waters of Indian life—the steady impact of alien ideas on an ancient and obsolescent civilization; the more or less imperfect assimilation of those ideas by the few; the dread and resentment of them by those whose traditional ascendency they threaten; the disintegration of old beliefs, and then again their aggressive revival; the careless diffusion of an artificial system of education, based none too firmly on mere intellectualism, and bereft of all moral or religious sanction; the application of Western theories of administration and of jurisprudence to a social formation stratified on lines of singular rigidity; the play of modern economic forces upon primitive conditions of industry and trade; the constant and unconscious but inevitable friction between subject races and their alien rulers; the reverberation of distant wars and distant racial conflicts; the exaltation of an Oriental people in the Far East; the abasement of Asiatics in South Africa—all these and many other conflicting influences culminating in the inchoate revolt of a small but very active minority which, on the one hand, frequently disguises under an appeal to the example and sympathy of Western democracy a reversion to the old tyranny of caste and to the worst superstitions of Hinduism, and, on the other hand, arms, with the murderous methods of Western Anarchism, the fervour of Eastern mysticism compounded in varying proportions of philosophic transcendentalism and degenerate sensuousness.

In so far as this movement is directed to the immediate subversion of British rule, we need not exaggerate its importance, unless the British Empire were involved in serious complications elsewhere which might encourage the seditious elements in India to break out into open rebellion. We are too often, in fact, inclined to underrate the strength of the foundations upon which our rule rests. For it alone lends—and can within any measurable time lend—substantial reality to the mere geographical expression which India is. A few Indians may dream of a united India under Indian rule, but the dream is as wild to-day as that of the few European Socialists who dream of the United States of Europe. India has never approached to political unity any more than Europe has, except under the compulsion of a conqueror. For India and Europe are thus far alike that they are both geographically self-contained continents, but inhabited by a great variety of nations whose different racial and religious affinities, whose different customs and traditions, tend to divide them far more than any interests they may have in common tend to unite them. We have got too much into the habit of talking about India and the Indians as if they were one country and one people, and we too often forget that there are far more absolutely distinct languages spoken in India than in Europe ; that there are far more profound racial differences between the Mahratta and the Bengalee than between the German and the Portuguese, or between the Punjabee and the Tamil than between the Russian and the Italian ; that, not to speak of other creeds, the religious antagonism between Hindu and Mahomedan is often more active than any that exists to-day between Protestants and Roman Catholics, even, let us say, in Ulster ; and that caste has driven into Indian society lines of far deeper cleavage than any class distinctions that have survived in Europe.

We do not rule India, as is sometimes alleged, by playing off one race or one creed against another and by accentuating and fostering these ancient divisions, but we are able to rule because our rule alone prevents these ancient divisions from breaking out once more into open and sanguinary strife. British rule is the form of government that divides Indians the least. The majority of intelligent and sober-minded Indians who have a stake in the country welcome it and support it because they feel it to be the only safeguard against the clash of rival races and creeds, which would ultimately lead to the oppressive ascendency of some one race or creed; and the great mass of the population yield to it an inarticulate and instinctive acquiescence because it gives them a greater measure of security, justice, and tranquillity than their forbears ever enjoyed.

There are only two forces that aspire to substitute themselves for British rule, or at least to make the continuance of British rule subservient to their own ascendency. One is the ancient and reactionary force of Brahmanism, which, having its roots in the social and religious system we call Hinduism, operates upon a very large section—but still only a section—of the population who are Hindus. The other is a modern and, in its essence, progressive force generated by Western education, which operates to some extent over the whole area of India, but only upon an infinitesimal fraction of the population recruited among a few privileged castes. Its only real *nexus* is a knowledge, often very superficial, of the English language and of English political institutions. Though both these forces have developed of late years a spirit of revolt against British rule, neither of them has in itself sufficient substance to be dangerous. The one is too old, the other too young. But the most rebellious elements in both have effected a temporary and unnatural alliance on the basis of an illusory "Nationalism" which appeals to nothing in Indian history, but is calculated and meant to appeal with dangerous force to Western sentiment and ignorance.

It rests with us to break up that unnatural alliance. We may not reconcile aggressive Brahmanism to Western civilization, but we can combat the evil influences for which it stands and which many enlightened Brahmans have long since recognized; and we can combat them most effectively by rallying to our side the better and more progressive elements which, in spite of its many imperfections, Western education and the contact with Western civilization have already produced. To that end we must shrink from no sacrifices to improve our methods of education. The evils for which we have to find remedies have been of slow growth, and they can only be slowly cured. But they can be cured by patient and sustained effort, and by carrying courageously into practice the principle, which none of us will challenge in theory, that the formation of character on a sound moral basis, inseparable in India from a sound religious basis, is at least as important a part of the educational process as the development of the intellect.

That, however, is not all. If we are to save and to foster the better elements, we must stamp out the worse. Do not let us be frightened by mere words. To talk, as some do, of the Indian Press being "gagged" by the new Press Act is absurd. It is as free to-day as it has always been to criticize Government as fully and fearlessly, and, one may add, often as unjustly, as party newspapers in this country are wont to criticize the Government of the day. It is no longer free to preach revolution and murder with the cynical audacity shown in some of the quotations I have given various Nationalist organs. "Repression" in India, whether of the seditious press, or of secret societies, or of unlawful meetings, means nothing more cruel or oppressive than the application of surgery to diseased growths which threaten to infect the whole organism—and especially so immature and sensitive an organism as the semi-Westernized, semi-educated section of Indian society to-day represents. This surgical treatment will probably also have to be patient and sustained, for here too we have to deal with evils of no sudden growth, though some of their worst outward manifestations have come suddenly upon us. Even if the improvement be more rapid than we have any right to expect, do not let us throw away our surgical instruments, but rather preserve them against any possible relapse. We have to remember not only what we owe to ourselves, but what we owe equally to the many well-meaning but timid Indians who look to us for protection against the insidious forms of terrorism to which the disaffected minority can subject them [24]. The number of our active enemies may be few, but great is the number of our friends who are of opinion that we are more anxious to conciliate the one sinner who may or may not repent than to encourage the 99 just who persevere.

We want the Western-educated Indian. We have made him, and we cannot unmake him if we would. But we must see that he is a genuine product of the best that Western education can give, and not merely an Indian who can speak English and adapt his speech to English ears in order to lend plausibility to the revival in new forms of ancient religious or social tyrannies. We must remember also that even the best type of Western-educated Indian only speaks at present for a minute section of the population of India, and that, when he does not speak, as he often naturally does, merely in the interests of the small class which he represents, he has not yet by any means proved his title to speak for the scores of millions of his fellow-countrymen who are still living in the undisturbed atmosphere of the Indian Middle Ages. One of the dangers we have to guard against is that, because the Western-educated Indian is to the stay-at-home Englishman, and even to the Englishman whose superficial knowledge of India is confined to brief visits to the chief cities of India, the most, and indeed the only, articulate Indian, we should regard him as the only or the most authoritative mouthpiece of the needs and wishes of other classes or of the great mass of his fellow-countrymen with whom he is often in many ways in less close touch than the Englishman who lives in their midst.

The weak point of the recent political reforms is that they were intended to benefit, not wholly, but mainly, that particular class. In so far as they may help to satisfy the legitimate aspirations of the moderate Indian politician they deserve praise; and in that respect, as far as one can judge at this very early stage, they are not without promise. In effect they have also helped to give other important interests opportunities of organization and expression. Apart from the great Mahomedan community, whose political aspirations are largely different from, and opposed to, those of Hinduism, there are agricultural interests, always of supreme importance in such a country as India, and industrial and commercial interests of growing importance which cannot be adequately represented by the average Indian politician who is chiefly recruited from the towns and from professions that have little or no knowledge of or sympathy with them. The politician, for instance, is too often a lawyer, and he has thriven upon a system of jurisprudence and legal procedure which we have imported into India with the best intentions, but with results that have sometimes been simply disastrous to a thriftless and litigious people. Hence the suspicion and dislike entertained by large numbers of quiet, respectable Indians for any political institutions that tend to increase the influence of the Indian *vakeel* and of the class he represents. Our object, therefore, both in the education and in the political training of Indians, should be to divert the activities of the new Western-educated classes into economic channels which would broaden their own horizon, and to give greater encouragement and recognition to the interests of the very large and influential classes that hold entirely aloof from politics but look to us for guidance and help in the development of the material resources of the country. We have their support at present, but to retain it we must carefully avoid creating the impression that political agitation is the only lever that acts effectively upon Government, and that in the relations of India and Great Britain—and especially in their fiscal and financial relations—the exigencies of party politics at home and the material interests of the predominant partner must invariably prevail.

Whilst, subject to the maintenance of effective executive control, we have extended and must continue steadily to extend the area of civil employment for Indians in the service of the State, there would certainly seem to be room also for affording them increased opportunities of military employment. It is a strange anomaly that, at a time when we have no hesitation in introducing Indians into our Executive Councils, those who serve the King-Emperor in the Indian Army can only rise to quite subordinate rank. A good deal has no doubt been done to improve the quality of the native officer from the point of view of military education, but, under present conditions, the Indian Army does not offer a career that can attract Indians of good position, though it is just among the landed aristocracy and gentry of India that military traditions are combined with the strongest traditions of loyalty. By the creation of an Imperial Cadet Corps Lord Curzon took a step in the right direction which was warmly welcomed at the time, but has received very little encouragement since his departure from India. Something more than that seems to be wanted to-day. Some of the best military opinion in India favours, I believe, an experimental scheme for the gradual promotion of native officers, carefully selected and trained, to field rank in a certain number of regiments which would ultimately be entirely officered by Indians—just in the same way as a certain number of regiments in the Egyptian Army have always been wholly officered by Egyptians. Indeed, we need not go outside India to find even now, in the Native States, Indian forces exclusively officered by Indians. The effect upon the whole Native Army of some such measure as I have indicated would be excellent; and though we could never hope to retain India merely by the sword against the combined hostility of its various peoples, the Native Army must always be a factor of first-rate importance, both for the prevention and the repression of any spasmodic outbreak of revolt. It is no secret that reiterated attempts have been made to shake its loyalty, and in some isolated cases not altogether without success. But the most competent authorities, whilst admitting the need for vigilance, deprecate any serious alarm, and it is all to the good that British officers no longer indulge in the blind optimism which prevailed among those of the old Sepoy regiments before the Mutiny.

One point which Englishmen are apt to forget, and which has been rather lost sight of in the recent political reforms, is that more than a fifth of the population of our Indian Empire—about one third of its total area—is under the direct administration not of the Government of India, but of the Ruling Chiefs. They represent great traditions and great interests, which duty and statesmanship equally forbid us to ignore. The creation of an Imperial Council, in which they would have sat with representatives of the Indian aristocracy of British India, was an important feature of the original scheme of reforms proposed by the Government of India. It was abandoned for reasons of which I am not concerned to dispute the validity. But the idea underlying it was unquestionably sound, and Lord Minto acted upon it when he drew the Ruling Chiefs into consultation as to the prevention of sedition. Some means will have to be found to embody it in a more regular and permanent shape. If we were to attempt to introduce what are called democratic methods into the government of British India without seeking the adhesion and support of the feudatory Princes, we should run a grave risk of estranging one of the most loyal and conservative forces in the Indian Empire. The administrative autonomy of the native States is sometimes put forward as an argument in favour of the self-government which Indian politicians demand. It is an argument based on complete ignorance. With one or two exceptions, far more apparent than real, the Native States are governed by patriarchal methods, which may be thoroughly suited to the traditions and needs of their subjects, but are much further removed than the methods of government in British India from the professed aspirations of the Indian National Congress. Just as the Ruling Chiefs rightly complained of the effect upon their own people of the seditious literature imported into their States from British India before we were at last induced to check the output of the "extremist" Press, so they would be justified in resenting any grave political changes in British India which would react dangerously upon their own position and their relations with their own subjects.. When we talk of governing India in accordance with Indian ideas, we cannot exclude the ideas of the very representative and influential class of Indians to which none are better qualified to give expression than the Ruling Chiefs. One furthur suggestion. The policy of annexation has long since been abandoned, and the question to-day is whether we might not go further and give ruling powers to a few great chiefs of approved loyalty and high character, who possess in British India estates more populous and important than those of many whom we have always recognized as Ruling Chiefs. The objections to so novel a departure are, I know, serious, and may be overwhelming—foremost among them being the reluctance hitherto shown by the people themselves whenever, for purposes of administrative convenience, any slight readjustment of boundaries has been proposed that involved the transfer to a native State of even a few villages until then under British Administration.

The political reforms with which Lord Minto's Viceroyalty will remain identified are only just on their trial. All that can safely be said at present is that they are full of promise, and it would be rash to predict whether and when it may be safe to proceed further in the direction to which they point. It is difficult even to say yet awhile what share they have had, independently of the "repressive" measures that accompanied them, in stemming at least temporarily the tide of active sedition. Time is required to mature their fruits whether for good or for evil. One may hope that, though they address themselves only to the political elements of the present unrest, they will tend to facilitate the treatment of the economic and social factors of the Indian problem. It is these that now chiefly and most urgently claim the attention of the British rulers of India. To rescue education from its present unhealthy surroundings and to raise it on to a higher plane whilst making it more practical, to promote the industrial and commercial expansion of India so as to open up new fields for the intellectual activity of educated Indians, to strengthen the old ties and to create new ones that shall bind the ancient conservative as well as the modern progressive forces of Indian society to the British *Raj* by an enlightened sense of self-interest are slower and more arduous tasks and demand more patient and sustained statesmanship than any adventures in constitutional changes. But it is only by the successful achievement of such tasks that we can expect to retain the loyal acquiescence of the Princes and peoples of India in the maintenance of British rule.

The sentiment of reverence for the Crown is widespread and deep-rooted among all races and creeds in India [25]. It is perhaps the one tradition common to all. It went out spontaneously to Queen Victoria, whose length of years and widowed isolation appealed with a peculiar sense of lofty and pathetic dignity to the imagination of her Indian peoples. It has been materially reinforced by the pride of personal acquaintance, since India has been twice honoured with the presence of the immediate successor to the Throne. The late King's visit to India has not yet faded from the memory of the older generation, and that of the present King-Emperor and his gracious Consort is, of course, still fresh in the recollection of all. How powerful is the hold which the majesty of the Crown exercises upon Princes and peoples in India was very strikingly shown by the calming effect, however temporary, which the presence of the Prince and Princess of Wales had in Bengal four years ago, at the very moment when political agitation in that province was developing into almost open sedition; and it was shown once more this year by the hush of subdued grief that passed over the whole of India at the sudden news of King Edward's death. Only such rabid papers as Tilak's old organ, the *Kesari*, ventured an attempt to counteract the deep impression produced by that lamentable event, and it could only attempt to do so, very ineffectively, by a spiteful and ignorant depreciation of the position and personality of the Sovereign, and of the part played by him in a Western democracy.

In spite of the traditional prestige attaching to the Crown, we cannot, however, reasonably look for loyalty from India in the sense in which we look for it from our own people or from our kinsmen beyond the seas. There can never be between Englishmen and Indians the same community of historical traditions, of racial affinity, of social institutions, of customs and beliefs that exists between people of our own stock throughout the British Empire. The absence of these sentimental bonds, which cannot be artificially forged, makes it impossible that we should ever concede to India the rights of self-government which we have willingly conceded to the great British communities of our own race. And there is another and scarcely less cogent reason. The justification of our presence in India is that it gives peace and security to all the various races and creeds which make up one-fifth of the population of this globe. To introduce self-government into India would necessarily be to hand it over to the ascendency of the strongest. That we are debarred from doing by the very terms on which we hold India, and that is what Lord Morley must have had in his mind, when, in supporting the Indian Councils Act last year, he specifically excluded all possibility of such assemblies ever leading to the establishment of Parliamentary government in India The sooner that is made perfectly clear the better. But just because executive self-government is inconceivable in India so long as British rule is maintained, we must recognize the special responsibility that consequently devolves upon us not only to do many things for India which we do not attempt to do for our self-governing Dominions, but, above all, not to force upon India things which we should not dream of forcing upon them, and especially in matters in which British material interests may appear to be closely concerned. We must continue to govern India as the greatest of the dependencies of the British Crown, but we must do our utmost to satisfy Indians of all classes and castes and beliefs that we govern them as none of their race could govern them, with an equal and absolutely impartial regard for all law-abiding communities, with an intelligent appreciation of their peculiar interests, and with genuine consideration for all their ideas, so long as those ideas are compatible with the maintenance and security of British rule.

The retirement of Lord Morley has been announced just as these last pages are going to press. The announcement has been received with genuine and widespread regret at home, where criticism of certain details and aspects of his administration has never detracted from a genuine recognition of the lofty sense of duty and broad and courageous statesmanship which he has displayed throughout a very critical period in the history of our Indian Empire. It will assuredly be received with the same feeling in India by all those who have at heart the destinies of the British *Raj* and the interests of the countless peoples committed to our charge. Lord Morley's tenure of office will remain for all times memorable in Anglo-Indian annals. He has set for the Indian ship of State a new course upon which she will be kept with increasing confidence in the future if we keep steadily before us the wise words which, with his own singular felicity of speech, he addressed two years ago to the Indian Civil Service:—"We have a clouded moment before us now. We shall get through it—but only with self-command and without any quackery or cant, whether it be the quackery of blind violence disguised as love of order, or the cant of unsound and misapplied sentiment, divorced from knowledge and untouched by any cool consideration of facts."

NOTES

NOTE 1 (*page* 15).

THE NATIVE PRESS.

Not a single Indian member of the Imperial Council made any serious attempt to controvert the following description given by Sir Herbert Risley of the demoralization of the native Press when he introduced the new Press Bill on February 4, 1910 :—We see the most influential and widely-read portion of the Indian Press incessantly occupied in rendering the Government by law established odious in the sight of the Indian people. The Government is foreign, and therefore selfish and tyrannical. It drains the country of its wealth ; it has impoverished the people, and brought about famine on a scale and with a frequency unknown before ; its public works, roads, railways, and canals have generated malaria ; it has introduced plague, by poisoning wells, in order to reduce the population that has to be held in subjection it has deprived the Indian peasant of his land ; the Indian artisan of his industry, and the Indian merchant of his trade ; it has destroyed religion by its godless system of education ; it seeks to destroy caste by polluting maliciously and of set purpose, the salt and sugar that men eat and the cloth that they wear ; it allows Indians to be ill-treated in British Colonies ; it levies heavy taxes and spends them on the army ; it pays high salaries to Englishmen, and employs Indians only in the worst paid posts—in short, it has enslaved a whole people, who are now struggling to be free.

My enumeration may not be exhaustive but these are some of the statements that are now being implanted as axioms in the minds of rising generation of educated youths, the source from which we recruit the great body of civil officials who administer India. If nothing more were said, if the Press were content to—

"let the lie
Have time on its own wings to fly"

things would be bad enough. But very much more is said. Every day the Press proclaims, openly or by suggestion or allusion, that the only cure for the ills of India is independence from foreign rule, independence to be won by heroic deeds, self-sacrifice, martyrdom on the part of the young, in any case by some form of violence. Hindu mythology, ancient and modern history, and more especially the European literature of revolution, are ransacked to furnish examples that justify revolt and proclaim its inevitable success. The methods of guerilla warfare as practised in Circassia, Spain, and South Africa; Mazzini's gospel of political assassination; Kossuth's most violent doctrines; the doings of Russian Nihilists; the murder of the Marquis Ito; the dialogue between Arjuna and Krishna in the "Gita," a book that is to Hindus what the "Imitation of Christ" is to emotional Christians—all these are pressed into the service of inflaming impressionable minds. The last instance is perhaps the worst. I can imagine no more wicked desecration than that the sacrilegious hand of the Anarchist should be laid upon the Indian song of songs, and that a masterpiece of transcendental philosophy and religious ecstasy should be perverted to the base uses of preaching political murder.

The consequences of this ever-flowing stream of slander and incitement to outrage are now upon us. What was dimly foreseen a few years ago has actually come to pass. We are at the present moment confronted with a murderous conspiracy, whose aim it is to subvert the Government of the country and to make British rule impossible by establishing general terrorism. Their organization is effective and far-reaching; their numbers are believed to be considerable; the leaders work in secret and are blindly obeyed by their youthful followers. The method they favour at present is political assassination; the method of Mazzini in his worst moods. Already they have a long score of murders or attempted murders to their account. There were two attempts to blow up Sir Andrew Fraser's train and one, of the type with which we are now unhappily familiar, to shoot him on a public occasion. Two attempts were made to murder Mr. Kingsford, one of which caused the death of two English ladies. Inspector Nanda Lal Banerji, Babu Ashutosh Biswas, the Public Prosecutor at Alipore, Sir William Curzon-Wyllie, Mr. Jackson, and only the other day Deputy Supdt. Shams-ul-Alum have been shot in the most deliberate and cold-blooded fashion. Of three informers two have been killed, and on the third vengeance has been taken by the murder of his brother in the sight of his mother and sisters. Mr. Allen, the magistrate of Dacca, was shot through the lungs and narrowly escaped with his life. Two picric acid bombs were thrown at His Excellency the Viceroy at Ahmedabad, and only failed to explode by reason of their faulty construction. Not long afterwards an attempt was made with a bomb on the Deputy Commissioner of Umballa.

These things are the natural and necessary consequence of the teachings of certain journals. They have prepared the soil in which anarchy flourishes; they have sown the seed and they are answerable for the crop. This is no mere general statement; the chain of causation is clear. Not only does the campaign of violence date from the change in the tone of the Press, but specific outbursts of incitement have been followed by specific outrages.

And now, Sir, I appeal to the Council in the name of all objects that patriotic Indians have at heart to give their cordial approval to this Bill. It is called for in the interests of the State, of our officers both Indian and European, and most of all of the rising generation of young men. In this matter, indeed, the interests of the State and the interests of the people are one and the same. If it is good for India that British rule should continue, it is equally essential that the relations between Government and the educated community should be cordial and intimate, and that cannot long be the case if the organs of that community lay themselves out to embitter those relations in every sort of way and to create a permanent atmosphere of latent and often open hostility. In the long run people will believe what they are told, if they are told it often enough, and if they hear nothing on the other side. There is plenty of work in India waiting to be done, but it will be done, if the energies of the educated classes are wasted in incessant abuse and suspicion of Government. As regards the officers of Government the case is clear. At all costs they must be protected from intimidation and worse. And it is our Indian officials who stand in most need of protection, for they are most exposed to the danger. The detailed work of investigation and detection necessarily falls upon them, and they are specially vulnerable. through their families. They have done most admirable work during the troubles of the last few years, and have displayed under most trying conditions courage and loyalty that are beyond all praise. We are bound in honour to protect them from threats of murder and outrage which sooner or later bring about their own fulfilment.

To my mind, Sir, the worst feature of the present situation is the terrible influence that the Press exercises upon the student class. I was talking about this about a month ago with a distinguished Indian who is in close touch with schools and colleges in Bengal. He took a most gloomy view of the present state of things and the prospects of the immediate future. According to him the younger generation had got entirely out of hand, and many of them had become criminal fanatics uncontrollable by their parents or their masters.

I believe, Sir, that this Bill will prove to be a wholesome and beneficial measure of national education, that it will in course of time prevent a number of young men from drifting into evil courses and ruining their prospects in life, and that in passing it this Council will earn the lasting gratitude of many thousands of Indian parents.

NOTE 2 (*page* 29).

THE SUPERIORITY OF HINDU CIVILIZATION.

In an " Open Letter to his Countrymen," published at the Sri Narayan Press in Calcutta, Mr. Arabindo Ghose has in so many words proclaimed the superiority of Hindu to Western civilization. " We reject," he writes, " the claim of aliens to force upon us a civilization inferior to our own or to keep us out of our inheritance on the untenable ground of a superior fitness."

NOTE 3 (*page* 44).

SEDITIOUS PLAYS.

One of the most popular of these plays is *The Killing of Kichaka* (*Kichaka-vadd*). The author, Mr. Khadilkar, was assistant editor of the *Kesari* until Tilak was arrested and convicted in 1908, and he then took over the chief editorship. The play has been acted all over the Deccan as well as in Bombay City to houses packed with large native audiences. The following account of it appeared in *The Times* of January 18 last :—

Founded upon the Mahabharata, *The Killing of Kichaka* seems at first sight a purely classical drama. It will be remembered by Oriental students that Duryodhan, jealous of his cousin Yudhistira, Emperor of Hastinapura and the eldest of the five Pandava brothers, induced him to play at dice with a Court gambler called Sakuni. To him the infatuated monarch lost his wealth, his kingdom, his own and his brother's freedom, and lastly that of Draupadi, the wife of all the brothers. Eventually, at the intercession of Duryodhan's father, it was agreed that the Emperor, in full settlement of his losses, should with his brothers and Draupadi abandon Hastinapura to Duryodhan for 13 years. Of these 12 were to be spent in the forest and one in disguise in some distant city. Should, however, the disguise of any be penetrated, all would be obliged to pass a further 12 years in the forest. When the 12 years had expired, the brothers fixed on Viratnagar, the capital of Virata, King of the Malyas, in which to spend their year of concealment. Yudhistira took the name of Kankbhat, a professional dicer, and Bhima that of Ballava, a professional cook. Under their pseudonyms all five brothers obtained posts in the King's service, while Draupadi, styling herself a *sairandhri*, or tirewoman, entered the service of the Queen Sudeshna. Before the year of concealment ended Kichaka, the brother of Queen Sudeshna and commander-in-chief of the Malya forces, returned from a visit to Duryodhan at Hastinapura. Duryodhan had given him as presents Yudhistira's regalia and Draupadi's jewels, and Kichaka boasted that, as Duryodhan's friend, he would one after the other kill the five Pandavas in single combat and then wed their queen. While telling King Virata's Court of his reception, his eye fell on Draupadi, and learning that she was a *sairandhri* and being struck with her beauty, he formally requested the King Virata that she might be sent to his harem. The King consenting, Yudhistira was faced with the dilemma of suffering his queen's dishonour or of revealing his identity. Eventually his brother Bhima solved the difficulty by secretly killing Kichaka.

It is out of this story that Mr. Khadilkar has sought for the materials of his play. It opens with the return of Kichaka to Viratnagar and his passion for the beautiful *sairandhri*. The latter seeks in turn the protection of the King and his queen, and of Kichaka's wife Ratnaprabha; but Kichaka, who as commander-in-chief and on account of the number of his followers is all-powerful in Malya, becomes daily more insistent. He reminds the King of his past exploits, and threatens to leave his service, taking his followers with him. Finally, Virata is driven to make a feeble compromise. He will not himself hand over the *sairandhri* to Kichaka, but he will have her sent to a temple of Bairoba outside the town, washing his hands of all responsibility as to subsequent events. All this time the rescue of Draupadi has been repeatedly discussed between Yudhistira and his brother Bhima. The former is all for mild methods, feeling sure that justice will ultimately prevail. The mighty Bhima wishes to strangle Kichaka regardless of consequences. At last Bhima and Draupadi together extract from him a most reluctant permission. Bhima goes secretly to the Bairoba temple, and removing from its stand the god's idol, he takes its place. So hidden, he is present when Draupadi, abandoned by the King's guards, is seized upon by Kichaka. In vain Draupadi appeals to the latter for mercy. He laughs alike at tears and menaces, and is about to carry her off in triumph when the god Bairoba is seen to rise from his pedestal. It is Bhima. He seizes the terrified Kichaka, hurls him to the floor, and strangles him at Draupadi's feet.

Its Allegorical Meaning.

These things are an allegory. Although his name is nowhere uttered on the stage or mentioned in the printed play, every one in the theatre knows that Kichaka is really intended to be Lord Curzon, that Draupadi is India, and that Yudhistira is the Moderate and Bhima the Extremist Party. Every now and again unmistakable clues are provided. The question, indeed, admits of no doubt, for since the play first appeared in 1907 the whole Deccan has been blazoning forth the identity of the characters. Once they have been recognized, the inner meaning of the play becomes clear. A weak Government at home, represented by King Virata, has given the Viceroy a free hand. He has made use of it to insult and humiliate India. Of her two champions, the Moderates advocate gentle—that is, constitutional—measures. The Extremists, out of deference to the older party, agree, although satisfied of the ineffectiveness of this course. Waiting until this has been demonstrated, they adopt violent methods, and everything becomes easy. The oppressor is disposed of without difficulty. His followers—namely, the Anglo-Indians—are, as it is prophesied in the play and as narrated in the Mahabharata, massacred with equal ease. And the Extremists boast that, having freed their country, they will be able to defend it against all invaders, thus averting the calamities which, according to Lord Morley, would overtake India on the disappearance of the British.

It may be said that all this is mere fooling. But no Englishman who has seen the play acted would agree. All his life he will remember the tense, scowling faces of the men as they watch Kichaka's outrageous acts, the glistening eyes of the Brahmin ladies as they listen to Draupadi's entreaties, their scorn of Yudhistira's tameness, their admiration of Bhima's passionate protests, and the deep hum of satisfaction which approves the slaughter of the tyrant.

NOTE 4 (*page* 48).

SHIVAJI'S EXHORTATIONS.

In the *Kesari* just a week before the Poona murders, the following verses were put into the mouth of Shivaji :—

" I delivered my country by establishing ' Swaraj ' and saving religion. I betook myself to the Paradise of Indra to shake off the great exhaustion that came upon me from my labours. Why, O my beloved ones, have you awakened me ? I planted in the soil of Maharashtra virtues that may be likened to the Kalpavriksha (one of the five trees of Indra's Paradise that yields whatsoever may be desired) ; sublime policy based on strong foundations, valour in the battlefield like that of Karma, patriotism, genuine unselfishness, and unity, the best of all . . . . Alas, alas ! all I see now is the ruin of my country. Those forts of mine to build which I poured out money, to acquire which torrents of fiery blood streamed forth, from which I sallied forth to victory roaring like a lion —all those are crumbling away. What a desolation is this ! Foreigners are dragging out Lakshmi (the goddess of Good Fortune) by the hand of persecution. Along with her Plenty has fled, and with Plenty, Health. The wicked Akabaya (the goddess of Misfortune) stalks with Famine at her side through the country, and relentless Death scatters foul diseases.

" Say, where are those splendid ones who promptly shed their blood on the spot where my perspiration fell ? They eat bread once in a day, but not even enough of that. They toil through hard times by tightening up their bellies. O People, how have you tolerated in the sacred places the carrying off to prison of those holy preceptors, those religious teachers of mine, those saintly Brahmans whom I protected—who, while they devoted themselves to their religious practices in times of peace, exchanged the Darbah (sacrificial grass) in their hands for weapons which they used manfully when occasion required. The cow, the foster-mother of babes when their mother leaves them, the mainstay of the hard-worked peasant, the importer of strength to my people, whom I worshipped as my mother and protected more than my life, is taken daily to the slaughter-house and ruthlessly butchered by the unbelievers. . . . . . . How can I bear this heartrending spectacle? Have all our leaders become like helpless figures on the chess-board? What misfortune has overtaken the land!"

NOTE 5 (*page* 49).

TILAK IN THE CIVIL COURTS.

The Tai Maharaj case came up once more in September on the Appellate side of the Bombay High Court on appeal against the decision of the Lower Courts. It was contended on behalf of Tai Maharaj, the widow, that her adoption of one Jagganath was invalid owing to the undue influence brought to bear upon her at the time by Tilak and one of his friends and political associates, Mr. G. S. Khaparde, who were executors under the will of her husband, Shri Baba Maharajah. Mr. Justice Chandavarkar, in the course of his judgment reversing the decisions of the Lower Courts, said that on the one hand they had a young inexperienced widow, with a right of ownership but ignorant of that right, and led to believe that she was legally subject to the control of the executors of her husband's will as regarded the management of the estate which she had by law inherited from her son, prevented from going to Kolhapur even to attend a marriage in a family of relations, and anxious to adopt a boy from Kolhapur as far as possible. On the other hand they had two men of influence learned in the law, taking her to an out-of-the-way place ostensibly for the selection of a boy, and then, as it were, hustling her there by representing that everything was within their discretion, and thereby forcing her to adopt their nominee. In these circumstances they came to the conclusion that the adoption was not valid, because it was brought about by means of undue influence exercised over Tai Maharaj by both Tilak and Khaparde.

Mr. Justice Chandavarkar is a Hindu Judge of the highest reputation, and the effect of this judgment is extremely damaging to Tilak's private reputation as a man of honour, or even of common honesty.

NOTE 6 (*page* 62).

KHUDIRAM BOSE'S CONFESSION.

A similar confession was made by Khudiram Bose, the author of the fatal bomb outrage at Muzafferpur. When he was brought before the District Magistrate on May 1, 1908, within twenty-four hours of the crime, he stated :—

I came to Muzafferpur five or six days ago from Calcutta to kill Mr. Kingsford. I came of my own initiative, having read in various papers things which incited me to come to this determination. These papers were the *Sandhya*, *Hitabadi*, *Jugantar*, and many others. They wrote of great *Zoolum* done to India by the English Government. Mr. Kingsford's name was not specially mentioned, but I determined to kill him because he put several men in gaol. Besides reading the papers I heard the lectures of Bpin Pal, Surendranath Banerjee, Gisputty Kabyatirtha, and others. There were lectures in Beadon-square and College-square [in the student quarter of Calcutta], and they inspired me to do this. There is also a Sanyasi who lectures in Beadon-square, who is very strong.

NOTE 7 (*page* 84).

RELIGION AND POLITICS.

On this point a very important piece of evidence has been recently produced in Court in the course of the Dacca Conspiracy trial. It is a letter, of which the authenticity is beyond dispute, written by Mr. Surendranath Banerjce to one of the extremist leaders, in which he suggests means for carrying out the proposed celebration of the "boycott" anniversary on August 7 in spite of the prohibition of public meetings under the Seditious Meetings Act. "My suggestion," writes this distinguished politician, who is also the head of Ripon College, one of the most popular colleges in Calcutta, "is that you should organize a religious ceremony on the 7th of August such as *Shakti-puja* and *Kali-puja*, and have *Swadeshi katka* or *jatra* and *Swadeshi* conversation by having a sort of conference. Give a religious turn to the movement. As for the Muhammedans, if you can get them to your side, why not have a *waz* followed by *Swadeshi* preaching? Kindly let me know what you do. But something must be done." *Shakti* rites and the worship of Kali are associated with some of the most libidinous and cruel of Hindu superstitions. The simultaneous attempt to attract Mahomedans by grafting "*Swadeshi* preaching" on to one of their accustomed religious services betrays Mr. Surendranath Banerjee's cynical indifference to any and every form of religious creed so long as it can be exploited in the interest of his political creed.

NOTE 8 (*page* 97).

THE "REMOVAL OF INFORMERS."

Shortly after the murder of Shams-ul-Alam, the following "Appeal" was printed and issued in Calcutta with reference to the "removal of informers":—

HATYA NOY JAGNA.
(Not Murder but Sacrifice.)

Cash price: the head of a European or the heads of two informers.
50th issue Calcutta, Sunday, 6th Chaitra, 1316.

Tempted by gold, some native devils in form of men, the disgrace of India—the police—arrested those great men Barendra Ghose and others who worked for the freedom of their country by sacrificing their interests and dedicating their lives in the performance of the sacred ceremony of *Jagna*, preparing bombs. The greatest of these devils in human form, Ashitosh Biswas, began to pave for these heroes the way to the gallows. Bravo, Charu! [the murderer of Biswas] all honour to your parents. To glorify them, to show the highest degree of courage, disregarding the paltry short span of life, you removed the figure of that monster from the world. Not long ago, the Whites by force and trick, filched India from the Mahomedans. That mean wretch Shams-ul-Alam, who espoused the cause of the enemies of Alamghir Padshah, who put a stain on the name of his forefathers for the sake of gold—to-day you have removed that fiend from the sacred soil of India. From Nuren Gossain to Talit Chakravarti, all turned approvers through the machinations of that fiendish wizard Shams-ul-Alam and by his torture. Had you not removed that ally of the monsters, could there be any hope for India ?

Many have raised the cry that to rebel is a great sin. But what is rebellion ? Is there anything in India to rebel against ? Can a Feringhee be recognized as the King of India, whose very touch, whose mere shadow compels Hindus to purify themselves ?

These are merely Western Robbers looting India. . . . . Extirpate them, ye good sons of India, wherever you find them, without mercy, and with them their spies and secret agents. Last year 19 lakhs of men died of fever, smallpox, cholera, plague, and other diseases in Bengal alone. Think yourselves fortunate that you were not counted amongst those, but remember that plague and cholera may attack you to-morrow, and is it not better for you to die like heroes ?

When God has so ordained, think ye not that at this auspicious moment it is the duty of every good son of India to slay these white enemies ? Do not allow yourselves to die of plague and cholera, thus polluting the sacred soil of Mother India. Our *Shastras* are our guide for discriminating between virtue and vice. Our *Shastras* repeatedly tell us that the killing of these white fiends and of their aiders and abettors is equal to a great ceremonial sacrifice (*Asyamedh Jagna.*) Come, one and all. Let us offer our sacrifice before the altar in chorus, and pray that in this ceremony all white serpents may perish in its flames as the vipers perished in the serpent slaying ceremony of *Janmajog*. Keep in mind that it is not murder but *Jagna*—a sacrificial rite.

NOTE 9 (*page* 99).

BENGALEE LAWLESSNESS.

A very striking, and at the same time sober, picture of the conditions produced by Bengalee methods of agitation is to be found in the speech delivered at the opening of the Provincial Legislature of Eastern Bengal at Dacca on April 6, 1910, by Sir Lancelot Hare, the Lieutenant-Governor appointed in succession to Sir Bampfylde Fuller. "We have had abundant experience," he said, "in the last three years that the advocacy of the boycott at public meetings is invariably followed by acts of tyranny and brutality and illegal interference with the rights of a free people to buy and sell as they, and not as a particular set of agitators, prefer. No district officer anxious to maintain the peace of his district can allow a recrudescence of these disturbances. I have seen it denied that there have been such cases, but the state calendar of crime is there to refute such an assertion ; and you and I well know that the cases which have been brought to trial bear a very small proportion to the cases which have arisen but which the raiyats have been afraid to press home. When we remember the enormous power of the zemindar following from the unfortunate absence of any record of right upon which the tenant can lean and rely, we can well understand how a raiyat hesitates to oppose his landlord's will. I have seen it claimed that such advocacy of the boycott is a constitutional right. The extraordinary fallacy of this assertion hardly needs refuting. With a democratic Government an appeal to the public is an appeal to the Government, as it is an appeal to the voter who appoints the member of Parliament who appoints the Government. Such a condition does not exist in this country, and when an agitator who wishes to press his views on Government says that the boycott will be preached until Government takes a particular course which Government has decided is not for the good of the people, and has announced that it will not adopt, such an appeal is not a constitutional act nor an appeal to Government but an act of defence and open resistance to Government. This Government now as always will do what it believes to be in the best interests of the people. It will always give such regard as it can to respectful representations, even when they come from a small minority only of the population; but appeals to force and violence, appeals to the mob for race hatred, malice, and all uncharitableness, do not constitute constitutional agitation. I would say a few words on the mischief of the boycott agitation. The boycott agitation has been the curse of this province for the past five years, causing endless suffering and unrest, obstructing the path of progress, exciting ill-feeling between Government and the people, and hindering their co-operation in the work of reconstitution and reform. The agitation has displayed itself in many evil forms, all tending to oppression and lawlessness.

" MANY-HEADED MISCHIEF."

It is difficult to review this many-headed mischief in a few words, but its main features may readily be brought to mind. First there is the economic disturbance which resulted from the enforcement of the boycott whether by persuasion or by intimidation or by force. This has been a very real mischief and a very real suffering in many parts of the country where the cultivators found themselves unable to obtain the products to which they were accustomed at prices which they could afford to pay. Next is to be noted the violent scenes in the bazaars, where the sale of British goods was sought to be obstructed by organized force. The deplorable riot at Jamalpore, with its terrible sequel, is only one among many such scenes. A closely allied evil was the picketing of the bazaars by students and other young men, which became an intolerable nuisance until it was put down with a strong hand. The case at Jhalakati, where the young boycotters practically took possession of the bazaar, is a prominent typical instance. Then followed the numerous cases of interference with individuals with the accompaniment of assault and mischief and criminal restraint. The long list of crimes of this nature that have been punished in due course would be wearisome to repeat. No less mischievous and perhaps even more widespread and more common have been the cases of criminal intimidation, in which notices have been posted, or letters have been sent, threatening vendors or purchasers individually or collectively with arson or murder or other outrage. Wealthy zemindars and bankers, shopkeepers of all grades, and villagers and townsfolk have alike prayed to be protected from such interference in the lawful pursuit of their ordinary avocations; and too often it has been impossible to afford this protection. That these threats were not mere idle extravagance has been proved to the hilt by the grave incidents that have actually taken place. More widespread, more difficult to deal with, and causing even greater suffering than these violent methods has been the social persecution which has been exercised upon those who have failed to bow down to the orders of the boycotters. This is one of the most serious chapters in the whole history of the agitation, and Government has again had to deplore the sufferings to which quiet and law-abiding persons have been subjected. The constitution of Hindu society lends itself with great readiness to this form of compulsion, and no weapon is more feared than social ostracism when ruthlessly used in pursuance of a political object. Another most grave aspect of the boycott agitation has been the constant attempt to excite disaffection against Government by public meetings, speeches, propagandist tours, newspapers, pamphlets, songs, flaunting and noisy processions, and dramatic performances. Every effort has been made to try and persuade the people that the Government is hostile, callous, and neglectful and that boycott, and its kindred measures, are the means by which to bring it to a better course. Some of the worst offenders have been prosecuted under the law and have paid the penalty of their crimes, but it is impossible by such means to counteract or nullify the mischief that they and others have caused.

Youths and Politics.

There remains another point which is at the present time of the most sinister significance. The promoters of the agitation conceived the deplorable idea that their propaganda might best be spread, and that their designs might best be carried out by the youths of the country. From this selection has arisen what is now the worst feature of the situation. It is impossible to condemn too strongly the use of the students and other youths to foster political aims. It has resulted in a wave of excitement amongst immature and impressionable minds throughout the affected districts. In this province in the first instance this evil exhibited itself in the constant appearance of youths in the forefront of political demonstration, however hostile and objectionable in character. This phenomenon was naturally accompanied by numerous instances of indiscipline among students which Government has repeatedly been obliged to denounce. The effect on the minds of the most impressionable youths, and especially among those who had a ready means of livelihood and an available occupation, has reached a pitch which was doubtless never contemplated by the more sober among those who initiated this regrettable movement. Nevertheless a series of crimes in which youths belonging to the respectable classes have been known to participate must be regarded as directly attributable to the excitement of political agitation. It is impossible to avoid mentioning in this connexion the system of national schools which was to be lauded in all three of the prohibited Conferences, and which has been encouraged in other similar meetings that are taking place.

During the past few years in this Province the record of these schools is an evil one. They were established in open hostility to the State system of education, which is the true national system, and several of the most important were opened for the purpose of receiving boys expelled from or punished in other schools for taking part in political demonstrations of a most reprehensible character. Their subsequent history has accorded with the spirit in which they were founded and their close connexion with forms of political agitation most unhealthy for young minds has been evinced in many a regrettable incident.

The Outlook.

If we review the present position we find that during the past year there has been some subsidence of the acute stage of the malady, or rather it has taken a different turn. The bulk of the reasonable inhabitants have become wearied of the senselese agitation which brings annoyance and suffering without doing them good. There is less active boycott and the ordinary citizen has become less amenable to the leaders of the agitation. But in spite of this, two circumstances stand out—first, the local leaders have not in general abated one tittle of their efforts to enforce the boycott, and where in any locality they showed signs of resting, their chiefs are ready to urge them forward; secondly, the perversion of our young men has reached a most alarming stage, not merely from the point of view of the crime and the sense of insecurity that it engenders, but also from the more general aspect of the character and prospects of the rising generation. Many parents have most bitter reason to lament their failure to guide, control, and restrain their children. On the 7th August boycott celebrations occurred at the headquarters of each district of the Dacca division, and at a number of places in the interior. The boycott vow was everywhere renewed and at several meetings speeches were delivered, the tendency and object of which was to excite renewed disaffection and to stir up zeal for the cause. The observances for the 16th October were prescribed in an order of the chiefs published in the Calcutta papers, and the local leaders did their best to carry out these instructions. Rakhibandan bathing, abstinence from cooked food, and the solemn renewal of the boycott vow were the principal features. In some places public meetings were held and again the tone of several speakers was most reprehensible. District conferences and other similar meetings played their usual important part in the year's programme. In the Dacca division, Jhalakati, Faridpur, and Pangsa were selected as the theatres of those performances. The resolutions were varied in character, but however guarded and mild their phraseology, the speeches advocated boycott in its most blatant form, and sentiments were expressed tending to keep alive the most pernicious and dangerous characteristics of the political and social situation. Similar conferences, in which the boycott played a prominent part, and in which ill-feeling against the Government was excited, were held in August and September at Pabna and Dinajpur, and in the Sylhet district in October a series of meetings took place. In a portion of the Faridpur district, the unsettled condition of which has for some time been a cause of anxiety, the inhabitants are mostly Namasudras. The ostensible object of these meetings was to raise the social condition of the people, but it appears from the accounts published in the Press that the Anti-Partition agitation and the boycott of foreign goods were urged and the promise of social privilege was only made as a reward or return for promising to take the boycott vow. This condition of affairs could not be permitted to continue indefinitely, and it became evident that sooner or later—and the sooner the better—the mischief must be stopped and the people of the province given the opportunity which they need and desire to settle down to their normal life and to co-operation with the Government for their material and moral progress.

NOTE 10 (*page* 103).

SACRIFICING "WHITE GOATS"

The term occurs, for instance, in one of the most violent fly-sheets issued only a few months ago from a clandestine press in India, under the heading *Yagantar*, killing no murder :—

Rise up, rise up, O sons of India, arm yourselves with bombs, despatch the white *Asuras* to Yana's abode. Invoke the mother Kali ; nerve your arm with valour. The Mother asks for sacrificial offerings. What does the Mother want ? The cocoanut ? No. A fowl or a sheep or a buffalo ? No. She wants many white *Asuras*. The Mother is thirsting after the blood of the Feringhees who have bled her profusely. Satisfy her thirst. Killing the Feringhee, we say, is no murder. Brother, chant this verse while slaying the Feringhee white goat, for killing him is no murder : With the close of a long era, the Feringhee Empire draws to an end, for behold ! Kali rises in the East.

NOTE 11 (*page* 125).

HINDUS AND MAHOMEDANS IN GOVERNMENT SERVICE.

Some statistics have been collected lately by the Moslem League with reference to the relative numbers of Hindus and Mahomedans employed in Government service in India. The figures are still subject to revision, and therefore can only be given as approximately correct. Moreover, the classification adopted does not seem to have been precisely the same in the different provinces. But even if a considerable margin is allowed for discrepancies which may yet have to be rectified, the figures quoted below for several important branches of the service are instructive :—

EXECUTIVE OFFICERS OF THE RANK OF DEPUTY COLLECTORS, DEPUTY MAGISTRATES, ASSISTANT COMMISSIONERS, &c.

	Hindus.	Mahomedans.
Bombay	53	9
Madras	61	7
Bengal	265	59
Eastern Bengal	136	49
Central Provinces	60	24
United Provinces	125	98
Punjab	74	68

SUB-DEPUTY COLLECTORS, SUB-DEPUTY MAGISTRATES, &c.

	Hindus.	Mahomedans.
Bombay	186	3
Madras	151	11
Bengal	165	33
Eastern Bengal	107	39
Central Provinces	52	16
United Provinces	122	106
Punjab	142	90

SUB-DEPUTY JUDGES AND MUNSIFFS.

	Hindus.	Mahomedans.
Bombay	109	2
Madras	132	1
Bengal	195	17
Eastern Bengal	21	1
Central Provinces	117	6
United Provinces	111	35
Punjab	81	52

EDUCATIONAL DEPARTMENT.

	Hindus.	Mahomedans.
Bombay	39	17
Madras	127	10
Bengal	110	16
Eastern Bengal	56	15
Central Provinces	23	2
United Provinces	58	5
Punjab	53	6

NOTE 12 (*page* 126).

INDIAN NATIONAL CONGRESS SUBSIDIES TO ITS SUPPORTERS IN ENGLAND.

The following resolutions passed by the Indian National Congress show that considerable financial support has been regularly given by that body towards the expenses of its London organ, *India*, and of the British committee it co-operates with.

MADRAS, 1898.

"That a sum of Rs.60,000 be assigned for the expenses of the British Committee and the cost of the Congress publication *India*, and also for the expenses of the Joint-General Secretary's Office, and that the several circles do contribute, as arranged, either now or hereafter in Committee for the year 1899."

AHMEDABAD, 1902.

"That with a view to meet the balance required to defray the expenses of *India* and the British Committee a special delegation fee of Rs.10 be paid by each delegate in addition to the usual fee now paid by him with effect from 1902."

MADRAS, 1903.

"That a sum of Rs.10,500 be assigned for the expenses of the British Committee and that the several Congress circles do contribute the amount allotted to each."

BOMBAY, 1904.

"That a sum of £700 be assigned for the expenses of the British Committee and that the several Congress circles do contribute the amount allotted to each."

NOTE 13 (*page* 145).

AN ENGLISH SOCIALIST "MANIFESTO."

The support given to Indian Nationalists by a certain class of politicians in England goes sometimes to such lengths that the tolerance extended to them is open to very serious question. For instance, in a London newspaper which calls itself "the Organ of Social Democracy," *Justice*, there appeared on August 27 a "Manifesto" headed "The Infamies of Liberal Rule in India," which contained, along with much indiscriminate denunciation of British tyranny, the outrageous statement that Savarkar, who is now undergoing trial in Bombay on grave charges, including the abetment of murder, had been arrested in England "for an alleged political offence, and in order that he might not have a fair trial defended by Council, and safeguarded by public opinion in this country, he was sent back to India, where, innocent or guilty, his condemnation could be officially ensured." In conclusion, it was stated :—"We, at any rate, shall take care that this little manifesto of ours shall be distributed in the native languages throughout Hindustan, in order that the population of that great Empire may know that there is an active and growing party in this island which has neither part nor lot in the outrages and crimes committed by our rulers, and that its members heartily sympathize with the legitimate efforts of Indians of all races, castes, and creeds to emancipate themselves finally from the monstrous domination under which they suffer to-day."

Many loyal Indians, and indeed the disloyal ones too, may very reasonably ask whether it is right and just to allow language of this kind to be used and circulated with impunity in this country when, if it were used and circulated in India, it would at once give rise to a crimimal prosecution.

NOTE 14 (*page* 153).

INDIAN STUDENTS IN ENGLAND.

An Indian Correspondent of *The Times* who has made a special study of the condition of his fellow-countrymen studying in England writes that it would be almost impossible for an Englishman who has never been in the East to realize the enormous difference between the life to which the student has been used and the life to which he has come. In many instances his home is in some far off lonely village. He may have been to some town to study in a Government or missionary school or college. But that has not given him an insight into English life. In the Government institution he sees little of his English teacher or professor outside lessons or lecture hours. He never has the chance of knowing an English lady. The student has little time for more than his studies, so numerous are the subjects and the prescribed text-books for Indian examinations. In the vacations the Professors go to the hills, or sail for England, and the student goes back to his village. He has acquired little or no knowledge of the English. He comes to England feeling there is a gulf between the East and the West, save in the case of a missionary interest in his soul. He is by nature extremely sensitive. On board ship he and his brother Indians keep together. The English passengers, fatigued after a period of hard work in a hot climate, have no energy left for the effort of trying to draw out and know this batch of silent Orientals. So the gulf gapes wide. If they tarry in Marseilles or Paris there are those who are anxious and ready to widen this gulf between the Indians and English. Then the student arrives in London, where a man can be more lonely than anywhere in the world. Here he has to find a dwelling. The man from a dreamy, lonely, Eastern village, from the land of the sun has to select an abode in London. Hotels and boarding houses and lodgings there are in abundance; but the hotel or boarding house or lodging suitable to this man's need—fitted to introduce him to English life, may exist, but how is he to find it? He is not only bewildered, he is terribly home-sick. His wish to come to England has been gratified, but oh! for a sight of his own people and his simple home. He must drown this longing as best he may. There are many ways of drowning it in London. There are many who will assist him to forget what he had better never forget—his village home. But after all there are some English people who will know him. He has found lodgings, and the landlady and her family make themselves most agreeable. He knows no other English people. He wants friendliness so far away from home, so these and theirs become his friends.

In London the majority of Indian students gain admission to the Inns of Court. The new regulations, which come into force in January next, were intended to render admission more difficult to attain ; but they will fail of their purpose, for success in the Oxford and Cambridge senior local examinations is a qualification for admission, and these examinations are held in various parts of India. Students will in future avoid entering the Indian Universities, but will get private coaching, and sit for these examinations in India, with a view to gaining admission to one or other of the Inns. It never seems to have occurred to the Honourable Societies of the Inns to take any steps to look after the well-being of these numberless students, who bring hundreds of pounds to their coffers every year. So different is their position from that of the English student that their case merits special attention. To look after them might be unusual, it would certainly be expedient. The eating of a few dinners and attendance at certain lectures are no tax on the student's time. He puts off real study to the last moment. It is so easy to learn all the subjects just before each examination. With a few exceptions the English and Indian students do not speak to each other. So the Inns do not provide the Indian with society. A youth from the East, dwelling in a London lodging, finding himself for the first time in command of a banking account, with abundance of leisure, and no English friends of his own standing —can he become a loyal, useful citizen of our Empire ?

Some of them go to Oxford and Cambridge. They have heard in India, from some Indians who were up at these Universities from ten to fifteen years ago, how delightful the life is—how sociable the undergraduates, how hospitable the dons. Surely then at these ancient seats of learning they will find friendliness, and will come to know the English. They go up only to find disappointment. The numbers have largely increased and all sorts and conditions of men come. Colleges are reluctant to admit them. The English undergraduate accepts any man who is good at games and ready to enter into the University life, but leaves severely alone the man of any nationality who has had no opportunity of learning English games, and who is too shy and sensitive to show what he is worth. Those who are good at games get on, the others are far from being happy. A few gain admission to colleges, the rest are "unattached." Lodging-house existence at Oxford or Cambridge is preferable to that in London ; but it does not assist to a knowledge of the English. Foreigners at the Universities take the trouble to try and know the Indian, and extend to him that friendship which the English undergraduate, through youthful lack of thought, withholds. The Imperial instinct is lacking in the youth of to-day ; else would they realize that it is an important duty to try and know fellow-subjects from a distant part of the Empire. There is nothing that Orientals will not do to make the stranger to their country feel at home. They cannot understand the reserved Occidental who leaves the stranger to his Western country all alone. Some of the Indian students think that the only way to bid for the English undergraduate's acquaintance is by a lavish expenditure on wine parties ; and so he spends largely, and acquires an acquaintance, but not with the typical Englishman. If Indian students at the old Universities are only to know each other or foreigners, how are they to be bound by a loyal attachment to

England ? At Edinburgh the gulf is wide indeed. A number of Colonial students help to make it wider. The two sides seldom or never meet. They just tolerate each other's presence. So the Indian student is tempted to seek for company in circles which do not help his education or tend to elevate him. Should such a state of things continue ?

Engineering and medical students are in better case than others. Their work is so hard and exacting, if they do it aright, they have no time to feel solitude. The one complaint of engineering students is that they find it enormously difficult to gain opportunities for learning the practical side of their work. Firms are most reluctant to admit them as apprentices. France and Germany welcome them, and Continental firms extend to them the aid the English firms deny. Is it always to be so ? Other nations gaining that esteem and gratitude which England should so jealously acquire and guard. Americans, too, are winning the good will of the Indian student both in India and abroad. They have well-equipped schools and colleges all over India. They spare no efforts to make the Indian student feel they are there solely for him. They are with him in and out of school and college hours. They inspire him with their enthusiasm. Wherever they meet him they give him a grip of the hand which leaves him in no doubt as to their frank friendliness. Yet it is not to America nor to any other nation that India belongs, but to England. But there is no security in mere possession. The only safety lies in the constant effort to hold—to hold pleasantly, gaining the heart and head.

Surely the fact that many influences are at work systematically striving to estrange these students from England should rouse the English to effort. It may not be an easy task to gain these men. It will need patience and zeal. There must be no touch of patronage in the attempt. Their deep-rooted belief that no real friendship can exist between the English and the Indian has to be overcome ; the much misrepresentation which has made the Indian student misjudge the English character has to be counteracted and set right. It must be remembered that he is a being far away from home, excessively sensitive, situated in extremely unusual surroundings, and in most cases having lost that religious belief without which no Oriental is really happy or able to live and be his best. He is, in truth, not himself. Such is the student who is to be won to attachment. The difficulty of the task should appeal to the English nature.

What is required is not a sudden and indiscriminate rush to seek out and know the Indian student. That would not last and would lead to much disappointment on both sides. The great need of the present is workers who know both sides and who will judiciously draw them together. Connecting links to bring the right Indians into touch with the right English. They will need very special qualifications, these workers, if they are to succeed. There is enough to be done to employ the full time of exceptionally energetic men. Wonders could be worked if England only realized her duty to these men. The Indian student would return to his home at any rate with no feeling of bitterness. He would have his chance of seeing the real English, and of being influenced aright. Misconceptions would be banished. He would live in an atmosphere better adapted to hard work. He would attain a higher standard in his studies and examinations. He would be better fitted to be a useful citizen. Friendliness would, at any rate, have blunted antagonistic tendencies. And what a difference it would make to his people ! The father who has spent so much on him would no longer feel that his son has lost and not gained by crossing the seas. The mother who, though behind the purdah, has eagerly been watching his career, dwelling lovingly on the weekly news, counting the days to his return, would no longer need to weep that it is not well with her son, who has come back so different from all she had hoped. Whole families would bless the England which had made their member manly, upright, better for his sojourn there, fitted to earn a living honourably, and possessed of grit to strive to do his best. And he, the student, stirred by memories of kindness in the West, would win those with whom he comes in contact to a friendlier feeling for the British race. The seditionist would find no soil here ready for his seed. Could anything be better worth accomplishing ?

NOTE 15 (*page* 171).

THE VICEROY'S EXECUTIVE COUNCIL.

A Mahomedan gentleman, Mr. Ali Imam, has been appointed to succeed Mr. Sinha as Indian member of the Viceroy's Executive Council. He too is a leading member of the Bengal Bar, and, like Mr. Sinha, will take charge of the Legal Department. Though the selection of a Mahomedan in succession to a Hindu cannot fail to gratify Indian Moslems, Mr. Ali Imam's appointment should not be altogether unacceptable to the Hindus. For when the details of the reforms' scheme were being worked out in India, he adopted, on the subject of separate electorates for the Mahomedan community, a line of his own which was applauded by the Hindus, but was very much resented by the vast majority of his co-religionists. The Government of India seemed inclined to favour his proposals, and he proceeded to England to press them upon Lord Morley. But the Secretary of State wisely decided that the pledges originally given by Lord Minto to the Indian Mahomedans must be scrupulously and fully redeemed, so as to secure to them substantial representation in the new Councils.

NOTE 16 (*page* 171).

The first Indian Member of the Bengal Executive Council is expected to be Mr. R. N. Mookerjee, a partner in the well-known Calcutta firm of Messrs. Martin and Co., to whom I have referred (page 258) as "the one brilliant exception" amongst Western-educated Bengalees, who has achieved signal success in commerce and industry and has shown the possibility and the advantages of intelligent and business-like co-operation in those fields between Englishmen and Indians.

NOTE 17 (*page* 212).

THE WASTAGE IN INDIAN UNIVERSITIES.

The most striking feature about the number of graduates at the Indian Universities is not the magnitude of their total or any increase in it, but the very high proportion of wastage. It takes 24,000 candidates at Matriculation to secure 11,000 passes, it takes 7,000 candidates at the Intermediate examination to secure 2,800 passes, and it takes 4,750 candidates for the B.A. degree to secure 1,900 passes.

There are 18,000 students at college in order to supply an annual output of 1,935 graduates. This means that a very large number fall out by the way without completing successfully their University career. The phenomenon, peculiar to India, of candidates for employment urging as a qualification that they have failed at a University examination (meaning that they have passed the preceding examination and added thereto some years of study for the next) is due to two causes, the large number of students whom the University rejects at its examinations before it grants the B.A. degree to the remainder, and the dearth of graduates. (*Quinquennial Report on the Progress of Education in India for* 1902-1907, by Mr. H. W. Orange, Director-General of Education.)

NOTE 18 (*page* 220).

ENGLISH HISTORY IN INDIAN SCHOOLS.

At the opening of an Educational Conference held last April in Bombay under the joint auspices of the Director of Public Instruction and of the Teachers' Association, the Governor, Sir George Clarke, alluded to some of the effects of Western education on the younger generation of Indians:—

"It is widely admitted by the thoughtful Indians that there are signs of the weakening of parental influence, of the loss of reverence for authority, of adecadence of manners and of growing moral laxity. The restraining forces of ancient India have lost some of their power; the restraining forces of the West are inoperative in India. There has thus been a certain moral loss without any corresponding gain. The educated European may throw off the sanctions of religion; but he has to live in a social environment which has been built up on the basis of Christian morality, and he cannot divest himself of the influences which have formed his conscience. The educated or partially educated Indian who has learned to look on life and the affairs of men from a Western standpoint has no such environment and may find himself morally rudderless on an ocean of doubt. The restraints of ancient philosophies, which have unconsciously helped to shape the lives of millions in India who had only the dimmest knowledge of them, have disappeared from his mental horizon. There is nothing to take their place. Ancient customs, some of them salutary and ennobling, have come to be regarded as obsolete. No other customs of the better sort have come to take their place, and blindly to copy the superficial customs of the West is to ignore all that is best in western civilization."

Commenting on his Excellency's speech, the Bombay *Examiner*, a weekly paper very ably conducted in the interests of the Roman Catholic missions, drew attention in the following terms to some of the causes of the mischief.

(1) The study of English history in schools reveals a gradual transition from an unlimited monarchy to a limited monarchy differing barely from a republic, the gradual transfer of political power from kings and aristocracy through the barons and then through the burghers and finally to the whole people. In reality this process took almost a thousand years, but in the schoolroom it is compressed into a term. The gradualness of the process, the long preparation of each class of citizens, the slow political education of the masses, all of which forms a long historical perspective, is through the medium of the text-book thrown upon the screen at once as a flat picture. It may not occur perhaps to the young mind to apply the precedent to his own country; but as soon as he falls under the influence of the political agitator the question suggests itself:

If the English people thus fought their way to supremacy, why should not the Indian people do the same? Losing sight of the perspective of history, it seems to him feasible that India should achieve in one bound what it took nearly a thousand years for the English people to bring about.

(2) In studying political economy and social science he meets with such principles as these—that the ruler is merely the delegate and representative of the people, from whose will he derives all his power. This power is to be exercised for the well-being of the people who have conferred it, and according to their will in conferring it. The old idea that all power, even that conferred through the people, is ultimately derived from God and exercised in His Name, is of course never heard of. The ruler is a public servant of the collective nation, and that is all. To introduce this notion among a people whose idea of government has run for thousands of years on the lines of absolute monarchy and hereditary if not divine right is nothing short of revolutionary. All idea of the sacredness of authority is at once gone. The Government is a thing to be dictated to by the people, to be threatened and bullied and even exterminated if it does not comply with the nation's wishes. Hence as soon as the political agitator appears on the scene, nothing seems more plausible to the raw mind of the student than an endeavour to upset the existing order of things. This cannot, of course, all be done at once; but at least a beginning can be made. Let us agitate for the redress of this or that grievance, for the increase of native appointments, and the like; and if we do not at once get what we ask for, let us try what bullying and intimidation can do—aspiring ultimately to substitute a representative for a monarchical form of government, and having secured this, wait the opportune moment for driving the foreigner into the sea. Thus a change which, to be successful, would require the gradual education of the people for generations, is to be forced on at once; and "if constitutional means are not sufficient to achieve our ambition, why not try what unconstitutional means will do?"

NOTE 19 (*page* 223).

A SHAMELESS APPEAL.

Perhaps the most audacious defence of the enlistment by Hindu politicians of schoolboys and students in the service of a lawless propaganda occurs in an article in the *Bengalee* of August 2, 1906, shamelessly appealing to the language of Christ. The *Bengalee*, which is published in English, is Mr. Surendranath Banerjee's organ:—

"In all great movements boys and young men play a prominent part, the divine message comes first to them; and they are persecuted and they suffer for their faith. 'Suffer the little children to come unto Me,' are the words of the divinely-inspired Founder of Christianity; and the faith that is inseparable from childhood and youth is the faith which has built up great creeds and has diffused them through the world. Our boys and young men have been persecuted for their *Swadeshism*; and their sufferings have made *Swadeshism* strong and vigorous."

NOTE 20 (*page* 241).

THE BRAHMANS AND WESTERN EDUCATION.

The special caste grievances of Brahmans against Western education are very frankly set forth in a speech on "The Duties of Brahmans,"

23

delivered in Bombay at the beginning of this year to his fellow caste-men by Rao Sahib Joshi, a distinguished and very enlightened member of the Yajurvidi Palshikar sept of Brahmans. Mr. Joshi, who laid great stress upon the duty of loyalty to the British *Raj*, began by recalling the patent conferred upon them by a British Governor of Bombay at the beginning of the eighteenth century for the protection of their privileges, especially in connexion with the teaching of medicine. But their community had gradually lost ground from various causes, and amongst those which he enumerated, he laid the chief stress upon the diffusion of secular education. He fully recognized the benefits of English education, but "all education being of a secular character, it made the new generation a class of sceptics. People brought up with English ideas, and in the atmosphere of secular education, now began to pay less respect to their Gurus and hereditary priests. In former days when the Guru or head priest came to one's house people used to say:—'I bow down to the Guru; the Guru is Brahma, the Guru is Vishnu, the Guru is Shiwa; verily the Guru is the Sublime Brahma!' This idea, this respect the secular English education shattered to pieces, and so the income and importance of the hereditary priests dwindled down."

NOTE 21 (*page* 252).

FEMALE EDUCATION.

In his quinquennial review of the progress of education in India, Mr. H. W. Orange quotes the following remarks by Mr. Sharp, Director of Public Instruction in Eastern Bengal, on the position of female education, adding that they describe the prevailing, if not quite universal, state of affairs:—

"All efforts to promote female education have hitherto encountered peculiar difficulties. These difficulties arise chiefly from the customs of the people themselves. The material considerations, which have formed a contributing factor in the spread of boys' schools, are inoperative in the case of girls. The natural and laudable desire for education as an end in itself, which is evinced by the upper and middle classes as regards their sons, is no match for the conservative instincts of the Mahomedans, the system of early marriage among the Hindus, and the rigid seclusion of women which is a characteristic of both. These causes prevent any but the most elementary education from being given to girls. The lack of female teachers and the alleged unsuitability of the curriculum, which is asserted to have been framed more with a view to the requirements of boys than those of girls, form subsidiary reasons or excuses against more rapid progress. To these difficulties may be added the belief, perhaps more widely felt than expressed, that the general education of women means a social revolution, the extent of which cannot be foreseen. 'Indian gentlemen,' it has been well said, 'may thoroughly allow that when the process has been completed, the nation will rise in intelligence, in character and in all the graces of life. But they are none the less apprehensive that while the process of education is going on, while the lessons of emancipation are being learnt and stability has not yet been reached, while, in short, society is slowly struggling to adjust itself to the new conditions, the period of transition will be marked by the loosening of social ties, the upheaval of customary ways, and by prolonged and severe domestic embarrassment.' There is, it is true, an advanced section of the community that is entirely out of sympathy with this view. In abandoning child-marriage they have got rid of the chief obstacle to female education ; and it is among them, consequently, that female education has made proportionately the greatest progress in quantity and still more in quality. But outside this small and well-marked class, the demand for female education is much less active and spontaneous. . . . In fact the people at large encourage or tolerate the education of their girls only up to an age and up to a standard at which it can do little good, or, according to their point of view, little harm."

NOTE 22 (*page* 255).

THE THEORY OF THE "DRAIN."

The Master of Elibank, then Under-Secretary of State, included in his Indian Budget speech on Aug. 5, 1909, a brief but effective refutation of the "drain" theory :—

"If the House will allow me, I wish to digress for a moment to deal with a charge that is constantly made, and has recently been repeated, to the effect that there is poverty in India which is largely due to the political and commercial drain on the country year by year, the political, it is asserted, amounting to £30,000,000 and the commercial to £40,000,000. These figures have been placed even higher by those who wish to blacken the Indian Administration in order to bolster up a malicious agitation against this country. I think it is incumbent upon the representative of the Indian Government in this House to deal with the statement. I may at once say that it has no foundation in fact. (Hear, hear.) Its origin is to be found, no doubt, in the fact that India makes annually considerable payments in England in return for services rendered, such as the loan of British capital ; but there is no justification for describing these payments as a drain, and their amount is only a fraction of the figures which I have just quoted. Let me deal first with the question of amount. As the method by which India makes her payments in England is that she exports more than she imports, all calculations as to the amount of payments must necessarily be based on the returns of Indian trade, which show by how much the Indian exports exceed her imports. If the trade returns are examined for 1904, 1905, and 1906, after making due allowance for the capital sent to India in connexion with Government transactions, the average excess of exports over imports, or in other words payments by India to England for services rendered, is £23,900,000 per year during the three years that have been mentioned. This payment is made up of, first, £21,200,000, being the average annual amount of the Government remittance during three years, which corresponds to the alleged political drain of £30,000,000 ; and, secondly, £2,700,000, the average annual amount of private remittances during the same period, which total has been most carefully examined and corresponds to the alleged commercial drain of £40,000,000. Now let us examine for a moment the nature of these two remittances. The Government remittance is mainly for the payment of home charges—namely, those charges in England which are normally met from revenue. These charges, in the three years to which I have referred, averaged £18,250,000, made up in the following manner :—Interest on debt, £9,500,000 ; payments for stores, ordered and purchased in this country, which cannot be manufactured in India, £2,500,000 ; pensions and furlough pay to civil and military officers, £5,000,000 ; and miscellaneous, £1,250,000. It will thus be seen that after deducting £5,000,000 for pensions and furlough pay, the bulk of the remittance represents interest for railway developments and other matters with which the interests of the peoples of India are intimately bound up. Besides the home charges proper, certain sums were remitted to England by the Government to defray capital charges. These bring the Government remittances to the total of £21,200,000 already mentioned. Now let us turn for a moment to the supposed commercial drain of £40,000,000 per year, which, as I have endeavoured to show, is in reality £2,700,000, being the difference during the period referred to between the private remittances from India, representing private profits, savings, &c., sent home to England, and the private remittances to India representing the transmission of English capital to that country. We can therefore say definitely that whatever India may have sent to England within the three years, she received from England as capital a sum falling short of that amount by £2,700,000 a year; and perhaps I might incidentally remind the House that at the end of 1907 the capital outlay on railways alone in India amounted to £265,000,000 sterling, the bulk of which is British capital, but by no means represents the full amount of British capital invested in India, which has taken its part in commercially developing its resources and providing employment for the masses of people in that great continent. Hon. members who have followed a recent discussion in the pages of the *Economist* as to whether £300,000,000 or £500,000,000 was the amount of British capital invested in India for its commercial and industrial development and for providing employment of the people in that land, will agree that the sum could not be placed lower than £350,000,000."

NOTE 23 (*page* 306).

THE SECRETARY OF STATE AND THE VICEROY.

This issue was raised, for instance, during the Viceroyalty of Lord Northbrook, when Lord Salisbury was Secretary of State, Mr. Bernard Mallett's memoir of Lord Northbrook contains the following noteworthy remarks upon the subject by Lord Cromer, who, as Major Baring, was Private Secretary to Lord Northbrook :—

There can be no doubt that Lord Salisbury's idea was to conduct the government of India to a very large extent by private correspondence between the Secretary of State and the Viceroy. He was disposed to neglect and, I also think, to underrate the value of the views of the Anglo-Indian officials. . . . This idea inevitably tended to bring the Viceroy into the same relation to the Secretary of State for India as that in which an Ambassador or Minister at a foreign Court stands to the Secretary of State for Foreign Affairs. . . . Lord Northbrook's general view was the exact opposite of all this, and I am strongly convinced that he was quite right. . . . He recognized the subordinate position of the Viceroy, but he held that Parliamant had conferred certain rights not only on the Viceroy but on his Council which differentiated them in a very notable degree from subordinate officials such as those in the diplomatic service. . . . Lord Northbrook regarded the form of government in India as a very wise combination which enabled both purely English and Anglo-Indian experience to be brought to bear on the treatment of Indian questions.

He did not by any means always follow the Indian official view; but he held strongly, in the first place, that to put aside that view and not to accord to the two Councils in London and Calcutta their full rights was unconstitutional in this sense that, though the form might be preserved, the spirit of the Act of Parliament regulating the government of India would be evaded. In the second place, he held that for a Viceroy or a Secretary of State without Indian experience to overrule those who possessed such experience was an extremely unwise proceeding, and savoured of an undue exercise of that autocratic power of which he himself was very unjustly accused.

NOTE 24 (*page* 326).

THE DIFFICULTIES OF LOYAL HINDUS.

A Hindu gentleman who has taken a considerable part in the struggle against Brahmanical disloyalty and intolerance in the Deccan has sent me a copy of a letter addressed to the *Times of India* in which he explains the peculiar difficulties with which loyal Hindus find themselves confronted :—

Englishmen hardly appreciate the true magnitude of the difficulties we have to contend with in any attempt to expose sedition. All the social forces that exist in Hindu society run counter to anti-Brahminical movements. The influence which the Brahmins exercise on the popular mind is still considerable. A man who is damned by the village-priest or the Brahmin kulkarni is doomed for good. Loyalty has been rendered odious to the ordinary mind by this as well as by many other influences. Loyalty is flattery. This is a dictum now almost universally recognized in the Deccan. A supporter of the Government is a "Johukum," a "hireling," or a "traitor." The Press has of late become sufficiently powerful to make or mar the reputation of a man so far as the native public is concerned. Every advocate of Government measures—even of the best of them—is held up to ridicule by the Press. This is immediately reflected in the most exaggerated form in what we may call public opinion in the land. Certainly very great courage is necessary in one who is called upon to bear calumny such as this from his society and his castemen. But there are other forces more threatening still. The rowdier section of the people never fails to hoot the man out on every possible occasion and even the women of his family may be subjected to indignities. The vakils are a very powerful class in the Deccan. Many of them do not openly dabble in politics; but you can hardly find many among them who do not sympathize with extremist politics. The landholders, traders and agriculturists in general are always in need of the services or, as they think, of the favour of the legal profession whose prejudices will never be wounded by the classes mentioned. The vakils, I may say, are to be propitiated by every one who wishes to conduct any public movement. But a loyal movement can never save itself from condemnation at the hands of this powerful class.

Although reluctantly, I must add that the lower services of the Government are filled by men who passively help extremism. They form the bulk of the total constituency of our public Press. That is a fact to show their political inclinations. Even they do not hesitate to use their little arts to worry a man known to be "anti-political" whenever he happens to come in contact with them. An agriculturist friend of mine who belonged to the caste to which I have the honour to belong once came to me and asked me why I was taking a particular step connected with the political movements in Kolhapur. The reason he gave for his attempt to dissuade me from participation in any anti-Brahmanical movement was that every Jain would be put to immense trouble in his dealings with pleaders and clerks simply because another Jain (in this instance myself) was against the leaders of their caste! Another class which always forms a check on a pro-government man is composed of the chiefs, sirdars, landholders, &c., who belong to the agitators' caste and who certainly cherish admiration for the doings of the "patriots." Many of us have to come in contact with some one or other belonging to this class and if he be known to favour anything against the great figures of the city-politics, his business is sure to be spoilt.

This is in brief the doleful tale of the loyalist in the Deccan. I shall briefly touch upon one or two things with reference to what will strengthen the hands of the loyal citizen. The first thing is that the Government should boldly come forward to help on the coming into existence of a bigger class of educated men among the backward or lower classes of the Deccan. The suspicion that they too will join hands with the agitator must vanish once for all. The half-heartedness due to such lurking suspicion gives a fine tool in the hands of Government's enemies. The English people should realize the probable danger of this and should use their vast resources to create a strong body of educated men from the ranks of the loyal castes. H. H. the Maharaja of Kolhapur, in his attempts to break down Brahmanical supremacy, found nothing so useful as the bringing into being of such a class and for this he is doing the best he can. Unless this example is followed by the Government, there is no hope of a strong loyal party coming forth to combat the evil work done by Extremists. The strengthening of the loyal Press such as it exists and adding to it is another measure the Government might wisely adopt.

NOTE 25 (*page* 331).

HINDU THEORIES OF GOVERNMENT.

Englishmen are apt to ignore the hold which ancient Hindu traditions concerning the rights and duties of kingship and the old Hindu theories of government derived from the sacred books of Hinduism still have on the Indian mind. They have been recently reviewed in an article contributed to *The Times* from a very scholarly pen.

The ancient Hindu theory of government is fully disclosed in the *Mahabharata*, the most majestic work ever produced by the human intellect, a work, too, which is to-day as popular with Indians as when 40 centuries ago it was chanted to instruct the youth and beguile the tedium of the princes of Hastinapura. Unlike all systems of government known to the West, the Hindu system contains no popular element whatever. In it we find no Witanagemote in which the nobles may advise the monarch; still less has it any place for a *comitia centuriata*, with its stormy masses of spearmen, to scrutinize and control the encroachments of the Royal prerogative. In the kingdoms described in the *Mahabharata* the inhabitants are rigidly divided into four wholly distinct and separate classes (*Udhyog Parva*, p. 67, Roy's translation). First come the Brahmans whose duty it is to study, to teach, to minister at sacrifices—receiving in return gifts from "known" or, as we should say, respectable persons. Then follow the *Kshattriyas* or the warrior class, whose whole life has to be spent in fighting and in warlike exercises. Thirdly come the *Vaisyas* who acquire merit by accumulating wealth through commerce, cattle-breeding, and agriculture. Fourthly, we have the *Sudras*, or serfs, who are bound to obey the other three classes, but who are forbidden to study their scriptures or partake in their sacrifices.

High over all classes is the King. He is the living symbol of strength and power. He is "the tiger among men," the "bull of the Bharata race," and his form and features bear the visible impress of the Most High. The whole arduous business of government rests on his shoulders. He cannot appeal to his subjects to help him in carrying out good administration nor can he leave his duties to others. For to beseech and to renounce are both against the laws of his order (*Vana Parva*, p. 457). At the utmost he can employ counsellors to advise him, but their numbers must never exceed eight (*Çanti Parva*, p. 275). In any case they only tender advice when asked (*Udhyog Parva*, p. 100), and the full responsibility of all acts rests on the King only. It is he who must keep up the arsenals, the depôts, the camps, the stables for the cavalry, the lines for the elephants, and replenish the military storehouses with bows and arrows. It is he who must maintain in efficient repair his six different kinds of citadels—his water citadels, his earth citadels, his hill citadels, his human citadels, his forest citadels, and his mud citadels (*Çanti Parva*, p. 277). It is he who must see that the capital has abundant provisions, impassable trenches, impenetrable walls; that it teems with elephants, cavalry horses, and war chariots. He must maintain an efficient staff of spies to ascertain the strength of neighbouring monarchs and do his utmost to cause dissension among their servants (*Çanti Parva*, p. 224). The War Office and the Foreign Office are alike under his immediate headship. It is for him to conclude treaties, to lead to battle his armies, and during peace to keep them prepared for war (*Çanti Parva*, p. 228). But the duty which comes before all others is to protect his subjects. That, indeed, is imposed on him as a religious duty. "For having protected his Kingdom a King becomes sanctified and finally sports in Heaven" (*Çanti Parva*, p. 68). "Whether he does or does not do any other religious acts, if only he protects his subjects he is thought to accomplish all religion." (*ibid.*, p. 193).

In return for the proper discharge of his innumerable tasks, he is regarded by his subjects as the incarnation of Indra. He is entitled to a sixth share of the gross revenue of the country. Fearful penalties attach to the infringement of his rights. "That man who even thinks of doing an injury to the King meets with grief here and Hell hereafter" (*Çanti Parva*, p. 221). "He will be destroyed like a deer that has taken poison." On the other hand, should the King fail to meet his obligations—and above all, if he does not protect his subjects—he offends grievously. "These persons should be avoided like a leaky boat on the sea, a preceptor who does not speak, a priest who has not studied the Scriptures, a King who does not grant protection" (*Çanti Parva*, p. 176). "A King who does not protect his kingdom takes upon himself a quarter of its sins" (*Drona Parva*, p. 625). In the last resort his subjects will be freed from their allegiance. "If a powerful King approaches kingdoms torn by anarchy from desire of annexing them to his dominions the people should go forward and receive the invader with respect."

In a similar manner the entire civil administration must be conducted by the King. He must see to it that wide roads, shops, and water conduits are constructed. He must look after the streets and by-paths. He must treat all classes impartially, and, above all, scrutinize carefully the work of the Courts of Justice. "The penal code properly applied by the ruler maketh the warders [*i.e.*, Judges] adhere to their respective duties, and leadeth to an acquisition by the ruler himself of virtue." (*Udhyog Parva*, p. 383). But although the subjects have the right to expect justice they cannot expect kindness or even easy condescension. "The heart of a King is as hard as thunder" (*Çanti Parva*, p. 57). "Knowledge makes a man proud, but the King makes him humble" (*Çanti Parva*, p. 223). "When the King rules with a complete and strict reliance on the science of chastisements, the foremost of ages called the Kirta is said to set in" (*ibid.*, p. 228). "The King must be skilful in smiting" (*ibid.*, p. 174). "Fierceness and ambition are the qualities of the King" (*ibid.*, p. 59). "The King who is mild is regarded as the worst of his kind, like an elephant that is reft of fierceness" (*ibid.*, p. 171). Indeed, failure to treat subjects with rigour is visited with penalties as tremendous as failure to protect them. "They forget their own position and most truly transcend it. They disclose the secret counsels of their master; without the least anxiety they set at nought the King's commands. They wish to sport with the King as with a bird on a string" (*ibid.*, p. 172). And in the end they destroy him. "The King should always be heedful of his subjects as also of his foes. If he becomes heedless they fall on him like vultures upon carrion" (*Çanti Parva*, p. 289).

Here we have commended as a pattern of administration a despotism such as the West has never experienced. It is inquisitorial, severe—sometimes, perhaps, wantonly cruel. But from the fearful pitfalls that encompass weakness it is certain to be sleeplessly vigilant and in the highest degree virile, forceful, and efficient. Now it will be asked what bearing the doctrines of a work four thousand years old have on the problems of the present day. But it must be remembered, as that eminent scholar, the late Mr. Jackson, the victim of the abominable Nasik outrage, pointed out, that Hindu civilization and Hindu thought are at bottom the same now as in the days of Yudhisthira.

The *Mahabharata* is the constant companion from youth to age of every educated Indian. Its tales have provided matter for the poetry, the drama, and the folk-songs of all ages and of all languages. No Hindu will live in a house facing south, as it is there that lives Yama, the god of death. No Hindu will go to sleep without murmuring *Takshaka* as a preventive against snake-bite. For Takshaka rescued the snakes from the vengeance of Janamajaya, the great-grandson of the *Mahabharata* hero Arjuna. The independent Indian Princes conduct their administration exactly on the lines indicated in the *Mahabharata*, and even States as enlightened as Baroda and Kolhapur still adhere to the Council of eight Ministers recommended in that immortal work. Indeed, its teachings really explain the puzzle of Indian loyalty to the British Government. According to Western ideas, no amount of *pax Britannica* would compensate the conquered for foreign rule. The Poles still sigh for the bad old days of independence and misrule, and are in no way comforted by the efficiency of German administration. But the Indian's allegiance to his native kings was, as the *Mahabharata* lays down, released by their weakness, and he readily transferred his loyalty to those who, although foreign, had yet shown that they could govern vigorously.

INDEX